W9-CKH-252

PAKISTAN

TRANSITION FROM MILITARY TO CIVILIAN RULE

Golam W Choudhury

SCORPION PUBLISHING LTD

954.91
C

© G W Choudhury 1988

All rights reserved. No part of this publication may be reproduced, stored in a retrieval system, or transmitted in any form or by any means, electronic, mechanical, photocopying, recording or otherwise, without the prior permission of the copyright owner.

First published in 1988 by Scorpion Publishing Ltd
Victoria House, Victoria Road, Buckhurst Hill, Essex, England
ISBN 0 905906 68 3
General Editor: Leonard Harrow
House Editor: John Orley
Assistant Editor: Kay Larkin
Art Direction and Design: Colin Larkin
Studio Assistant: Andrew Nash
Production Assistants: Susan Pipe and Doreen Channing
Typeset in Linotype Bembo 10 on 12 point
Printed and Bound in England by Biddles Ltd

WHITE PLAINS PUBLIC LIBRARY

To
my father
the late
Golam Mawla Choudhury

9 CT1CC989 0 t4CT 9

Preface

My first two books – *Constitutional Development in Pakistan* (1st and 2nd editions, 1959 and 1970) and *Democracy in Pakistan* (1963) were devoted to constitutional and political developments in United Pakistan (1947–1970). Then came the tragic events of 1971 culminating in the dismemberment of Pakistan on 16 December 1971. I gave a full account of the events of 1971 in my *The Last Days of United Pakistan* (1974). I had to pay a heavy price for publishing this impartial and objective story of the disintegration of Pakistan. I became a 'stateless person' and lived 'a new life in a new homeland' – the USA – for more than a decade. During that period I was not allowed to visit either Bangladesh or Pakistan under Mujibur Rahman and Z A Bhutto respectively. My book was banned in both countries.

I had, therefore, turned my research and publications to a new area – the People's Republic of China – which I visited six times for my research and publications.

I returned to my homeland, Bangladesh, in 1984 and also began to visit Pakistan regularly from 1977. On a visit to China, where my wife, Dilara, and I were invited by the Chinese People's Institute of Foreign Affairs in April 1987, I stopped over in Pakistan for about two weeks. I met President General Mohammad Zia-ul-Haq and other leaders of his government as well as my former colleagues and friends in the Pakistani government and in academic circles. I was greatly impressed and fascinated to see the process of Islamization of Pakistani society and government as well as the peaceful transition from military to civilian rule in Pakistan. As a result of my visits to Pakistan I decided to write a book on the great experiment of 'Islamic democracy' in Pakistan. The prestigious British publishing company, Scorpion Publishing Limited, offered me a contract to publish the proposed book. This is the background of this work. I made several trips to Pakistan during this period of preparation and research for the work. I also went to the United States to acquire materials on the theoretical aspects of the work.

In expressing my gratitude and thanks for being able to produce this volume I should first mention the name of President Zia-ul-Haq who, in spite of his busy schedule, was never tired of giving his time for my work. I greatly appreciate his kind help and co-operation in my work, particularly by giving me unique research materials and data without which the book probably would not have seen the light of day. I am also grateful to his staff, in particular Lieutenant-General (Retired) Syed Refaquat Hussain, Chief of Staff to President Zia. I would be failing in my acknowledgements if I did not make reference to the co-operation and help I received from the unnamed Pakistani officials in the Ministries of Information and Broadcasting, Law and Foreign Affairs. They helped me greatly in getting my research materials and data.

Last but not least, I must express my feelings for the affectionate encouragement I received from my family – my wife, Dilara, my two sons, Pappu and Sayeed, and the new member of my family, Lipi, my daughter-in-law. Sayeed during his 1988 summer vacation helped me greatly in the proof reading of the typed manuscript.

I sincerely hope this volume will stimulate further studies and publications on the great experiment of the synthesis of Islamic and democratic values and traditions that is going on in Pakistan under President Zia.

G W CHOUDHURY, DHAKA, JULY 1988

Contents

Introduction   6

Chapter I   Military Intervention in Pakistan   27

Chapter II   Military Withdrawal from Politics in Pakistan   50

Chapter III   The State and Religion in Islam:

          The Islamic State in Pakistan   77

Chapter IV   *Nifaz-i-Nizam-i-Islam*:

          The Process of Islamization   113

Chapter V   Parliamentary vs. Presidential System   153

Chapter VI   Federalism in Pakistan   183

Chapter VII   Ingredients of Democracy   202

Chapter VIII   Conclusion   231

Epilogue   239

Appendix I   245

Selected Bibliography   250

Index   254

Introduction

Pakistan was established on 14 August under the Indian Independence Act 1947. Why did the Muslims of India want a separate state of their own? Why could not the unity of India, which was considered as the greatest achievement of British rule in India, be maintained? The Indian Muslims were afraid of being a permanent and stagnant minority in a caste-ridden Hindu society in India.

When the British government in 1892 introduced, in a rudimentary way, the principle of election and representative institutions, the Muslims expressed their apprehension of being dominated by a majority with whom they differed in every sphere of life. The Muslim leader of this period, Sir Syed Ahmed, warned the Muslims against the dangers of majority rule in India contending that 'the larger community would totally over-ride the interests of the smaller community.' This fear of domination by the Hindus governed Muslim policies and actions; the Muslim minority in undivided India considered itself to be in perpetual danger of domination by an intolerant majority.

There were a number of attempts to bring about a rapprochement between the two communities. The Lucknow Pact of 1916 is an example in point; in 1928, the Muslims of India under the leadership of Jinnah, the founder of Pakistan, made sincere attempts to solve the Hindu–Muslim problem. Their demands were modest: a true federal form of government with autonomy for the provinces so that the Muslims could govern their affairs in those areas where they were in a majority. The Congress leaders failed to appreciate the honest aims of Jinnah who was known, at that time, as the ambassador of Hindu–Muslim unity, and his efforts to solve India's constitutional problems by an honourable agreement between the two major communities came to a sad end.

Then, in 1937, came the opportunity for constructive co-operation between the two communities, when responsible government was introduced in the Indian provinces under the Government of India Act 1935. Unhappily, the Muslims' offer of coalition government was turned down by the Congress, which then seemed to be intoxicated with power as a result of its victory in the elections. The result – total exclusion of the Muslims under the first experiment of parliamentary democracy, with its principle of majority rule – was disastrous. The Congress rule in the provinces from 1937 to 1939 was a real threat to the Muslims' political and economic interests and to their culture and cherished way of life. The Congress rule was marked by such systematic attacks on Muslim rights and their culture that the Muslims observed a 'Day of Deliverance' when that rule came to an end with the outbreak of the Second World War.

From this bitter experience of majority rule in undivided India, the Muslims were driven to one alternative: a separate Muslim state. The vision of a separate state had already been expressed by the poet-philosopher Allama Iqbal in 1930, but it remained a 'poet's vision' until the implications of majority rule in India were made clear to the Muslims by the Congress rule in the provinces in 1937–39.

The demand was formally proclaimed on 23 March 1940, and Jinnah declared that Hindus and Muslims were two nations by any definition or test of a nation. Pakistan was claimed as a homeland for Indian Muslims on the principle of the right of self-determination. But the idea of a separate Muslim state was totally abhorrent and repugnant to the Congress leaders, for whom the unity of India was an article of faith. For the Muslims it was a struggle for survival; for the Hindus it was to avoid 'vivisection of the motherland'. When the British government finally decided to grant self-rule to India in 1945, the two communities were engaged in a bitter struggle involving violence and communal riots on a vast scale.

Finally, the partition of India was accepted and a new state, Pakistan, was carved out of it. Under section 8 of the Indian Independence Act 1947, the Government of India Act 1935 became, with certain adaptations and modifications, the interim constitution of Pakistan. The interim constitution was supposed to exist till a new constitution was framed by the constituent assembly of Pakistan. While India was successful in framing a constitution by 1950–51, constitution-making in Pakistan became a highly complicated task. In its thirty-one year history, Pakistan has had a unique record of constitution-making.[1]

There were three constituent assemblies (the first one in 1947–54, the second one in 1955–56 and the third in 1972–73). Then a constitution was promulgated in 1962 by executive decree by Pakistan's first military ruler, Field Marshal Mohammad Ayub Khan, which was subsequently abrogated in 1969. Then followed a period of martial law (1969–72). During the second martial law regime, no attempt was made to frame a constitution. The expectations were that a new constituent assembly would be set up by holding a free and fair election. In order to hold the proposed elections, the martial law regime promulgated a Legal Frame Work Orders (LFO), president's order no.2 of 1970 on 30 March 1970. Though the LFO did not frame a constitution yet it did spell out the fundamental principles of the proposed constitution and the structure and composition of the national and provincial assemblies.

The elections were held under the Legal Frame Work Order of the second martial law regime in December 1970. This was the first and last general election in undivided Pakistan (1947–71). Elections were held simultaneously for both national and five provincial assemblies. By any criteria, elections were free and fair. There was no interference from the government; it maintained strict neutrality showing no favour or discrimination for or against any political parties. The members of the ruling council of ministers were debarred from participating in the elections. There were no allegations of rigging of the elections as is often alleged in elections held in the countries of the third world. In Pakistan itself, there were hardly any fair elections during the era of parliamentary democracy (1947–58). In fact there was not a single general election in Pakistan during the first eleven years of its existence.

But the results of the first and the last general elections in 1970 were simply disastrous from the standpoint of national unity and demonstrated the failure of national integration in Pakistan. There was no single national party in the country which enjoyed the confidence of the people of Pakistan, both East and West Pakistan. Two regional parties – the Awami League under the leadership of Mujibur Rahman in East Pakistan (now Bangladesh) – won 160 out of 162 seats allotted for East Pakistan. But in West Pakistan it could not secure a single seat and the percentage of votes secured by the Awami League in the four provinces of West Pakistan were: 0.07 (Panjab), 0.07 (Sind), 0.2 (North West Frontier Province) and 1.0 (Baluchistan).

In West Pakistan, the Pakistan People's Party (PPP) under the leadership of Z A Bhutto won 81 out of 138 seats for West Pakistan. But the PPP did not even dare to set up a candidate in East Pakistan. The remaining 57 seats of West Pakistan were shared by seven parties and there were fifteen independent candidates. None of the West Pakistani political parties, like the PPP, could win a single seat in East Pakistan. So the election results demonstrated political polarization of the country between the two wings, East and West Pakistan.

Serious negotiation began in January–March 1971 between the two major regional leaders – Mujib and Bhutto – and the ruling military government under President General Yahya Khan. But the tripartite negotiation for an agreed federal or even a confederal constitution was a dismal and total failure. The two regional leaders, Mujib and Bhutto, were inordinately ambitious and unscrupulous politicians. Mujib was more interested in creating a separate state for Bengalis, Bangladesh. He could never trust the ruling elite of West Pakistan. He was convinced, rightly or wrongly, that only under a separate state of their own would the interests of Bengalis be safe and secure. The present author had many lengthy discussions with Mujib and it was quite evident from those discussions that Mujib was not interested in becoming the prime minister or president of a united Pakistan. His ambition was to become the founder of a new state, Bangladesh. He also seemed to have entered into a secret deal with India for the secession of East Pakistan. India, thanks to its consistently and persistently hostile attitude towards Pakistan, was gladly ready to help Mujib in his secession plan.

On the other hand, Bhutto was more interested in getting power, no matter whether in a united or divided Pakistan. In fact he realised that in a united Pakistan, he had little chance of becoming either prime minister or president. The present author had also lengthy discussions with Bhutto before and after the 1970 election. It was quite clear from those discussions that if Bhutto had to make a choice between the two 'Ps' (power or Pakistan), he would choose the former. He was more interested in getting a 21-gun salute as the head of the state than in the maintenance of the unity of Pakistan.[2]

The army ruler, General Yahya Khan, was politically honest though his personal life had many 'colourful' aspects. He was the first head of the state in Pakistan who was honest and sincere in meeting the legitimate demands and aspirations of the people of East Pakistan. But he was not a man of great vision or capabilities. He was unable to deal with the highly explosive situation in Pakistan in 1970–71. Moreover, he had to deal with two unscrupulous leaders.

The result was the failure of the tripartite negotiation and Pakistan was plunged into a bloody civil war lasting for nine months (March–December 1971). The 1971 civil war in Pakistan was not merely an internal conflict between East and West Pakistan. It was a case of 'foreign-linked factionalism' where 'there are linkages between internal political factions and the international environment.'[3]

The disintegration of Pakistan and the birth of Bangladesh were mainly due to internal political squabblings in Pakistan and the ruthless atrocities of the Pakistani army against the innocent Bengali population of East Pakistan. Yet the Indo-Pakistan war on Bangladesh in 1971 was not merely a regional conflict between the two countries – 'it was not only another phase in the long religious conflict between the Muslims and the Hindus, not merely a moral conflict between Pakistan's vicious suppression of the Bangladeshi rebels and India's calculated military aggression to dismember the Pakistani state. Back of all this, there was a power struggle between China and the Soviet Union, and a strategic struggle between Moscow and Washington.'[4]

The dismemberment of Pakistan in 1971 was linked with a wider conflict involving the five most populous countries in the world – China, the Soviet Union, the United States and India and Pakistan.

Thus ended an important era of the largest Muslim state, Pakistan. A new and smaller Pakistan emerged on 16 December 1971. Why could not Pakistan survive as a united country? The inordinate delay in framing a constitution giving birth to a stable political order and the eclipse of democracy in Pakistan were largely responsible for the break up of the country in 1971. Before we begin the story of 'new' Pakistan's political developments since 1972, we shall give a resumé of the almost unique conditions which complicated constitutional advance in Pakistan and of the rise of military rule there.

Constitution-Making Dilemmas

It took nine years (1947–56) for two constituent assemblies to frame a constitution for Pakistan. The inordinate delay in producing a stable political order under which the people of both East and West could participate in the decision-making process on important national issues was a major, if not the major, factor for the failure of national integration in Pakistan. Constitution-making in Pakistan was unduly delayed by the political intrigues and squabblings which characterised the Pakistan political scene after the deaths of the two ablest leaders – Quaid-e-Azam Mohammad Ali Jinnah, the founder of the state, and Liaquat Ali Khan, the first prime minister of the country – within a couple of years of the creation of Pakistan. India was fortunate to have the guidance of a leader like Jawaharlal Nehru in its formative phase; the existence of a broad-based political party, the Indian National Congress, was also helpful for the success of democracy in India. By contrast Pakistan had no able political leadership after the deaths of Jinnah and Liaquat, and its national party, the counterpart of the Indian National Congress, the Muslim League, was also in a sad state of affairs soon after the creation of Pakistan. Constitution-making became a tool in the hands of unscrupulous politicians who were engaged in 'palace intrigues' making and unmaking the cabinet. The task of framing a stable constitution was sacrificed at the altar of power politics, which ultimately led to the military's involvement in politics.

It is, however, true that apart from political intrigues, there were certain fundamental issues facing the framers of the constitution in Pakistan.[5] First, the framers of the constitution had to decide the role of religion, Islam, in the country's constitution. Pakistan, it was claimed, was established because of the desire of Indian Muslims to preserve and foster Islamic values and ideals. What is an Islamic state? Is it compatible with a modern democratic state? What would be the status of non-Muslim minorities in an Islamic state? The relationship between state and religion in Islam was widely debated inside and outside the constituent assemblies. While there was general agreement that the constitution of Pakistan should be based on Islamic ideology and principles, there were differences about the exact place of Islam in the political system of the country. The framers of the constitution had to spend considerable time and energy in arriving at a commonly accepted concept of an Islamic state. The debate on the relationship between state and religion is not yet over in Pakistan even after the separation of East Pakistan in 1971. It is still a big and challenging issue facing the country. We shall discuss in detail the process of Islamization of the Pakistan constitution in our subsequent chapters. Here we conclude by saying that the role of Islam in the country's political order was a big issue facing the framers of the constitution when the first constitution of the country was adopted in 1956.

The more complicated issues of constitution-making in Pakistan were, however, related to the federal structure of the constitution. From the beginning Pakistan was created constitutionally as a federation. The Pakistan (Provincial Constitution) Order 1947 established the federation of Pakistan. From the very inception of Pakistan, it was decided that Pakistan should form a federation. This decision in favour of a federation constitution was regarded as the 'dictate of geography', and it was accepted without any controversy. But serious differences were raised over the structure and shape of the federal system in Pakistan. Before the creation of Bangladesh in

1971 Pakistan could be described as geographically unique; it consisted of two parts, commonly known as East and West Pakistan, separated by a thousand miles of foreign (Indian) territory.

East Pakistan comprised one-seventh of the total area, but its population exceeded the total population of all other provinces and states of West Pakistan. There were other complicating factors: whereas East Pakistan consisted of the single province of East Bengal, in the West the territory was divided into a number of provinces and states. Economically the eastern region was a compact area, but its economy was no organic part of that of the western region. The western part was industrially more advanced.

The cultural and linguistic differences were also important. Geographical separation finds expression in other differences – those of racial complexion, language, habits of life, and culture. The people of the western region speak different languages – Panjabi, Pushtu, Sindhi, Baluchi; yet most of them look upon Urdu as their common heritage. In East Pakistan, Bengali was the cherished language. West Pakistan is predominantly Muslim; East Pakistan had important non-Muslim minorities. These difficulties and differences were exploited by a group of disgruntled politicians, in both East and West Pakistan, who encouraged provincialism and did considerable harm to feelings of national unity. They found in the delay in constitution-making an excellent opportunity for endeavours to disrupt the state.

Apart from the problems peculiar to Pakistan, the organization of a federal state is usually complex. A federation comes into existence to overcome differences; it therefore has to work out a compromise between the desire for union and the anxiety to safeguard the interest of the federating units. If a federation has homogeneity of population, its difficulties are lessened. In the case of Pakistan, there was not only lack of homogeneity between East and West Pakistan; even in West Pakistan, there are differences among the different sectors of the population.

The first constituent assembly set up a committee to work out the structure of the proposed federal constitution. The committees, known as the Basic Principles Committee (BPC), worked hard to find an acceptable federal system. To work out a federal system for a country like united Pakistan with so many differences, particularly between the then East and West Pakistan, was a very difficult task. The BPC published its first draft constitution in 1950. The first point of controversy related to the quantum of representation of the various federating units in the legislature of the proposed federation.

The first draft constitution prepared by the BPC was presented in 1950 by the first Prime Minister Liaquat Ali Khan. Among the problems which were dealt with by the report was the problem of the quantum of representation of the various units in the proposed federal structure. The first draft constitution provided that there should be a federal legislature consisting of two houses – the House of the Units, representing the units, and the House of the People to be directly elected by the people on the basis of adult franchise.

It further laid down that the two houses of the federal legislature should have equal powers and, in the case of dispute on any question, a joint session of both the houses should be summoned for taking a final decision thereon.

The committee further recommended that the ministries should be responsible to both houses of the legislature. Provision was thus made for a bicameral system with equal representation of the various units in the upper house and equality of powers between the two houses.

The draft constitution as published in 1950 animated strong protest in East Pakistan. It was opposed on the ground that it did not provide for the province with the larger population an overall majority in the legislature and might even have converted it into a minority in a joint session of the two houses. The provision of equality of powers for both houses was also objected to, especially since all provinces would have equal representation in the upper house.

The opposition from East Pakistan led the constituent assembly to drop this draft and the assembly was engaged in producing a new version of the constitution.

The second draft constitution was presented to the constituent assembly by the second Prime Minister, Khawaja Nazimuddin, in 1952. It brought forth the principles of parity between East and West Pakistan as its most important contribution towards solving the problem of representation. Under the second draft constitution there were to be two houses of parliament as in the first report; the House of Units would consist of 120 members of whom 60 would come from East Pakistan and 60 from West Pakistan. Similarly, of the total membership of 400 in the House of the People, half would be elected from the East and half from the West. The House of the People was to have real authority; the House of the Units would enjoy only the privilege of recommending revision in hasty legislation. The Council of Ministers was to be responsible collectively to the House of the People.

The fate of the second draft constitution was, however, no more favourable than that of its predecessor. This time the reaction was adverse particularly in West Pakistan. The press of West Pakistan, with few exceptions, joined in a chorus of protest. The West Pakistan leaders saw no logic in treating one single province, East Pakistan, as being equal in importance to all other units put together. They even regarded it as a violation of the federal principle under which each unit should be given equal representation in the upper house and cited the example of federation in the United States.

All these criticisms against the second draft constitution led the constituent assembly, once more, to postpone its deliberations for an indefinite period and it seemed that the country faced a constitutional dilemma and no solution seemed to be acceptable to both East and West Pakistan. In order to appreciate fully the situation, one has to look also into the political intrigues and manoeuvrings which were going on over constitution-making in Pakistan. Honest efforts at a compromise were frustrated through political moves so as to give the opportunists a chance to come into power. The process of constitution-making, as stated earlier, was greatly affected by the scramble for power among the politicians.

The third prime minister, Mr Mohammad Ali, presented the third draft constitution in 1953. He evolved a formula popularly known as the 'Mohammad Ali Formula' to overcome the constitutional deadlock over the quantum of representation in the proposed federal legislature. Neither the first draft constitution of 1950 nor the second draft of 1952 could solve this problem and as such was not accepted by the constituent assembly. Mohammad Ali's 'Formula' was, however, accepted by the constituent assembly in 1954. While this formula maintained the principle of parity between East and West Pakistan, it brought a substantial departure from the parity clauses of the second report. The main features of the formula were as follows:

a   The upper house was to consist of 50 members distributed geographically. As West Pakistan had a greater part of the country's territory, it was given a clear majority in the house of units.

b   The lower house was to consist of 300 members; the majority was to come from East Pakistan since it had the absolute majority of the country's population.

c   The distribution of seats was made in such a way as to ensure parity between the two zones in the joint session of the houses:

	U House	L House	J Session
East Pakistan	10	165	175
West Pakistan	40	135	175

Important measures like a vote of confidence in the cabinet or the election of the Head of State were to be decided only in joint sessions.

The second major issue relating to the federal structure was the distribution of powers between the federal and the provincial governments. This problem was not peculiar to Pakistan; it has to be faced in framing any federal constitution. But in Pakistan the problem was more complicated because of the growing mistrust and conflicts between East and West Pakistan. How did the framers of the constitution try to solve it? Though Pakistan was constituted as a federation from the very beginning in 1947, in practice, the government has highly centralized – Pakistan had, in reality, a highly centralized government.

Under the interim constitution (the 1935 Act) a highly centralized federal system was established in Pakistan. The Government of India Act 1935 provided adequate provisions and processes to ensure full predominance of the central authority. Those provisions and processes were fully utilized. The central government's hold in the legislative, financial, administrative and political spheres was so great that for practical purposes, the country's governmental structure could hardly be described as truly federal. The grave and abnormal situation with which the country was faced immediately after its inception led the central government to apply emergency measures which in turn tightened its hold over provincial governments. Similarly the inadequate financial resources of the provinces made them more and more dependent on the central government.

But more significant than anything else was the political control of the central authorities in provincial politics. The provincial governor was appointed by the central authorities and held office during the pleasure of the governor-general. The central government exercised considerable pressure and influence in the provincial political scene through its powers of appointment and dismissal of provincial cabinets through the provincial governors. Many changes in the provincial cabinet took place under dictates from the centre. The centre in several instances virtually nominated provincial chief ministers and in one case a person was 'nominated' as the chief minister of a unit before that unit was created.

The highly centralized structure of the dominant party, the

Muslim League, also contributed towards centralization of powers and influence in Pakistan. Another source of federal government supremacy lay in the fact that senior civil servants employed in the provinces were under the administrative control of the federal government. The senior civil servants were the members of the civil service of Pakistan. There was only a single higher service recruited common to all levels of government and controlled by the federal government, enjoying special rights and protections guaranteed by the constitution itself.

The highly centralized federal structure of Pakistan as described above was soon attacked and subjected to severe criticism and strain. The centrifugal forces seemed to be getting much stronger than the centripetal ones. Unlike the federal systems of the United States or Australia the sense of distinct nationality was getting stronger and the sense of common nationality getting weaker in Pakistan. To explain the peculiar development of federalism in Pakistan, one has to look back to the history of the country during the first one and a half decades.

It was rather curious that the demand for maximum provincial autonomy came from the largest unit, East Pakistan, which under normal circumstances should not have had any fear of domination, but unfortunately this fear was deeply rooted in East Pakistan as a result of certain unfortunate developments particularly in the economic sphere. The people of this region had legitimate reasons to feel neglected by the central government as they did not have their reasonable, fair and adequate share in the central government's administration. Consequently, any increase of the power of the centre was viewed with distrust and disapproval in East Pakistan whose people had once given the most inspiring support to the establishment of Pakistan. The problem in East Pakistan was not merely political, it was largely economic. At the time of partition Pakistan was a poor and underdeveloped country producing raw materials, having very little industry and not much control over commerce. It was not fully developed administratively or economically. This was true of both East and West Pakistan. The governments, both central and provincial, applied themselves vigorously to the task of economic development. Progress had been made particularly in industrialization of the country. But the most unfortunate feature of the economic development was that East Pakistan continued to be a neglected area. The first five-year plan of Pakistan, published by the central government in May 1956, admitted this fact in a statement: 'East Pakistan has made appreciable progress since 1947. The rate of development, however, has not been as high as in West Pakistan.'[6] There was a deep conviction among the East Pakistanis that the economic disparity between East and West Pakistan had widened instead of being narrowed down as a result of the economic policies and programmes of the central government. These feelings had great impact on the interaction of centrifugal and centripetal forces in Pakistan.

An analysis of the various constitutional drafts as presented to the country since the first draft constitution of 1950 clearly showed trends towards decentralization. In the draft constitution as prepared by the first constituent assembly we, however, find that the stress was on the national government. A national convention was held in Dacca on 4 and 5 November 1950 which demanded that only three powers, viz. defence, foreign affairs and currency, should be given to the centre and the rest should be vested in the provinces. This demand for maximum autonomy in East Pakistan gained further impetus with the formation of the new political party, the United Front, which secured an overwhelming victory in the provincial election in 1954. A considerable opinion grew up in favour of giving more powers to the East Pakistan provincial government. It had been felt that in view of the experience gained under the interim constitution the province could best be administered in many respects by the provincial government rather than by the geographically distantly situated central government in West Pakistan.

The draft constitution as finally passed by the first constituent assembly in 1954 gave adequate powers to the national government, though it made some minor concessions to demands from East Pakistan for maximum autonomy for that province.

Another highly emotional and explosive issue facing the framers of the constitution was the language problem. The third prime minister was apparently successful in bringing about a compromise on the language issue which had been agitating the country since the beginning and had a great impact on constitution-making. Pakistan was a bilingual state where the majority of the population spoke Bengali. It was declared in the first draft constitution of 1950 that Urdu which was, generally speaking, the language of West Pakistan (although there are regional dialects within West Pakistan) was accepted as the official language of Pakistan. This was bitterly resented in East Pakistan; and as such Mohammad Ali brought about a compromise giving equal status to both Urdu and Bengali as official languages, although hope was expressed for the development and growth of a common language without mentioning what it should be. In the meantime English was to continue as the official language of the state for a period of twenty years. The net result of Mohammad Ali's language formula was to postpone the language controversy for the next twenty years.

With the successful handling of the problems of representation and language, and distribution of powers between the federal and the provincial governments, the framers of the constitution proceeded faster towards adopting a constitution and by September 1954 the constituent assembly was successful in adopting a draft constitution. The constitution bill was reported to have been ready and only the formality of enacting it into law remained. Prime Minister Mohammad Ali even announced the date of promulgation of the new constitution, viz. 25 December 1954.

The first constituent assembly of Pakistan could not, or rather was not allowed to, complete its mission. Within ten days of the adoption of the final draft of the constitution it was dissolved by the governor-general in a most undemocratic and arbitrary manner. The dissolution of the first constituent assembly involved Pakistan in a series of legal disputes and in a period of constitutional crises and confusion. The judiciary in Pakistan played a very important role during this period of constitutional crisis and cleared the way for summoning the second constituent assembly in 1955.

The second constituent assembly produced quicker results than its predecessor. It was inaugurated in July 1955 and on 8 January 1956 it presented a (fourth) draft constitution to the country which with certain changes and amendments was finally adopted on 29 February 1956. Pakistan's first constitution was the 1956 constitution.

The Failure of Democracy and Rise of Military Rule in Pakistan

After nine years of frustration and effort Pakistan was successful in framing a constitution which was implemented on 23 March 1956. However, the constitution, like many other constitutions of various countries, was not perfect and could not satisfy the different groups of people in Pakistan. Instead of giving due representation to the people of East Pakistan which constituted the majority of the population, it introduced parity of representation. There was a single chamber legislature at the national level. The national assembly was to consist of 300 members, half elected by constituencies in East and half by constituencies in West Pakistan. The principle of parity was never fully approved by the people of East Pakistan. It continued till 1970 when the second military president, General Yahya Khan, restored the democratic principle of 'one man, one vote', thereby giving East Pakistanis the majority of seats in the national assembly. Apart from the defeats or limitations of the 1956 constitution, the fate of democracy in Pakistan had not improved since a democratic constitution was framed by the elected representatives of the people. Political bickerings and intrigues which began under the interim constitution after 1953, when a prime minister who had enjoyed the confidence of the legislature was arbitrarily dismissed by the governor-general, Ghulam Mohammad, and when a sovereign constituent assembly was also dissolved by the same governor-general in an undemocratic manner in 1954, continued to dominate the Pakistan political scene even after the adoption of a democratic constitution in 1956. During two and a half years of its existence, there was not a single general election as under the interim constitution (1947–56). There were seven prime ministers in Pakistan during the era of parliamentary democracy (1947–58). With the exception of the first prime minister, Liaquat, none of the remaining six prime ministers were elected as a result of any election or even as a result of the vote of confidence in the legislature. They were the products of 'palace intrigues' by the two governor-generals – Ghulam Mohammad and Iskander Mirza. There was a cabinet, there was a parliament, but the real powers were exercised by the governor-general with the help of a ruling elite, composed of the top civil and military officials. The constitutional forms and trapping of democracy had only provided a cloak for rule by the few who had been able to draw power into their own hands.

Parliamentary institutions, or more accurately the parody of them, were brought to an end on 7 October 1958 when President Mirza and General Mohammad Ayub Khan, Chief of the Army, imposed martial law in the country by abrogating the 1956 constitution. National and provincial assemblies were abolished, the cabinets, both at the centre and in the provinces, were dismissed, fundamental rights of the citizen were suspended. The country began to be governed by an authoritarian system under martial law regulations – President Mirza was removed within three weeks on 27 October 1958. The army chief, Ayub, became the Chief Martial Law Administrator and the president. Martial law continued for four years (1958–62).

Why was democracy a failure in Pakistan while in neighbouring countries like India and Sri Lanka democracy is working rather successfully? A constitution commission, headed by a former chief justice, Mohammad Shahabuddin, was appointed in 1960 to examine the causes of the failure of democracy in Pakistan. According to the constitution commission, the main reasons for the failure of parliamentary democracy in Pakistan were: (i) lack of proper elections, (ii) undue interference by the heads of the state with the ministers and political parties and by the central government with the functioning of the government of the provinces, (iii) lack of leadership resulting in the absence of well-organised and disciplined parties, lack of character in the politicians and their undue interference in the administration.[7] The present author was associated with the constitution commission as an honorary advisor. While he agreed with the reasons given by the commission for the failure of democracy in Pakistan, he feels that real threats and challenges to democracy in Pakistan came from an all-powerful and irresponsible executive in Pakistan which was aided and supported by the powerful bureaucracy.

In fact, the executive in Pakistan had been from its very inception very powerful and dominating. 'Since its emergence as a state the performance of the governmental functions in Pakistan had been dominated by the executive, bureaucracy and army.'[8] Political tradition in the Indo-Pak sub-continent was that of a strong executive, first under the oriental rulers, then under the British. The viceregal system of the British Raj had great impact on the political tradition which Pakistan inherited, and this tradition was not in tune with democratic ones. Some members of the bureaucracy in British India got key positions in the governmental machinery in Pakistan. Governor-General Ghulam Mohammad, President Iskander Mirza, fourth Prime Minister Chowdhury Mohammad Ali were all promoted to the highest office from the civil service. It was hardly expected that this powerful group should have any regard for democratic tradition and practices. Since the death of Liaquat Ali Khan, particularly after the arbitrary dismissal of the Nazimuddin cabinet in 1953, this group had full control and dominance in the governmental machinery, with perhaps a brief interval of thirteen months when Mr Suhrawardy became the prime minister. But even during this interval Mr Suharwardy had to rely on the all-powerful President Mirza and his party for his existence, and as such the grip of the group was not seriously undermined. This group had faith in

Pakistan and its destiny but had no faith in the ability of its people to govern themselves. The most ruthless of this group was Ghulam Mohammad, and the most outspoken was President Mirza who openly advocated 'controlled democracy' for Pakistan in 1954. He was a great believer in the British administrative system in India and was much more concerned to preserve and foster that system rather than maintain a democratic constitution to which he was sworn in as president of the republic. He was always in favour of dominance by the bureaucrats and preventing what he called the 'mess of things' by the elected representatives of the people. The policies and action of this powerful group constituted the greatest threat to the development and working of the nascent democracy in Pakistan. Among the most complex problems that rise to plague democratic government are those which relate to the extent and basis of executive power. To find a strong and vigorous executive, and at the same time to make it responsible and not autocratic, is not an easy task. There are those who maintain that strong and vigorous leadership is a dangerous proposition, while others, like the great political sociologists Mosca and Michels, have virtually asserted that leadership is by its very nature undemocratic. A powerful and vigorous executive is not necessarily incompatible with democratic government, as long as it is subject to restraint. The British executive, for instance, is one of the most powerful in the world but it operates within an area of consensus carved out by the party, vigilant electorate and a watchful parliament. None of these safeguards against the danger of arbitrary government existed in Pakistan. Further, it is recognised that political democracy requires an expert civil service but the civil service cannot be effective unless it is taken out of politics. There is always a need, as Professor Lindsay points out, for some democratic machinery to keep the efficient expert straight, to keep him as an instrument and not as a master.[9]

In the absence of a sound party system the leaders could not effectively control the authoritarian tendencies of the executive in Pakistan. The political leaders were not backed by parties with a wide following and sound foundation. As such they could not exert their influence or any effective control. The constitutional provisions, both under the interim constitution as well as under the 1956 constitution, contained many loop-holes which enabled the powerful executive to maintain and strengthen its grip on the country's administration and government. Since the time of Lord Cornwallis (1786), the constitutional machinery in British India provided for some crisis, government and emergency provisions.

These provisions were kept intact even after independence. The result was that the element of responsible government was often overshadowed by the element of crisis government. Ruthless exercise was made of section 92A of the interim constitution and article 193 of the 1956 constitution which suspended democratic institutions and replaced them by bureaucratic control. In fact the imposition of bureaucratic rule was a regular phenomenon in Pakistan politics. *The Times* (London) in making observations about the dyarchic pattern of government in Pakistan referred to the recurrent conflict in Pakistan between those who want the ablest leaders to exercise supreme power irrespective of popular support, and those who think it more important that the chief minister should be supported as widely as possible by the dominant party.[10]

Even while the popular governments were in operation, its leaders were constantly under the threat of emergency rule or disqualification from political life under the PRODA (Public and Representative Offices Disqualification Act).

The political order in Pakistan, therefore, could be termed as an oligarchy under a democratic constitution. In a recent study on the politics of the developing areas, Pakistan's political system was described as a 'modernizing oligarchy'.[11] There seems to be some truth in it and one cannot dismiss it altogether. The various government changes that took place in the country could be traced to the inordinate desire of this ruling oligarchy to perpetuate its power and position. It is, no doubt, true that this oligarchy could maintain its hold because of the lack of cohesion and integrity among the political parties and their leaders. This was much stressed by the constitution commission in its findings on the fate of parliamentary democracy in Pakistan. But this powerful oligarchy was determined to crush the democratic institutions in the country and it always encouraged splits and disintegrations of the parties whenever any of them constituted a threat to its hold and dominance. It was therefore the role and policy of this particular group, which had actual control of the governmental machinery, that was more responsible than any other factor in the unsatisfactory working of the democratic institutions in the country. As long as the grip of this powerful ruling oligarchy was not destroyed, the prospects for democracy remained bleak and uncertain. The only political machinery that could successfully challenge the hold of this group was the well-organized and widely based political parties. As long as, therefore, the parties were not developed on sound and proper lines, there was no prospect for the elimination of the control of the undemocratic elements in the governmental machinery.

Like any other military ruler, Ayub Khan also wanted to civilianize his military rule. As a first step towards civilianization, he introduced a comprehensive system of local self-government known as Basic Democracy.[12]

As local self-government institutions, Basic Democracy was quite good but Ayub also introduced the system of indirect election to the office of president and assemblies, both national and provincials, through eighty thousand Basic Democrats – forty thousand from East and forty thousand from West Pakistan under his 1962 constitution. The system of indirect election was greatly resented. The political agitation, which began in 1968–69, leading to the abrogation of his 1962 constitution and his exit from power, was mainly directed against the system of indirect election by the Basic Democrats.

The fall of Ayub and the emergence of a second military regime took place in March 1969. We have already discussed the dismal failure of the second martial law regime to negotiate a peaceful transfer from the military to civilian rule in Pakistan. As stated earlier, the failure of those negotiations led to a nine-month civil war in the country culminating in the dismemberment of Pakistan and the emergence of Bangladesh in December 1971.

Beginning of a New Era (1972–77)

After the emergence of Bangladesh in December 1971, the former West Pakistan, comprising four provinces – Panjab, North West Frontier, Baluchistan and Sind – became the new state of Pakistan. The Pakistan army was thoroughly discredited for the loss of East Pakistan, and also for the defeat in West Pakistan in the third Indo-Pakistan war in 1971. Obviously army rule could not continue; Yahya had to quit. The powers were handed over to Mr Z A Bhutto whose party became the single largest majority party in West Pakistan in the 1970 general election held under the LFO, framed by the second military regime. Bhutto, however, did not restore democracy. Pakistan, for the first time, had a civilian martial law administrator and the country continued to be governed under martial law till August 1972. Under the provisional constitutional order, 1972, the 1962 constitution became the interim constitution of Pakistan till a new constitution was framed and adopted in 1973.

The 1973 constitution, with some major amendments made under the 8th amendment of the same constitution effected by the national assembly in December 1985, is still the constitution of Pakistan. Unlike the first and second martial law regimes in 1958 and in 1969, the third martial law regime of 1977 did not abrogate the existing constitution; it only suspended it. We shall examine the various features of the 1973 constitution as it stands today in our subsequent chapters. Here we shall only give a brief resume of the political developments in Pakistan from 1973 to 1977 when Pakistan had its third martial law regime under President General Mohammad Zia-ul-Haq.

Pakistan had a civilian government under Z A Bhutto who adopted a democratic constitution in 1973. The 1973 constitution provided for a parliamentary system with all powers concentrated in the prime minister. He was also elected as the president of the national assembly. So there was total concentration of both executive and legislative powers in the office of the prime minister. Under article 48 of the original 1973 constitution the president of the country was bound by the advice of the prime minister, and it was mandatory that every order issued by the president must be countersigned by the prime minister and unless the prime minister had signed it, no order or decision of the president would have any legal sanction. To quote President Zia's words, 'The division of powers between the Prime Minister and the President was ludicrous, meaningless and downright comic'. Zia, while proposing amendments to the 1973 constitution, raised the question, 'What is the good of a helpless Head of the state or President who can take no action when he sees that the country is sliding into the quagmire of a serious crisis' as was the case in July 1977.[13]

Equipped with all the executive and legislative powers, Bhutto became a civilian dictator under the facade of a democratic government. From his role in the 1971 crisis, it was quite evident that Bhutto was a ruthless, unscrupulous and unduly ambitious politician. His rule as the all-powerful prime minister from 1973–77 was more undemocratic, more oppressive and more intolerable than the two martial law regimes which preceded his regime. Bhutto did not tolerate any dissenting voices even within his own parties. The leaders of the opposition parties were persecuted and prosecuted to an extent unknown even during the previous military rules in

Pakistan. Bhutto let loose a reign of terror and of oppression and suppression in the country. The economy of the country was ruined as a result of his undue zeal for so-called socialism. The law and order situation in the country was simply intolerable.

Bhutto was found guilty of causing the murder of an opposition political party leader by the highest courts of the country. Another prominent political leader of an opposition party, the Muslim League, Khawaja Khairuddin, told the present author in 1979 that one evening he was picked up by Bhutto's para-military force; he was forcibly taken by a boat to the sea and thrown out on an island along the Indo-Pakistan sea border. He was almost drowned by the tide of water but fortunately he was rescued by some fishermen who saw his helpless situation. There are many such cases of persecution of political leaders, both of the opposition parties as well as those of his own party.

Bhutto ruled the country for five years (1972–77). According to President Zia, the result of Bhutto's five years of arbitrary rule were – (i) the country reached the brink of a civil war, (ii) the national economy was ruined, (iii) normal life was totally disrupted, (iv) democracy was destroyed in the name of democracy, (v) the honour and dignity of womenfolk were violated by the so-called custodians of human dignity and honour, and thus (vi) the masses started despairing of the country's future.[14]

Bhutto remained in power for five years on the basis of the 1970 election held under the second martial law regime. Finally he had to hold general elections in 1977. The elections were a farce, mockery and fraud upon the electorate. The elections were noted for wide-spread riggings and malpractices. Bhutto managed to 'secure' a majority in the elections. But when the results were announced, there were violent protests and demonstrations in the streets all over the country. In spite of all his suppressive measures, the anti–Bhutto agitation was getting stronger and stronger. There was total breakdown of the machinery of law and order. Under these circumstances, the Pakistan army under Zia imposed martial law and thus began the third and the longest martial law regime in Pakistan from July 1977 to December 1985.

NOTES

1 For details see G W Choudhury, *Documents and speeches on the consitution of Pakistan*, Dhaka, 1967.
2 For details see G W Choudhury, *The Last Days of United Pakistan*, Bloomington, Indiana, 1974.
3 See Alan Dowty, 'Foreign-linked Factionalism as a Historical Pattern', *The Journal of Conflict Resolution*, vol. xv, no. 4, 1971.
4 J Raston, 'Who won in India?', *The New York Times*, December 4 1971.
5 For details see G W Choudhury, *Constitutional Development in Pakistan*, second edition, London, 1969.
6 *The First Five Year Plan (1955–60)*, Government of Pakistan, Karachi, vol , p. 1.
7 See *Report of the Constitution Commission*, Lahore, 1961.
8 Almand and Coleman, *The Politics of the Developing Areas*, Princeton, 1960, p. 572.
9 A D Lindsay, *The Essentials of Democracy*, Oxford, 1924, p. 65.
10 *The Times*, London, 26 April 1956.
11 Almand and Coleman, *The Politics of the Developing Areas*, Princeton, 1960, p. 572.
12 *The Basic Democracies Order*, Government of Pakistan, Rawalpindi, 1952.
13 *Constititutional Amendments Announced*, address to Nation (by) President Mohammad Zia-ul-Haq, Rawalpindi, March 2 1985, pp. 16–17.
14 *Political Plan Announced*, Seventh Session of Federal Council; address by President General Mohammad Mohammad Zia-ul-Haq, Islamabad, 12 August 1983, p. 14.

Chapter I
Military Intervention in Pakistan

Pakistan experienced direct military rule for nearly sixteen years (1958–62, 1969–71 and 1977–85) after it obtained independence from British rule in 1947. As we have already stated, the democratic process in Pakistan never had a strong foundation. Political developments in Pakistan, both under united Pakistan (1947–71) and in the 'new' Pakistan (1972–77), could give very little comfort to the friends of democracy. Military interventions in Pakistan have raised many queries and interpretations. It is often asked how does the Indian army, of which the Pakistan army was a part during the British Raj, maintain traditional aloofness from politics? What are the reasons for the repeated military involvement in Pakistani politics? The first Indian prime minister, J Nehru, was of the opinion that 'it is not the inordinate ambition or a special taste for the politics but the failure of the political classes to govern effectively that the military intervention takes place in Pakistan.'[1] It is, of course, true that there has been a section of the powerful Pakistan army who consider it 'the guardian of the national interests' (*Izzat* and *Gharat*),[2] and have, therefore moral obligations to intervene in politics whenever there occurs any political crisis or the governmental machinery comes to the verge of collapse; on each of the three occasions when the Pakistan army intervened in politics – October 1958, March 1969 and July 1977 – there was a real crisis in the country. When the first martial law regime under Ayub Khan emerged, Pakistan's socio-economic and political situation was simply intolerable. At the centre and in West Pakistan, a political party, the Republic Party, was in power because of repeated manipulations and violations of the then constitution (1956); it had no roots among the people; it was set up at the presidential palace as a result of political intrigues. The majority party in West Pakistan, the Muslim League, was prevented from coming into power by the arbitrary and undue interference of the president, Mirza. In East

Pakistan, two principal political parties, the Awami League and Krishak Sramik (peasants and workers) party, were engaged in bitter political bickerings and squabblings, so much so that inside the provincial legislature at Dacca (Dhaka) the deputy speaker was killed and the speaker was severely beaten. A number of the members of the two rival parties were also injured. Disrespect to the national flag was a regular phenomenon. The ruler of an acceded state in West Pakistan declared defiance of the central authority and removed the national flag. The country's economic condition was deteriorating fast; the State Bank of Pakistan revealed an alarming picture of the country's economic and financial conditions. Black marketeering, corruption, and profiteering became rampant; subversive and anti-national elements were flourishing. Ayub, while declaring martial law in October 1958, said 'There has been no limit to the depth of their [politicians'] baseness, chicanery, deceit and degradation. The result is total administrative, economic, political and moral chaos in the country.'[3]

Ayub began his martial law regime with wide support in the country, even in East Pakistan. People were so frustrated with the unsatisfactory working of the country's parliamentary democracy and the performance of politicians that they welcomed Ayub in the expectation that their basic problems and interests would be better served by an honest, efficient and stable regime. When he came to power in 1958, Ayub was regarded as the last hope for a united Pakistan. His political innovation, Basic Democracy, was acclaimed by many, including the historian Arnold Toynbee, as a 'plausible alternative between democratic and communist systems'.[4] The extensive rural development works under Ayub's Basic Democracy, especially in East Pakistan (Bangladesh), were described as 'an example of Jeffersonian democracy in action' by the leaders of the Harvard Advisory Group in Dhaka in 1968.[5] Pakistan under Ayub was cited as a model for developing countries. Similarly, Ayub's foreign policy and diplomatic moves earned him the title of the 'Asian or Muslim de Gaulle'. Ayub was credited with putting an end to Pakistan's subservient foreign policy to the United States. The *Economist* (London) wrote that 'Ayub wanted essentially what his brother soldier [de Gaulle] sought for France', an opportunity for national self-assertion and independence, meaning independence from the United States.[6]

Yet Ayub was removed from the presidency in March 1969 as a result of a scuffle between the students and the police over some allegedly smuggled goods. In November 1969, it appeared like an anomic movement; a sudden sporadic outburst of political activity engendered by the insecurity and frustrations usually characteristic of societies undergoing rapid change. How did the Ayub era come to such a dismal failure? There have been many interpretations of Ayub's fall. The main factors were that Ayub's economic policy and development projects had widened the gap between East and West Pakistan. More importantly, his political system under the 1962 constitution deprived the Bengalis of all opportunities of any participation in the decision making process on vital socio-economic as well as political matters. On any important national issue, the Bengalis would only react but not act; the vital decisions – whether related to defence, foreign affairs or economic policy – were decided at the Presidential House with the help of an inner cabinet composed of the top civil and military officials, all from West Pakistan. There was total exclusion of Bengalis from the decision making process. When Ayub came to power in October 1958 the condition of the country, as already stated, was totally intolerable. In spite of Ayub's many honest and remarkable socio-economic measures, the condition of Pakistan in March 1969, when Ayub had to quit, was no less tolerable.

The movement against Ayub was for the restoration of democracy and against his 'one man's' constitution with its indirect method of election and all-powerful presidential system as provided in the 1962 constitution. When the 1962 constitution was finally abrogated and Ayub resigned from the presidency, there was no restoration of democracy but the emergence of the second martial law regime under General Yahya Khan. Why did the military intervention take place and why was democracy not restored? Ayub, before his resignation, held round table conferences with the political leaders. He conceded their demands to abolish the indirect method of elections and to restore the parliamentary system instead of an all powerful presidential one. But the political leaders could not agree, and such an anarchic and explosive situation was created that there was no alternative to military intervention for the second time in Pakistan.

General Yahya began anew. He did not try, unlike Ayub, to make any significant socio-economic reforms or to introduce a new political order. His only aim was to transfer power to an elected representative body by holding a free and fair election. The general election, the first and last one in undivided Pakistan, was held, as already stated in the previous chapter, but instead of transfer of powers to an elected body, Pakistan was dismembered and a new country, Bangladesh, emerged out of the old East Pakistan. Why did the second martial law regime in Pakistan fail to achieve their objectives, and what led to their dismal failures?

Bhutto compared Pakistan when Yahya came to power in 1969 to 'a patient in the last stages of tuberculosis'.[7] Although he made this remark two years after Yahya had come to power and when the country was already heading towards break-up on the issue of Bangladesh, the remark contained truth. Apart from complicated political and constitutional issues, the country was beset with gargantuan problems in the socio-economic sphere. Whether the new military regime was capable of providing effective political leadership to meet the formidable challenges was very doubtful. In recent years, the social scientists in their new jargon have discussed extensively the role of the military in political developments and modernization in the new countries of the third world.[8] One conclusion drawn from a study of these recent volumes on military rule in new states was summed up by Robert Price:

> A striking characteristic of the literature on military rule in developing countries is the gap between theoretical expectations and political, social and economic reality. On the one hand, practitioners of comparative social and political theory have tended to view the military, at least in the non-Latin American area, as an organization capable of playing an important modernizing role. On the other hand, empirical researchers, often the very same individuals, who at a different time wear the same hat of theoretical practitioners, have found the performance of the military as political agents of modernization to have been rather dismal.[9]

Political and socio-economic realities in Pakistan in 1969–71 were not conducive to the Yahya regime performing any significant role. Further, the regime had its own weaknesses and deficiencies. One requisite for a military regime to achieve success is either to get broad support from the people as Nasser had done in Egypt and Ayub also in the initial years, or to have co-operation and assistance of powerful segments of society such as the bureaucrats, the business community and other important groups among the urban elite. The Yahya regime had the full support of the army, but Yahya was never the big boss among the armed forces that his predecessor had been.

The great debate on the synthesis of economic growth and social and distributive justice had already begun. The pertinent issue was whether such a synthesis could be achieved without fundamental changes in the political and economic order. Yahya's government, being a 'temporary' one, was neither capable nor willing to undertake such revolutionary changes in the economic system. As the former chief economist of the Planning Commission, Dr Mahbub Ul Haq, rightly pointed out:

> A mere reform of the capitalist system is no longer a viable solution. The capitalist system was rejected by the mass upsurge of 1969. The 'reformed' system which is being demanded by the public and politicians – with minimum wages for all workers, participation of the workers in profits, social responsibility of the capitalists, etc. – may be in operation in Sweden or Yugoslavia but cannot be built in Pakistan through an evolutionary process.[10]

But the explosive and vital problem on the economic front was that of regional distribution (between East and West Pakistan) rather than social distribution. Bengalis were not prepared to wait for an evolutionary process to remove the economic disparity by 'step by step' concessions. The political climate in East Pakistan in 1969–70 was not indicative of any compromise or waiting. Yet there was no 'magic lamp' to remove disparity by one or two five-year economic plans. The alternative was the division of the country. As stated earlier, the dismemberment of Pakistan took place on 16 December 1971 as a result of the role of two unscrupulous and inordinately ambitious politicians – Mujibur Rahman of East Pakistan (Bangladesh) and Z A Bhutto of West Pakistan. This led to a nine-month civil war, and ultimately, to the third Indo-Pakistan war in 1971. India took well-planned and calculated moves to cause the disintegration of Pakistan.

India's interest and involvement in political happenings in East Pakistan during 1969–71 were closely linked with her constantly tense and bad relations with Pakistan. As the UN Secretary-General U Thant pointed out in his Annual Report of 1971: 'The relations between the Governments of India and Pakistan are also major components of the problem [the Bangladesh crisis] . . . The crisis is unfolding in the context of the longstanding and unresolved difficulties which gave rise to open warfare only six years ago [i.e. in 1965].'[11] From the very beginning of the crisis, Pakistan complained of India's involvement and calculated wish to dismember Pakistan. Her fears were confirmed by the views expressed at a symposium organized by the Indian Council of World Affairs on 31 March 1971 (i.e. within six days of the outbreak of the revolt in East Pakistan) at which some Indians agreed with the candid statement of K Subrahmaniyam, Director of the Indian Institute of Defence Studies: 'What India must realise is that the break-up of Pakistan is in our interest, an opportunity the like of which will never come again.'[12] It was further stated at the same symposium that the Bangladesh crisis provided India with the 'opportunity of the century' to destroy her number one enemy, Pakistan.[13] Throughout 1970 All-India Radio had been broadcasting a programme every evening entitled *Apper Bangla and Opper Bangla* (This Side and the Other Side of Bengal), openly encouraging the secession movement in East Pakistan. All-India Radio is an official organ.

Even more significant, however, was the Indian government's immediate reaction to the crisis. Less than forty-eight hours after the Pakistan army action, Mrs Gandhi said in the Lok Sabha: 'We are deeply conscious of the historic importance of this movement . . . I would like to assure the honourable members who asked whether decisions would be taken *on time* [my italics], that obviously is the most important thing to do. There is no point in taking a decision when the time for it is over.'[14] The 'honourable members' were pressing for a decision for Indian intervention and Mrs Gandhi's answer was self-evident. In the Rayja Sabha on the same day she stated: 'We are interested in the matter for many reasons. First, as one member has said, Sh Mujibur Rahman has stood for the values we ourselves cherish . . .'[15] The head of a foreign government commented that just because the rebel leader subscribed to India's 'cherished values', India must therefore 'be interested' in the internal affairs of a neighbouring country. Then on 31 March 1971, the Indian Parliament passed a resolution introduced by Mrs Gandhi pledging full support to the rebel group: 'This House records its profound conviction that the historic upsurge of the 75 million people of East Bengal will triumph. The House wishes to assure them that their struggle and sacrifices will receive the wholehearted sympathy and support of the people of India.'[16]

What justification, if any, did India have for assuring 'support' to a federating unit which was rebelling against the national government in a neighbouring country? Was it not contrary to the UN Charter and to the 1950 and 1966 bilateral agreements between India and Pakistan, pledging not to interfere in each other's internal affairs? As pointed out earlier, the support of the Indian government, press and public for the armed uprising in East Pakistan was given long before her economy or society was burdened with the entry of a single refugee.

India complained that as a result of the Pakistan army's atrocities, 'three million' Bengalis took shelter in India. India's economy was adversely affected by the influx of the 'three million' refugees from Bangladesh, and that is why India had to attack Pakistan in November–December 1971, the third Indo-Pakistan war since the two countries gained independence in 1947. The Pakistani army was easily defeated in the Eastern front (Bangladesh) because of the effective help from Bengali Mukti Bahini (the Bengali freedom fighters) inside Bangladesh. In West Pakistan also, Pakistan's army's performances were poor compared with their heroic role during the 1965 Indo-Pakistan war. The Pakistan army was demoralized and disheartened by the nine-month civil war in Bangladesh where hundreds of Pakistani soldiers were killed while suppressing the revolt in Bangladesh.

The defeat of Pakistan in the third Indo-Pakistan war in 1971 and the dismemberment of the country disgraced the Pakistan army thoroughly. The army rule could continue no longer, Yahya had to quit and handed over power to Z A Bhutto. We have already described in the preceding chapter how Bhutto, the great champion of democracy in 1969–70, became a constitutional dictator under a democratic constitution (1973), and how as a result of the popular uprising against Bhutto's dictatorial rule, the army under President Zia came to power in July 1977. Thus began the third and longest martial law regime in Pakistan (1977–85).

Pakistan under President Zia

The third martial law regime under General Mohammad Zia-ul-Haq came into existence on 5 July 1977 and lasted till 30 December 1985. Zia's military regime was supposed to be the shortest one – 90 days – but it turned out to be the longest martial law regime in Pakistan. Unlike his two predecessors, Ayub and Yahya, Zia did not abrogate the existing constitution of the country (the 1973 constitution). He suspended it in abeyance. Under Chief Martial Law Administrator order no.1 of 1977 – the laws (continuance in force) order 1977, it was provided that (i) 'notwithstanding the abeyance of the provisions of the 1973 constitution, Pakistan shall subject to this order and any order made by the president and any martial law regulation or martial law made by the Chief Martial Law

Administrator (CMLA), be governed' as nearly as may be in accordance with the (1973) constitution, (ii) subject to the aforesaid, all courts in existence immediately before the commencement of this order 'shall continue to function and exercise their respective powers and jurisdictions.'

Under the new legal order as established by the laws (continuance in force) order no. 5 July 1977, any law might at any time be changed by the president and therefore there was no such thing as fundamental rights. The fundamental rights conferred under part 1, chapter 1 of the 1973 constitution and all proceedings pending in any court, in so far as they were for the enforcement of any of these rights 'shall stand suspended'.[17]

The new legal order was further clarified and elaborated under the Provisional Constitution Order 1981 (CMLA order no. 1 of 1981). Under the Provisional Order 1981, it was stated that the CMLA 'has already announced that endeavours will be made and are being made to restore as soon as possible democracy and representative institutions in accordance with the principles of Islam wherein the state of Pakistan exercises its power and authority through chosen representatives of the people and until then, interim measures are necessary.'[18] The powers of the judiciary were clarified under the Provisional Constitution Order 1981; under article 15 it was clearly stated that 'all presidential orders of the CMLA, including other orders amending the (1973) constitution made by the president or by the CMLA, martial law regulations, martial law orders and all other orders made on or after the fifth day of July 1977 are hereby declared, notwithstanding any judgement of any court, to have been validly made by competent authority and shall not be called in question in any court on any ground whatsoever.'[19]

With regard to political parties it was laid down that political activity would be permitted by the president – it may be added here that all political parties were banned with the imposition of martial law on 5 July 1977. It was further stated that only those defunct political parties would be entitled to function as were registered with the election commission – the election commission was already revived under the election commission, 1977 (President's order no. 4 of 1977) – or were declared by the commission to be eligible to participate in elections by 11 October 1979. All other political parties would 'stand dissolved', and all their properties and funds were forfeited. No new political party would be formed except with the previous permission of the election commission. It was further stated that if the president was satisfied that 'a political party has been formed or is operating in a manner prejudicial to the Islamic ideology or the sovereignty or integrity or security of Pakistan', the president might dissolve the political party in consultation with the chief election commissioner.[20] Similar restrictions on political parties were imposed under the Political Parties Act 1962, which was passed by the national assembly of Pakistan under the 1962 constitution on 15 July 1962.[21] The Political Parties Act 1962, was further amended by the political parties (Audit and Accounts Rules) 1979 by Zia's martial law regime. It provided elaborate provisions relating to the maintenance of accounts, submission of the audit report, etc., by the political parties.[22] A fully-fledged martial law regime was established with the curtailments of the powers of the judiciary with regard to judicial review of the constitution, fundamental rights, etc. Political parties were banned initially, but when revived, they were under similar restrictions as imposed by the first military ruler in Pakistan, Ayub Khan, in 1962.

President Zia's Socio-Economic and Religious Reforms

As already stated, Zia's martial law regime was expected to last only 90 days. The present author had his first lengthy meeting with President Zia in March 1979 – Zia explained why he had to prolong military rule. The country's economy, as a result of Bhutto's unrealistic and impractical policy of nationalization, was seriously affected. Zia wanted to stabilize the economy of the country. The widespread policy of nationalization was carried out without regard to the administrative and managerial capacity at the disposal of the public sector, and this led to a period of stagnation and slide back in the country's economy.[23] Pakistan was flooded with incomplete and inefficiently run projects; the result was hyper-inflation. Zia's government launched the Fifth Five-Year Plan (1978–83) with the aim of stabilizing the economy shattered by the reckless policy of nationalization during the era of Bhutto (1972–77). The fifth five-year plan, which was completed in June 1983, resulted in maintaining a consistent annual growth in gross national production (GNP) at 6.5% to around 5% by 1982–83.

The sixth five-year plan was launched in July 1983 envisaging an outlay of 210 billion Pakistani rupees for the period of July 1983 to June 1988. Its broad objectives were the rapid and equitable development of the country so that the benefits of economic growth would be widely shared by the people, particularly in lesser developed areas in Baluchistan and Sind. The principal instrument for development in the sixth five-year plan has been the creative energies of the private sector. The private sector got incentives from the government by a combination of programmes such as accelerated development of human resources through a five-fold increase in the expenditure on education, health, and technology development. There was also a substantial deregulation of the economy to dispense with discretionary controls, and to replace them with a policy framework that would protect both private initiative and social justice. The sixth plan was based on a new compact between the public and private sectors; policies of co-existence and co-operation were to be encouraged in all sectors of the economy. Zia's economic policy and programme are based on pragmatism rather than on any socialist or capitalistic ideology. Zia's stress on socio-economic reforms and policies was based on social justice and equitable distribution, which he strongly believes are based on Islamic ideology and principles, social justice as enunciated by Islam. While stressing the role of the private enterprise, the sixth plan also provided for a decisive breakthrough in the provision of physical infra-structure and social services to the rural areas. In order to help the poorer sections of the population, Zia introduced the system of *zakat* and *ushr* – *zakat* is an Islamic levy on saving and *ushr* is a levy on agricultural produce. The zakat and ushr were introduced 'with the prime objective of assisting the needy, the indigent and the poor, with a view to securing their economic well-being as also to help them becoming self-reliant.'[24] The introduction of zakat and ushr has raised great debates and controversy in Pakistan. On the one hand, it is claimed that zakat and ushr have helped considerably in promoting social welfare programmes throughout the country. The benefits of these two Islamic taxations were extended to 1.5–2 million deserving indigents during the sixth plan period; on the other hand, the urban elite, the middle class professional groups resent the introduction of zakat and ushr. They even refer to corruption and malpractices in the administration of them. The Shiah community, a minority Muslim section, has raised objections to zakat on the ground that they consider it 'un-Islamic', according to their interpretation of the Quran (the Holy Book of Islam). There were vigorous protests and even riots by the members of the Shiah community. As a result, they are now exempted from zakat.

The Islamization of the Banking and other Financial Institutions

After striking a pragmatic balance between private and public sectors in the fifth and sixth five-year plans, and after launching a programme aimed at striking a balance between growth and distribution, the Zia government began the process of Islamization of the country's financial institutions, particularly the banking system. We have already mentioned the introduction of the Islamic levies, zakat and ushr. According to strict interpretation of the *Shariah* (Islamic law) *riba*, interest, is forbidden in Islam. But modern Muslim scholars make a distinction between interest on personal loans by money-lenders to the poor and the needy, and the interest charged by modern banks for commercial and investment purposes. Whatever the correct position, President Zia followed the clear instruction in the Quran about interest, and took steps to eliminate riba. An interest-free banking system was first introduced in 1981 as a first step towards the Islamization of financial institutions in Pakistan. The Pakistani finance minister, in his budget speech for 1984–85, gave full details of the interest-free banking system, which was redefined as the 'profit and loss sharing system'. Under the new regulations, no banking company would accept any interest bearing deposits from 1 July 1985. As from that date all deposits accepted by a banking company, including all saving accounts regardless of the date of their opening, would be on the basis of participation in 'profit-loss' of the banking company, except deposits on current accounts on which no interest or profit would be given by the banking company.

These regulations would not, however, apply to the lending of foreign loans which would continue to be governed by the terms of the loan. Similarly these regulations would not apply to foreign currency deposits.

The following measures were adopted by the State Bank of Pakistan during 1984–85, to accelerate the process of Islamization of the financial system:

1 On 26 November 1984, the State Bank prescribed the method of calculating the maximum rate of service charges which a bank/development finance institution may recover on its loans other than *qarz-e-hasna* (interest-free loan to needy persons).

2 Instructions were also issued regarding minimum and maximum rates of return to be derived by a bank/development finance institution in respect of trade related and investment type modes of financing. These rates were revised on 10 December 1984 and 25 May 1985.

3 It was decided that, as from 1 January 1985, finance provided by a bank under the 'Export Finance Scheme' and the 'Scheme for Financing Locally Manufactured Machinery' should be only on the basis of any one of the non-interest modes of financing considered appropriate by the bank. In case of defaults by the exporters/suppliers/banks in fulfilling their obligations, a system of fines was introduced by the State Bank. The provision of refinance by the State Bank under 'Export Finance Scheme' and for 'Export Sales' under the 'Scheme for Financing Locally Manufactured Machinery', continued to be without interest or service charge. Later, on 25 May 1985, the State Bank advised the banks that, effective from the next day, its share in case of refinance under the Export Finance Scheme would be 50 per cent of the profits realised by banks from exporters. As for 'Export Sales' under the 'Scheme for Locally Manufactured Machinery', the State Bank's share in case of pre-shipment would be 50 per cent of the profits realised and 65 per cent in case of post-shipment finance. In the case of 'local sales' under the 'Scheme for Locally Manufactured Machinery', the State Bank would provide refinance on the basis of sharing profit and loss. The share of the State Bank in the profit would be 75 per cent. In the event of loss, the loss would first be met out of the reserves and credit balance in the profit-and-loss account of the bank, which have been created during the period of financing, and the balance, if any, shared by all the financiers in proportions to the respective finances provided by them.

4 A directive was issued on 26 November 1984 that from 1 January 1985, interest, wherever charged by a banking company/development finance institution (DFI) in any of the items of bank charges, would be replaced by a non-interest mode considered appropriate by it. Moreover, overdue penalty interest, or mark-up, would not be charged by a banking company/development finance institution as from that date. Instead, it may take legal steps for recovery of overdue finance.

5 It was decided that as from 1 January 1985, finance for meeting temporary liquidity difficulties (including telegraphic transfer discounting facilities) would be provided by the State Bank of Pakistan on a profit-and loss sharing (PLS) basis.

6 The banks/development finance institutions were advised that a banking company/DFI receiving PLS deposits shall declare rates of profit on various types of its PLS deposit on a half yearly basis, ending 30 June and 31 December each year, after obtaining clearance from the State Bank.

Deposits of scheduled banks, under the profit-and-loss sharing (PLS) scheme, had increased by Rs.7,942 million during 1983–84. The outstanding level of deposits under PLS system amounted to Rs.22,088 million as on 30 June 1984 (demand deposits Rs.8,264 million and time deposits Rs.13,824 million). At this level, PLS deposits formed about 18.7 per cent of the total bank deposits. During the year 1984–85, total PLS deposits registered a rise of Rs.16,008 million (demand deposits Rs.5,034 million and time deposits Rs.10,974 million). The outstanding level of PLS deposits, as at the end of June 1985, stood at Rs.38,097 million. Of the total, demand deposits accounted for Rs.13,299 million, and time deposits for Rs.24,798 million. At the end of June 1985, PLS deposits formed 27.6 per cent of total bank deposits.

For the six-month period ending June 1984, the commercial banks participating in the PLS deposits scheme announced the annual rates of return, ranging from 7.50 per cent to 11.25 per cent on saving deposits, and from 9.50 per cent to 19.50 per cent on term deposits. For the six-month period ending December 1984, the banks declared rates on special notice deposits for 7 to 29 days, ranging from 5.20 per cent to 6.60 per cent, and from 6.15 per cent to 7.85 per cent for deposits held for 30 days and over. These rates ranged from 7.10 per cent to 9.70 per cent on saving deposits, and from 9.00 per cent to 15.75 per cent on term deposits ranging from 3 months to 5 years. The rates of return declared by banks for the six-month period, ending June 1985, ranged from 4.90 per cent to 8.70 per cent on special notice deposits for 7 to 29 days, and from 5.60 per cent to 11.40 per cent for 30 days and over. The rates for saving deposits ranged from 7.50 per cent to 13.30 per cent, and from 8.60 per cent to 21.60 per cent on term deposits ranging from 3 months to 5 years.[25]

President Zia's process of Islamization was also extended to the country's legal system. Although the constitution of 1973, and every constitution that preceded it, provided for bringing the existing laws of Pakistan in conformity with the injunctions of Islam, and a council of Islamic ideology had also been provided for the purpose, no worthwhile steps were taken in this direction until President Zia embarked upon a policy of Islamization of the country's laws on a top priority basis. The Council of Islamic Ideology was consequently reactivated and the four Hudood Laws – pertaining to offences subject to Hadd (literally meaning hindrance, limit or restrictions, namely, intoxication, theft, *zinq*, unlawful sexual intercourse) were codified by the Council and enforced by the President/ CMLA in February 1979.

The enforcement of Hudood Laws (Islamic Penal Code) was followed by the establishment of Shariah benches in each high court and an appellate Shariah bench in the supreme court. The Shariah courts were empowered to dispose of appeals filed in them arising from judgements and orders of the sessions judges in cases tried under the Hudood Laws, and to decide on petitions made before them for determining whether, and in what respect, any existing law was repugnant to the Holy Quran and the Sunnah. The judgements of these benches were made binding subject to decisions on appeals filed against them in the Shariah appellate bench in the supreme court.

However, when it was found that the high courts could not dispose of such appeals and petitions speedily because of their normal judicial and other responsibilities, the federal Shariah court was constituted as an independent court on 26 May 1980, with a membership of five judges – one judge selected from each high court, and a chief justice with the status of a judge of the supreme court. In March 1981, three ulema judges were also included in the bench of the court, raising membership from five to eight. The jurisdiction exercisable by the Shariah benches of the high courts was conferred upon the federal Shariah court and all the pending matters, numbering 114, were transferred to it. By the beginning of 1981 almost all pending matters were decided and disposed of by the court.[26]

President Zia's Diplomatic Moves and Policies

Zia continued the basic objectives and aims of Pakistan's foreign policy. The prime one is a search for security. The search for security is a universal foreign policy goal of almost all countries, large or small, and even of the two super powers, the USA and USSR, but in the case of Pakistan, the search for security is very vital because of the corrosive quarrels and conflicts between India and Pakistan. They have fought three wars (1949, 1965 and 1971) since the two countries gained independence in 1947. Apart from three wars, there were many 'near-war' situations, concentrations of troops on the borders of the two countries causing grave concern. Pakistan, being smaller and comparatively militarily weaker than India, could not enjoy 'freedom from fear', freedom from fear of foreign aggression. After the defeat of Pakistan in the 1971 war, and the dismemberment of the country in the same year, Pakistan was considered almost as a 'lost case' vis-a-vis India. But soon Pakistan strengthened its defence capabilities. From 1977, Zia made it the top-most priority of Pakistan's foreign policy objective. Other foreign policy goals of Pakistan include securing maximum external economic assistance for its vast development projects, supporting the causes of the countries of the world of Islam, helping the anti-colonial and anti-apartheid struggle and promotion of an equitable international economic order.

Zia suffered some diplomatic setbacks in 1979 when Z A Bhutto was executed. Heads of many states and governments requested Zia to pardon Bhutto, but Zia adhered to the verdict of the supreme court which found Bhutto guilty of conspiring to kill an opposition leader. The setbacks were, however, temporary. Soon Zia emerged himself in the role of great statesman and highly successful diplomat. Pakistan's links with the world of Islam have always been close, cordial and warm. But Zia put special emphasis on Pakistan's growing links with the Muslim countries. He is never tired of speaking about the solidarity and unity of the ummah or the commonwealth of Muslim nations.

In October 1980, President Zia was accorded the unique honour of addressing the 1980 UN General Assembly on behalf of the entire Islamic world. As chairman of the Organization of Islamic Conference (OIC), he was the spokesman of 900 million fellow Muslims all over the world – from Indonesia in the east to Senegal in the west. While explaining the 'new spirit' in the Islamic world, Zia told the UN General Assembly, 'Living in different customs and political systems, speaking different languages and dialects, Muslims all over the world retain an abiding sense of Islamic affinity.'[27] Zia in his various speeches on many occasions talks about 'a new awakening, a new awareness, a new mood and a new vision in the world of Islam'.[28]

Relationships with the People's Republic of China and with the United States of America have been very important factors in Pakistan's external policies. Notwithstanding his Islamic zeal and his process of Islamization of Pakistan's political, social and economic order, Sino-Pakistan relations have grown both in depth and width. After his visit to China in May 1980, Zia said that 'Sino-political ties are so deep and solid that they do not have to be qualified or need further elaboration'; Zia added, 'China is the only country in Pakistan's experience which has stuck to its principles and whose policies are above any interests.'[29]

Zia had some initial difficulties and problems in the Pakistan-US relationship during the presidency of Jimmy Carter. Carter's obsession for human rights made him look towards Pakistan with indifference and coolness. Carter stopped all US aid, not only military but economic aid also, to Pakistan in April 1979, on the grounds that Pakistan had been secretly manufacturing an alleged 'Islamic atom bomb'. Carter was the only American president who visited the Indo-Pakistan sub-continent without any stop-over in Pakistan, 'America's most allied Asian ally' in the 1950s.

The Afghan Crisis and its Impact on Pakistan

The Soviet military intervention in Afghanistan in December 1979 had a profound impact on the balance of power in South Asia. The United States, which had followed a low profile policy towards the region since 1971, overnight changed its policy and began to plan a major involvement in the area through its former ally, Pakistan. President Carter felt strongly about the Soviet invasion of Afghanistan. Carter viewed Afghanistan as a watershed in East-West relations. The Afghan situation, according to the Carter administration, had elevated the status of the Gulf region to that of Western Europe, Japan, and South Korea – 'areas where Washington is prepared to risk a conflict to contain Soviet influence.'[30] This being the case, one of the few immediate moves open to Washington was to revive its military relationship with Pakistan. The Soviet military action in Afghanistan in December 1979 heightened long-standing Amerian concerns about Moscow's intentions toward South Asia and the Persian Gulf. It thrust Pakistan into the role of 'frontline state', Pakistan's status as an emerging leader of the non-aligned movement, and Chairman of the Organization of the Islamic Conference also made it an obvious partner in the American effort to rally third world opinion against the Soviet military intervention in Afghanistan.

As already stated, it was only in April 1979 that the Carter administration had stopped all US aid, economic and military. It was a delicate task for President Carter to propose military aid for Pakistan. But there was hardly any alternative option for Carter. Carter's National Security Adviser, Dr Brzezinski, dashed to Islamabad with the US offer of military aid. Zia, much to Washington's surprise, gave a cool reception to US overtones. He was reticent at first, and thereafter, reluctant to get involved with the aid offer of $400 million, of which only $200 million was for military aid. When Pakistani President Zia described the offer as 'peanuts', the US response was one of 'shocked incomprehension'.[31]

The whole situation was, however, changed with the change of administration in the United States. The Republicans under President Reagan came to power. Pakistanis have always felt that they get a fairer deal from the Republicans than from the Democrats.

After President Reagan's administration took office in January 1981, negotiations began on US economic and military aid to Pakistan. Pakistan's foreign advisor, Agha Shah, visited Washington in April 1981, and had lengthy discussions with the US Secretary of State, Alexander Haig. The US Under Secretary of State, James Buckley, visited Pakistan in June 1981. Finally, the US–Pakistan negotiations culminated in a September 1981 agreement on a six-year (1981–87) $3.2 billion programme of US economic and military assistance to Pakistan. The most significant aspect of the new military aid to Pakistan was the offer of selling 40 F-16 fighters. This would have great impact on the balance of power in the sub-continent between India and Pakistan.[32] James Buckley stated that 'the thrust of Reagan's administration is to recognize that arms transfers, properly considered and employed, represent an indispensable instrument of American policy that both complements and supplements the role of our own forces.'[33] Pakistan expressed satisfaction with the aid offer. The Carter administration's offer had not been commensurate with what Pakistan considered the magnitude of the threat. Pakistan believed in the Reagan administration's determination to give strong support to Pakistan's independence. Both sides insisted that the new military aid programme had no quid pro quo. It was not a formal treaty; Pakistan was not required to give any military base or any other facilities. Pakistan could continue as a non-aligned and as an Islamic block country. During the past decade, the US Pakistan security relationship has deepened steadily. US aid averaging more than $600 million per year has materially improved the fighting capabilities of

Pakistan's defence forces, contributed to the country's economic growth and helped bridge a major hard currency deficit. The United States has also played a role in promoting badly needed credits from the International Monetary Fund and development loans from the World Bank.[34]

For its part, Pakistan has maintained a strong stance against the Soviet military presence in Afghanistan despite considerable verbal pressure from the Soviet Union, and frequent shelling and air attacks across the Pakistan–Afghanistan frontier. Backed by the United States, Saudi Arabia and other Gulf countries, 'Pakistan has played a key role in providing a haven for the Afghan refugees and a channel for aid to the Afghan resistance.'[35]

The six-year-old US aid programme for Pakistan expired in 1987. The next six-year US aid was already worked out between the two governments. The post-1987 package would comprise \$2.28 billion in economic, and \$1.74 billion in military aid.

The aid is expected to be utilized for continuing modernization of Pakistan's armed forces which began with the previous assistance programme. At the top of Pakistan's post-1987 military shopping list would be an airborne radar and surveillance system as well as ground-to-air missiles and up-to-date armour. Islamabad has shown interest in an airborne warning and control system to improve the advance warning capability of its air force. Updating armour technology is also a priority.

The way Pakistan handled the Afghan crisis demonstrated the Zia regime's courage, statesmanship and adherence to principles. It did not succumb to Soviet threats and blackmailing. Pakistan continued its opposition to foreign aggression against a fellow Muslim and non-aligned country, Afghanistan. Pakistan took a leading part in condemning the Soviet aggression against Afghanistan at the UN General Assembly, at the Islamic Conference Organization (OIC) as well as at the non-aligned movement conference. The lengthiest UN sponsored talks at Geneva for a political settlement were ultimately successful on 14 April 1988. The Soviet Union was forced to agree to withdraw its occupation forces, numbering about 115,000 soldiers, from Afghanistan. This was possible because of the unique resistance movement by the Afghan freedom-fighters and due to the consistent and persistent support given by Pakistan to the Afghan freedom-fighters. Pakistan, backed by the United States, China, Saudi Arabia and other Gulf states, played a key role in providing a haven for three million Afghan refugees and in channelling American-Chinese-Saudi aid, including military aid, to the Afghan resistance. At the final stage of the UN-sponsored talks on Afghanistan in Geneva in March–April 1988, Pakistan did not sign the Geneva Accord till all the legitimate demands and aspirations of the people of Afghanistan were met. Pakistan was subject to crude pressure and threats from Moscow to sign the accord by the deadline – 15 March 1988 – but President Zia did not yield to any outside pressure. The present author was in Pakistan when the Geneva Accord was signed between Pakistan and Afghanistan, guaranteed by the two superpowers, the USA and the USSR, under the auspices of the United Nations on 14 April 1988. He had extensive discussions with Zia, and got a vivid and accurate picture of Pakistan's bold and courageous stand at the Geneva peace talks. Pakistan's image in the comity of nations was greatly enhanced by Pakistan's role in the Afghan crisis, culminating in the withdrawal of Soviet threats from Afghanistan. It was indeed a major achievement of the Zia regime.

President Zia had to inherit the unfortunate discord between India and Pakistan. It is most tragic that India and Pakistan have looked upon one another as enemies since their independence, and that relations with each other are charged with an envenomed load of bigotry, prejudice, religious and nationalistic hostility. This is a bitter disappointment, not only to the people of the two countries, but also to their friends and well-wishers all over the world. Instead of the peace and progress expected, the years since independence have brought warfare, vituperation, frustration and fear.[36] Instead of devoting all their resources to economic development, both countries have spent millions of rupees on defence against each other. The sub-continent was split by mutual consent, but the mistrust, antagonism and fear between the two successor states of the British Raj persisted. The brave aims of both countries to uplift their people's pitiably low standard of living have been greatly hampered by their corrosive quarrels and conflicts. There has been a lack of co-operation between these two new Asian countries in political, economic and financial matters; and not only a lack of co-operation, in many instances their policies have tended to aggravate mutual differences. Indeed Asia's ugliest unsolved problem has been the constant bad relations between India and Pakistan. As a foreign scholar has observed: 'The relations between India and Pakistan since the partition of 1947 have been characterised by extreme tensions much of the time, economic blockage on one occasion . . . periodic threats of war, and continuous ideological and political warfare which have produced, to put it mildly, a shambles in the relationship between these two countries.'[37] Bhutto used to talk in terms of a 'thousand years' war' with India, though after coming to power in 1972, Bhutto also tried to normalize relations with India. From the very beginning, President Zia sought to establish tension-free, good-neighbourly and co-operative relations with India in accordance with the UN charter and the principles of peaceful co-existence. Despite difficulties and set-backs, Pakistan perseveres in seeking a reduction in mutual tensions and a normalization of relations with India which are in the interests of peace and security. Zia paid a visit to India in 1982, and held discussions with India's late prime minister, Mrs Indira Gandhi. At this meeting, Pakistan made a proposal for a non-aggression pact between the two countries. India made a counter proposal of peace, friendship and a co-operation pact on the model of India's friendship treaty with the Soviet Union in 1971. Negotiations for the two proposals were, however, postponed by India in July 1984 on the grounds of India's baseless accusations that Pakistan was encouraging the Sikh movement for an independent homeland in East Panjab (India). Zia had two subsequent meetings with India's new prime minister, Rajiv Gandhi. The first meeting was held in New Delhi in November 1984, and the second meeting took place in Moscow in March 1985.

Zia made more than one visit to India; he went to India even to 'witness' a cricket match but the real purpose was to have further discussions with Rajiv Gandhi. Neither Mrs Gandhi nor Rajiv Gandhi had the courtesy to pay any visit to Pakistan; on the contrary, when the final round of UN sponsored talks on Afghanistan were to be held in March–April 1988, Rajiv asked Zia to go to India to discuss the Afghan crisis. This time President Zia gave a snub to Rajiv, and pointed out that there was 'nothing to discuss' with India about the Afghan issue. India and Vietnam are the only two non-aligned countries which did not support UN resolutions demanding the withdrawal of the Soviet troops from Afghanistan, and India supported the Soviet Union at all other international conferences where an overwhelming majority of third world countries as well as the Western countries condemned the Soviet aggression in Afghanistan, and demanded the withdrawal of the Soviet occupation army from Afghanistan. India is never tired of preaching against the so-called 'imperialism' of the Western countries, but whenever the Soviet Union resorts to any military intervention such as in Hungary in 1956 and in Czechoslovakia in 1968, India keeps her high moral principles in cold storage. When the present author asked

Zia about his refusal of Rajiv's invitation to go to Delhi in April 1988, during his interview with President Zia on April 13 1988, Zia's blunt reply was 'enough is enough'. Zia reminded the present author that he had been to Delhi several times; it was high time for Rajiv to return a visit to Pakistan.

India thought that Pakistan was a 'lost case' after the 1971 Indo-Pakistan war over Bangladesh. But Pakistan, under Zia, made remarkable progress in defence capabilities compared with India. The military balance of power in the subcontinent is still greatly in favour of India – India's military strength, thanks to massive Soviet military aid to New Delhi, is much stronger than that of Pakistan. But Pakistan in the 1980s is militarily stronger than ever in its history since 1947. The new security arrangement with the United States, two six-year, 1981–87 and 1988–94, military and economic assistance agreements between the United States and Pakistan, have helped Pakistan greatly in military capabilities. Pakistan also spent a large amount of its resources on a military build-up. The Zia regime has given top priority to the country's problem of defence and security.

Pakistan is also widely reported to have the capabilities of producing atomic bombs, though Pakistan maintains that its nuclear programme is not aimed at producing any atomic bomb. But from reliable sources, it is evident that Pakistan is not far from an ability to produce atomic bombs within a period of months, if not a matter of weeks. India had already exploded its first nuclear device in the mid 1970s. Pakistan cannot afford to allow itself to be blackmailed by India. So Pakistan's nuclear capabilities, regrettable from the standpoint of peace and stability in South Asia, is quite understandable in the context of consistent strained relationships between India and Pakistan. Pakistan is deeply conscious of the fact that international peace and security cannot be achieved and sustained in a world bristling with armaments. A halt to the ever increasing spiral of the arms race, particularly in the sphere of nuclear arms, is essential for world and regional peace and security. To prevent the spread of nuclear weapons in South Asia, Pakistan has offered specific disarmament proposals within the framework of the United Nations. Pakistan has also made several equitable and non-discriminatory proposals in the context of the region, by which Pakistan and India could keep the South Asian area free of nuclear weapons. These include:

1 Simultaneous accession by India and Pakistan to the Nuclear Non-Proliferation Treaty.
2 Simultaneous acceptance by both countries of full-scope International Atomic Energy Agency safeguards.
3 Mutual inspection of each other's nuclear facilities.
4 Joint declaration renouncing the acquisition or development of nuclear weapons.
5 Establishment of a nuclear weapons-free zone in South Asia.

Pakistan is also ready to accept any agreement or consultations, in the regional context or bilaterally, with India, which are aimed at keeping South Asia free of nuclear weapons. India has not responded to any of Pakistan's proposals.

Pakistan recognizes that economic deprivation and increasing poverty are among the basic causes of global instability. In such circumstances the arms race is a cruel contradiction as it consumes precious resources, diverting them from the noble goal of uplifting humanity from hunger and disease. Pakistan therefore recognizes the complementary relationship between disarmament and development. Pakistan fully endorses the view that precious material and human resources should not be squandered in the development of even more destructive weapons.

Pakistan under the third martial law regime has made remarkable progress in socio-economic areas as well as in national security and defence. Pakistan's per capita income today is higher than that of India, though at the time of the partition of India in 1947 Pakistan was less developed than India. Like any other country of the third world, Pakistan is beset with many socio-economic as well as political problems. The ethnic conflict among various racial groups in Pakistan is not yet solved. Ethnic riots and violence take place quite often. There are also allegations of corruption and malpractices. Notwithstanding all the current unresolved problems, Pakistan under Zia is in much better shape than ever before. The success of the third martial law regime has been remarkable.

NOTES

1 Lloyd J Rudolph and Susanne H Rudolph, 'Generals and Politicians in India', *Pacific Affairs*, spring 1964, cited in Talukder Maniruzzaman, *Military Withdrawal from Politics, A comparative study*, Cambridge, Massachusetts, 1987, p. 90.
2 Fazal Muqueem Khan, *The Story of the Pakistan Army*, Karachi, 1963, p. 63.
3 *Dawn*, Karachi, 8 October 1958.
4 Arnold J Toynbee, 'Communism and the West Asian Countries', *The Annals of the American Academy of Political and Social Sciences*, July 1961.

5 Quoted in an unpublished paper by Joseph Lelyveld for the Ford Foundation, New York, 1969.
6 The *Economist*, London, 15 August; for details see chapters 2 and 3 of *The Last Days of United Pakistan*.
7 Z A Bhutto, *The Great Tragedy*, A People's Party Publication, Karachi, 1971.
8 See M Janowitz, *The Military in the Political Development of New Nations*, Chicago, 1964; J J Jabuson (ed.), *The Role of the Military in Underdeveloped Countries*, Princeton, 1962; S E Finer, *The Men on Horseback*, London and New York, 1962; William F Cutteridge, *Military Institutions and Power in New States*, London, 1964.
9 Robert M Price, 'A Theoretical Approach to Military Rule in New States', *World Politics*, April 1972.
10 *Dawn*, Karachi, April 1969.
11 Extracts from the UN Secretary General's Introduction to the *Annual Report on the Work of the U.N. Organization Relating to the Situation in East Bengal*, Bangladesh, 17 September 1971.
12 The *Hindustan Times*, New Delhi, 1 April 1971.
13 Ibid.
14 See the text of Indira Gandhi's speech in Lok Sabha on 27 March 1971 in *Bangladesh Documents*, vol. 1, p. 669, New Delhi, Ministry of External Affairs, Government of India, n.d.
15 Ibid, p. 670.
16 Ibid, p. 672.
17 See the Text of the Laws (Continuance in Force) Order 1977, CMLA order no. 1 of 1977, Islamabad, Printing Corporation of Pakistan Press, 1981, pp. 19–23.
18 See the Text of the Provisional Constitution Order 1981, CMLA order no. 1 of 1981, Islamabad, Printing Corporation of Pakistan Press, 1981, pp. 1–15.
19 Ibid, p. 10.
20 Ibid.
21 See the text of the *Political Parties Act 1962* in *Election Commission of Pakistan: Election laws as modified up to 20th January, 1985*, Islamabad, Election Commission Office, January 1985, pp. 365–374.
22 Ibid, pp. 377–378.
23 For details see *Pakistan, 1986*, Islamabad, Ministry of Information and Broadcasting, Government of Pakistan, September 1986, chapter 8.
24 The *Tide*, special issue, Dhaka, September 1985, p. 52.
25 For details of the process of the Islamization of the financial system in Pakistan, see *Pakistan, 1986*, op. cit., pp. 90–94. See also Dr Justice Tanzil-ur-Rahman, *Islamization in Pakistan*, Council of Islamic Ideology, Government of Pakistan, Islamabad, May 1984, chapter 5.
26 Ibid, pp. 53–54.
27 *Dawn*, Karachi, 17 October 1980.
28 Based on the present author's interviews with the President on various occasions during 1979–1988.
29 Della Denman, 'Pakistan's Best Friend', *Far Eastern Economic Review*, 16 May 1980.
30 For details see Shirin Tahir-Kheli, *The United States and Pakistan: The Evolution of an Influence Relationship*, New York, 1982, chapter 4.
31 Ibid, p. 100.
32 Dilara Choudhury, 'Major Powers' Involvement in South Asia', *BIISS* (Bangladesh Institute of International and Strategic Studies), Journal, vol. 7, 3 November 1986, pp. 327–331.
33 *The United States and Pakistan: The Evolution of an Influence Relationship*, op. cit., p. 105.
34 'Major Powers' Involvement in South Asia', op. cit., pp. 329–330.
35 Richard P Cronim, *The United States, Pakistan and the Soviet Threats to Southern Asia*, Washington, DC, Congressional Research Service, Library of Congress, September 1985, pp. 2–4.
36 Paul Grimes, *New York Times*, 2 December 1962. Cited in G W Choudhury, *Pakistan's Relations with India*, London, 1968.
37 Michael Brecher in Selig Harrison (ed.), *India and the United States*, New York, 1961, p. 53.

Chapter II
Military Withdrawal from Politics in Pakistan

In the preceding chapter, we have described the various socio-economic and religious reforms as well as the steps taken for strengthening national security and defence in Pakistan under Zia's martial law regime and how the country has made remarkable progress under Zia. His greatest achievement, however, is the transition from military rule to a civilian one in Pakistan. A peaceful transfer of power from military rule to an elected representative government in a country like Pakistan, with a long tradition of authoritarian rule, is beset with great difficulties and challenges. Zia's successes in this task is, therefore, the most significant event in the history of contemporary Pakistan.

In the late 1950s, 1960s and early 1970s, military involvement in politics in the countries of the third world had become so commonplace that news of a military coup became increasingly less and less of a shock. But in the 1980s, the failure of military juntas in various Latin American countries led social scientists to examine the causes of the transition from military to civilian rule in the third world. Just as there is no single explanation for the rise of military rule, similarly we cannot offer any single interpretation of the transition from military rule to a civilian one as happened in Pakistan in 1985.

There are a number of factors involved when the ruling military junta decides to transfer power to an elected or to an ad hoc civilian authority: the transition may be partial in the form of civil military partnership or it may be genuine, when the real decision-making process is transferred to a duly elected civilian authority. Sometimes the military withdrawal is temporary or for some specific political needs. Sometimes the withdrawal is likely to be of longer duration. The pressure for military withdrawal may come from external and internal factors.

President Zia-ul-Haq of Pakistan is a dedicated professional soldier and seemed to have no special hunger for political power. The 1977 political crisis in Pakistan left the Pakistan army under him no choice but to intervene politically to save the country from a near civil war situation. There is almost a consensus that the 1977 political crisis in Pakistan forced Zia to intervene militarily.

What led President Zia to start a process of military disengagement in Pakistan? Were there any powerful internal or external pressures to make Zia move toward transition from military rule to a civilian one? The present author has had several long meetings with President Zia over the years – 1977 to 1987 – and had opportunities of discussing his plan for the ultimate withdrawal of the military from politics in Pakistan. In his first major speech on 12 August 1983 on his future plan for the transfer of power from the military to civilian authority, Zia claims that he formulated his plan for the restoration of democracy in Pakistan without any motive or pressure, and that it 'would be' a peaceful transition to what he terms an 'Islamic democracy in Pakistan'.[1] In another major speech to the Pakistan parliament on 17 October 1985 when the Pakistan constitution took its present shape and form by passing the 8th amendment bill, Zia claimed that he had implemented the plan for the transition from military rule to a civilian one 'under the umbrella of martial law . . . and got the honour of bringing back democracy to the country in an atmosphere of peace and through a gradual process . . . we have done this to bring an elected government into power. We have done all this so that the country instead of traversing the zigzag of martial law should travel on the high road of democracy.'[2]

Zia's Progress towards Restoration of Democracy

The first step towards some form of elected civilian institutions was taken in 1979 when elected local government institutions were revived after a long period of suspension. A fully representative local government was established in 1979 through elections on the basis of adult franchise. President Zia gives top priority to local government institutions in the country. Since Zia came to power in 1977, three elections to local bodies were held on a non-party basis – in 1979, 1983 and 1987. These elections were free and fair. There was no allegation of governmental interferences or rigging of the elections. The local government institutions in Pakistan, as in many of the 'new democracies' of Afro-Asian countries, are of considerable importance, and very useful in educating the general mass of the people in the art of managing their own affairs by co-ordinated effort. A strong and sound system of local self-government institutions helps greatly in providing an infrastructure of democracy. Lord Bryce, in his classic work, *Modern Democracies*, gave serious thought to the relation between successful democracy and the existence of a sound system of local self-government institutions. In a country like Pakistan, where the majority of people are illiterate and live in rural areas, the importance of local government institutions can hardly be exaggerated.

We shall give a resumé of the system and the functioning of local government institutions in Pakistan.

The representative local government system in Pakistan has been effected in accordance with the principle of policy laid down in article 32 of the 1973 constitution. It comprises 4,270 union councils, 93 district/agency councils, 298 town committees, 129 municipal committees, 13 metropolitan/municipal corporations and 39 cantonment boards. Out of the 77,107 local councillors, 68,778, i.e. 89.2 percent, belong to rural councils and 8,329 to urban councils.

There are nine local government laws for the different administrative units of the country:

1 The Panjab Local Government Ordinance 1979
2 The Sind Local Government Ordinance 1979
3 The NWFP Local Government Ordinance 1979
4 The Baluchistan Local Government Ordinance 1979
5 The Capital Territory Local Government Ordinance 1979
6 The Northern Areas Local Government Order 1979
7 The Azad Jammu and Kashmir Local Government Ordinance 1979
8 The Federally Administered Tribal Areas Local Government Regulation 1979
9 Cantonments Act 1924

Although each administrative unit has a local government law, there is a great deal of similarity in the structure and functions of local governments in different parts of the country. The following tiers of local government institutions exist in Pakistan:

Rural Areas:
Union Councils: For such, the number of members are determined on the basis of population of 1,000 per electoral unit.

Zila/District Councils: For each district, there is a zila/district council comprising such number of members as may be determined on the basis of population.

Urban Areas:

Town Committees: A town committee as a whole may represent a population of 5,000–30,000.

Municipal Committees: As the range of population of a municipal committee is wide, its membership also varies very much depending on population.

Municipal Corporations: Constituted in large cities. There are eleven municipal corporations in Pakistan.

Metropolitan Corporations: In the cities of Karachi and Lahore, metropolitan corporations have been constituted.

To ensure special representation for peasants, workers, women and minorities on various tiers of local government as required under the constitution of the Islamic Republic of Pakistan, provisions have been made in local government laws.

DELEGATION OF POWERS

The local councillors have been assigned a wide role, and been delegated a reasonable measure of authority in the fields of agriculture, communications, education, food, health, housing, industry, irrigation, law and order, manpower and social welfare.

In order to settle petty disputes arising locally, the councillors have been entrusted with powers of conciliation and arbitration in certain civil, criminal and family matters. In the province of Sind a panchayat system has been constituted. Panchayats are working in every electoral local unit (where the head is an elected councillor and its two other members are nominated by the local council concerned). There are at present 8,460 panchayats in Sind.

The chairmen of union and urban councils act as chairmen of arbitration councils under the Muslim Family Laws Ordinance 1961, which regulate procedure relating to marriage, divorce and maintenance of separated wives. Similarly, the chairmen of town committees, union councils and ward members of municipal committees and metropolitan corporations act as chairmen of the conciliation courts in order to settle petty criminal and civil disputes at the local level.

In order to maintain law and order at the local level in Sind province, the councillors who have passed the matriculation examination or possess equivalent qualifications have been appointed as justices of the peace, and are authorised to attest documents. The chairmen of local councils are ex-officio members of sub-divisional crime control committees. The justices of the peace have also been appointed from among local councillors in the Panjab and North West Frontier Province.

LOCAL FINANCES

The finances of rural and urban local councils are derived from taxes, remunerative projects, block or specific grants by the federal and the provincial governments and loans.

The rural local councils can levy taxes like hearth tax, property tax, tax on transfer of immovable property, professional tax, marriage tax, birth tax, advertisement tax, cattle tax, toll tax, licence fees, market fees, building construction fees, tax on fairs and exhibitions, sports tax, surcharge on any tax, cinema tax, water rate, drainage rate on facilities like electricity, and local rate.

The urban local councils can levy taxes like property tax, parking fees, schools fees, toll tax, octroi tax, fees on agricultural and industrial exhibitions, fees on the sale of cattle, advertisement tax, market fees, professional tax, water rate, vehicles tax, birth tax, fees on licences and permits, etc.

The income of all local government institutions during the year 1978–79 was Rs.1657 million and increased to Rs.5802 million during 1985–86.

All the provincial governments maintain institutions for the training of local councillors and the staff of local councils. In addition, the National Centre for Rural Development, Islamabad, and the Municipal Training and Research Institute, Karachi, have been established for the training of elected councillors and employees of local councils.

Four universities have been involved in local government training. Diploma courses in local government have been started in these universities.

President Zia's next move towards the civilianization of his military regime was taken on 24 December 1981. When he set up a nominated Majlis-e-Shoora (federal council) 'to aid and advise the Government', under article 4 of the Provisional Constitution Order

1981, there was a provision that 'there shall be a Federal Council/ Majlis-e-Shoora consisting of such persons as the President, may, by order, determine . . . and that the Federal Council shall perform such functions as may be specified in an order made by the President.'[3] In accordance with the provisions of the said Provisional Constitution Order 1981, President Zia issued an order – president's order no. 15 of 1981 – to set up the federal council. The federal council, known as the Majlis-e-Shoora, consisting of 350 nominated members, was established in early 1982. The federal ministers and ministers of state were ex-officio members of this consultative body. Subsequently, provincial councils were also established in the four provinces. These councils, both federal and provincial, continued to function till 1985, when elected national and provincial assemblies came into existence as a result of the first elections held under Zia's martial law.

In the absence of elected national and provincial assemblies, the consultative councils performed some useful functions in making a military regime understand public issues and problems as well as be responsible to public demands and aspirations. Zia gave the federal council significant importance. The members of his cabinet had to attend the sessions of the federal council, and the members of the council could ask any questions of the ministers. The role of a legislature in a modern democratic state is to extract information and to ventilate public grievances by exposing the ministers to parliamentary questions and answers.

Judged by that criteria, Zia's nominated legislature's performances were of some significance and importance. The council could consider and discuss, subject to such rules as might have been framed for the purpose, any matter specified in the legislative list (federal legislative list of the 1973 constitution), and recommend to the president the enactment of a law or the amendment of an existing law relating to that matter. The council was authorized to discuss the five-year development plan and make recommendations relating to it. It could also discuss the annual budget, after it was announced by the federal government, but the annual budget was not submitted to the council for approval or disapproval.[4] It could only discuss the budget and recommend any charges which were not binding on the government. But in practice, the council had impacts on the final formulation of the budget. The councils, both federal and provincial, were, no doubt, consultative and nominated bodies. They had no power of passing any law or to pass any vote of confidence or no confidence, for and against the cabinet. Yet the cabinet was asked to take into account seriously any suggestions or recommendations of consultative bodies.[5] The federal council set up a special committee to recommend 'the Form and System of Government in Pakistan from an Islamic point of view'. When Zia was engaged in formulating the various amendments to the 1973 constitution, the report of the federal council known as the Fida Commission Report was given due importance.

While President Zia was taking gradual steps, in an evolutionary manner, for the restoration of democracy in Pakistan, some of the opposition parties were engaged in political agitation for immediate restoration of democracy and for the ending of martial law. But the anti-Zia movement was neither effective nor well organized. The opposition parties were divided, though several parties formed an alliance for the movement for restoration of democracy (MRD). None of these parties had any genuine or wide support for their objectives. Bhutto's political party, the Pakistan People's Party (PPP), was the only strong opposition party, but its new leader, Benazir Bhutto, was not in a position to carry a successful or effective anti-Zia movement. She is a Western-educated young lady. In a conservative society like Pakistan's, people were not prepared to accept a Western-educated young lady as the head of an Islamic state. Moreover, the people of Pakistan are deeply religious. They greatly appreciate Zia's process of Islamization of the country. Zia himself is also a devoted Muslim. His process of Islamization – *Nifaz-i-Nizam-i-Islam* – is highly popular among the people. Zia, unlike his predecessors, not only talks about Islam but he is a practising Muslim. There is no gap between his profession and actual practice of Islam. In the past, Islam was exploited by politicians for the sake of remaining in power. Zia may be described as the first head of the state in Pakistan who not only preaches Islam, but also consciously practises it. His integrity, honesty, and uncorruptness are appreciated by the people of Pakistan who were tired of unscrupulous, corrupt, and dishonest politicians. So the anti-Zia movement was never a serious threat.

Similarly, there was no serious external pressure on Zia to restore democracy in Pakistan. Pakistan's single largest donor and supplier of military equipment, the United States, no doubt expressed the pious wish that the martial law should be lifted and representative civilian government should be restored. There were such voices in the US Congress occasionally. But the United States, as a result of the Afghan crisis, could hardly afford to lose Zia's friendship and co-operation. It was only during the Carter administration that the US government was not happy with the continued martial law regime in Pakistan. But Carter's main allegation against Pakistan, as stated in the previous chapter, was related to Pakistan's alleged nuclear capabilities to produce an 'Islamic atom bomb'.

So, Zia's plan for the peaceful transition from military to civilian rule was not due to any serious internal or external pressures. More important, Zia enjoys the full confidence of the Pakistani army. In the political dynamics of Pakistan, the army's role and support are vital for any political regime. Zia's claim that his plan for transfer of power to an elected civilian government was voluntary and not under any pressure, internal and external, is largely correct, and on 14 August (Independence Day) 1982 Zia announced that by the next Independence Day 1983 he would give to the nation a positive outline of an Islamic democratic system to be introduced in Pakistan.

Political Plan Announced

Addressing the 7th session of the Majlis-e-Shoora (the federal council) on 12 August 1983, President Zia announced his much awaited 'political plan' for the peaceful transition from military to civilian rule. He described his plan as a positive outline of a real Islamic state and the Islamic system of working.[6] Zia disclosed that his political plan for transfer of power to an elected civilian government had been widely and extensively discussed in political circles, various forums, newspaper columns and other institutions, both within and outside the country. Zia said, 'We studied all these views, took stock of them, and our endeavour to the best of our ability was to present to the nation a definite appropriate and realistic plan and programme.'[7] Zia narrated the process of formulating his political plan; he asked the council of Islamic ideology to make recommendations on the shape of the future government; he also set up a sub-committee of his cabinet to study the constitutional issues and to make recommendations. A special committee of the Majlis-e-Shoora was also set up for the same purpose. Finally, a special commission headed by a highly reputed scholar on Islam, Maulana Zafar Ahmad Ansari, was constituted to make recommendations for an 'Islamic democratic' system in Pakistan. Zia and his top advisers were engaged for months together examining and analysing the reports and recommendations of these commissions and committees. In the light of this extensive research and study, the political plan, as announced by President Zia on 12 August 1983, was given final form. Before he presented his political plan, Zia gave a lengthy background of the demand for an Islamic state in Pakistan. He quoted extensively from the speeches and comments of the founder of Pakistan, Quaid-e-Azam Muhammad Ali Jinnah, trying to prove that Jinnah was firmly committed to establishing an Islamic state when the Muslims of the Indian subcontinent were fighting for a separate state of their own. Similarly, Zia referred to the views of other leaders of the movement for Pakistan in the 1940s in favour of an Islamic state. There is, however, controversy about Jinnah's concept of an Islamic state for Pakistan. We shall examine it while we discuss the relationship between state and religion in Pakistan.

President Zia also extensively referred to the teaching and injunctions of the Muslims' Holy Book, the Quran, and the sayings of the Holy Prophet relating to the form of government in Islam. Finally, Zia gave his own concept of an Islamic state based on the verses of the Quran and the sayings of the Holy Prophet – all these issues relating to the concept of an Islamic state will be discussed in our two subsequent chapters.

Turning to Zia's political plan, he put forth the constitutional issues raised by the people, by various organizations and by the various committees set up for the purpose. The following constitutional problems and issues were involved:

1 Should the form of government be presidential or parliamentary?
2 Should the form of government be federal or unitary?
3 Should the 1973 constitution be restored as it is or after appropriate amendments? Or should it be abrogated and an altogether new constitution framed?
4 Is it necessary or not to hold a referendum to seek the endorsement of the people for the policies of the government?
5 What should be the respective powers of the president and the prime minister, and how should a balance be brought about between them?
6 What should be the constitutional role of the armed forces?
7 Should the present provinces be allowed to stay as they are or should new provinces be demarcated on the basis of the civil administrative divisions?
8 What is the role of political parties in an Islamic polity?
9 Should the next elections be held on a party basis or non-party basis?

10 What should be the mode of elections? Should there be proportional representation or elections by majority vote, separate or joint electorate?
11 From the Islamic standpoint, what should be the attributes or the qualifications of the candidates?
12 Is there a need or not for a change in the right of adult suffrage?
13 Will the local bodies be used as an electoral college or not?
14 What is the role of women in an Islamic polity?
15 What are the rights of the minorities in such a system, and how will their protection be guaranteed?[8]

Then Zia gave a resumé of the achievements of his martial law regime during the previous six years (1977–83):

> The performance of the development sector has been extra-ordinary during this period. A silent revolution has set in in the less-developed regions of the country. Hundreds of thousands of households have been illumined with bulbs powered by electricity. A network of roads spread over hundreds of miles has been constructed. Thousands of new schools have been opened, and old schools have been upgraded, and their accommodations improved. In the rural areas many health centres have been set up for mother care. There is hardly any walk of life where a beginning has not been made for its progress and reconstruction. The most important change that has taken place during this period of six years is that the Qibla (orientation of the people) has been set right. The process of the march towards an Islamic way of life which had been deliberately neglected some time back is now once again in evidence. People no longer feel ashamed of identifying themselves as Muslims and Pakistanis. They take pride in praying to God Almighty, and mosques now overflow with devotees. Now religious scholars, divines and thinkers of Islam are accorded a respect in our society.[9]

As regards the form of government, whether it should be of a presidential or parliamentary type, Zia again quoted Jinnah's views on it, and left no doubt that Zia himself was in favour of a presidential system, but he acknowledged that the majority of the people in Pakistan preferred the parliamentary system. So he gracefully accepted the majority view, but he was of the opinion that the parliamentary system, as provided in the 1973 constitution giving rise to dictatorial powers for the prime minister, must be abolished. A proper and pragmatic balance of powers between the president and the prime minister should be worked out. Zia then went on to point out three alternatives before the nation relating to the future constitution of Pakistan:

1 To restore the 1973 constitution as it was.
2 To abrogate the 1973 constitution, and to frame a new constitution and seek its endorsement by the people through a referendum.
3 To promulgate the 1973 constitution with necessary amendments.

Zia pointed out the defects of the first and second alternatives. If the original 1973 constitution without any amendments were adopted, the country, according to Zia, would face again a crisis as happened in July 1977. There was no adequate provision in the 1973 constitution to protect the country from any such catastrophe. The second alternative also carried a grave risk. As we have stated in our 'Introduction', constitution-making in Pakistan was a highly complicated process, and it took a long time to frame a constitution in Pakistan – it took nine years for two constituent assemblies to frame Pakistan's first constitution (1956). Zia was right in not allowing the country to plunge into a situation of uncertainty and to throw Pakistan's constitutional life back into the same position that obtained at the time of its creation in 1947.

So, after careful thought and considered views and opinions, Zia opted for the third alternative – to promulgate the 1973 constitution with necessary amendments. His amendments were announced in the revival of the constitution of 1973 order, 1985 – president order No. 14 of 1985. Zia made the following decisions for the restoration of democracy in Pakistan:

1 The constitution be restored but a balance be brought about between the powers of the president and prime minister, and the constitution harmonized with Islamic principles. In adopting these amendments due consideration will be given, apart from other proposals, to the opinion of the members of the Majlis-e-Shoora and the recommendations of the Ansari Commission.
2 There has been a lot of controversy with regard to the role of the armed forces. I would like to end this controversy too. The armed forces will have no new constitutional role. The recent accepted position in this matter will be maintained.

3 Elections will be held on the basis of adult suffrage.

4 The prime minister will be appointed by the president. But the person appointed must in the president's view command majority support in the national assembly. The prime minister, within two months of assumption of office, will be required to obtain a vote of confidence from the national assembly.

5 When the president feels that a need has arisen for seeking a fresh mandate of the electorate, he can dissolve the national assembly. But in such an event fresh elections will have to be held within 75 days.

6 The president will have the powers to return for reconsideration to the assembly and the house a bill which has already been passed.

7 The president will be the supreme commander of the armed forces. He will appoint the chairman of the joint chiefs of staff committee and the chiefs of staff of the three armed services and determine the terms and conditions of their appointments.

8 The appointment of the chief election commissioner and members of the commission will also be made by the president in consultation with the chief justice of Pakistan.

9 The provincial governors will also be appointed by the president.

10 Additionally, a national security council will be established. The government of the day will not be able to declare an emergency without the advice of the council. The composition and duties of the national security council will be announced later.

11 In order to improve the economic conditions of the country the private sector will be encouraged and protected.

In our order of priorities it would be our endeavour that the sixth five-year plan be properly executed. We attach great importance to this plan.[10]

Finally, in his political plan, Zia outlined an 18-month long programme for holding elections to representative institutions. Zia acknowledged that in the present-day world there is no alternative to elections. So elections must be held to restore democracy on an adult franchise. The elections would be held in two stages. In the first stage, elections for local bodies would be held – which were held in

1983. Zia attaches great importance to the role of local bodies. The 1983 elections to the local bodies were held on a non-party basis as was the case in the 1979 elections to local bodies. The character of local councils is fully democratic as all the councils are elected through adult franchise for a period of four years. The sections of population like peasants, workers, women and religious minorities not likely to get adequate representation due to various cultural and economic factors were provided with special representation in various fields of local government. The strength of membership of a local body is determined on the basis of the population of the respective areas.

As a result of the 1983 elections, 71,767 members were elected in 4,100 union councils, 84 district/agencies, 129 municipal corporations/committees, 285 town committees, and 39 cantonment boards. These included seats of 3,929 peasants, 472 workers, 7,539 women and 3,472 minorities.[11]

In the second stage, elections to the provincial and national assemblies and the senate would be held. In his 'political plan' Zia expressed the hope that elections to the legislatures would be completed by 23 March 1985. So his plan had 18 months intervening between 12 August 1983 and March 1985. Zia confirmed that when these stage-wise elections were over and the democratic process restored, martial law would automatically be lifted. One crucial missing link in Zia's 'political plan' as announced on 12 August 1983 was how the president of the country would be elected. This was elaborated in a subsequent order in December 1984. Some of Zia's critics and opposition political parties considered Zia's 18-month period was too long for the restoration of democracy, and it was alleged to be one of Zia's devices to prolong his martial law regime.[12] Zia justified his 18-month period for transfer of power on the ground that he would ensure 'a peaceful, orderly and smooth transfer of power so that the country is not deprived of the continuity that it needs.'[13] Zia also gave a stern warning to those elements who might try to subvert his 18-month long plan for the transfer of power. The whole process of transition from military to civilian rule would be done under the protection of martial law and no breaches of law and order would be tolerated. According to some foreign media there were arrests of political leaders who were organizing a civil disobedience movement. The movement, however, was not successful except in the province of Sind. In Sind, the movement was not for the immediate restoration of democracy; it turned into a form of secession movement and Pakistan alleged that it was encouraged and helped by India as she did during the movement for Bangladesh in 1971. As the movement in Sind was not only against Zia's military rule but also against the unity and territorial integrity of the country, the Sindi movement failed to get any support or sympathy from any other parts of the country, especially from Panjab which is the heart of power in Pakistan. The secession movement in Sind met its national death in due course, and it could not affect Zia's 'political plan'.

The Referendum, 1984

As already pointed out, an important missing point in Zia's 'political plan' of 12 August 1983 was the absence of any procedure to elect the president of the country. Zia fulfilled that missing link by the referendum order, 1984.

The main objective of the referendum was to seek a mandate from the people for Zia's various steps, already taken during the martial law period since 1977, towards the process of Islamization in Pakistan, and whether the process should be finalized under Zia's leadership. Zia felt that 'it is necessary that the ideology of Pakistan be preserved and the process [of Islamization] be completed in accordance with the will of the people'.[14] So in pursuance of the Provisional Constitution Order 1981, President Zia took steps to hold a referendum and the question referred to the referendum was 'whether the people of Pakistan endorse the process initiated by General Mohammad Zia-ul-Haq, the President of Pakistan for bringing the laws of Pakistan in conformity with the injunctions as laid down in the Holy Quran and Sunnah of the Holy Prophet (peace be on him), and for the preservation of the ideology of Pakistan, for the continuation and consolidation of that process and for the smooth and orderly transfer of power to the elected representatives of the people.'[15] The question was answered either by 'yes' or 'no'. The referendum was held on 19 December 1984.

If a majority of the votes cast in the referendum was in favour of the answer 'yes', the people of Pakistan would be deemed to have endorsed all steps taken by the president of Pakistan for bringing the laws of Pakistan into conformity with the injunctions of Islam – and for the preservation of the ideology of Pakistan, and for the continuation and consolidation of the process of Islamization, and the smooth and orderly transfer of power to the elected representatives of the people; General Mohammad Zia-ul-Haq would be deemed to have been elected president of Pakistan for a term of five years from the day of the first meeting of the houses of parliament in a first sitting.[16]

According to figures announced by the election commission which conducted the referendum, in an electorate of 33,992,425 those who cast votes in favour of the proposition were 21,253,757. The negative votes were only 316,918, giving a 97.7 per cent affirmative vote. As a consequence of the results of the referendum, Zia was elected as the president of Pakistan for five years (1985–90).

The official results giving Zia 97.7 per cent of the vote with almost 62 per cent of Pakistan's qualified electorate of 34 million casting their ballots were challenged by opposition political leaders and in some of the foreign media. Zia pointed out that polling patterns varied considerably with some polling stations registering less than 20 per cent and others, particularly rural Panjab, the largest and most populous province, with as many as 80 per cent of the voters showing up. The opposition parties had called for boycotting the referendum but as a Pakistan newspaper, *Wifaq*, pointed out, if the opposition boycott had succeeded there would have been riots in the streets. No one can get away with announcing fictional election results in Pakistan.[17] Apprehending such allegations, Zia had undertaken the precaution of going on a whirlwind tour of the country addressing large, cheering crowds to prove that he had genuine support. Zia enjoyed wide popularity among the rural population because of his zeal for Islamization and rural development schemes. Another Pakistani (left wing) paper, *The Daily Muslim*, said that Zia's support came from those groups who opposed Bhutto's regime during the 1977 political crisis. They included industrialists, landowners, religious leaders, and rightist political parties like Jamaat-e-Islam. Zia also got support from the Pakistan Muslim League led by *Pir* (spiritual leader) Pagara.[18] The results of the referendum made Zia's bargaining position stronger for making deals with political parties except, of course, Bhutto's Pakistan People's Party (PPP) and the opposition coalition the Movement for the Restoration of Democracy (MRD). They continued to oppose Zia's military rule and his political plan for the transfer of power from the military to a civilian regime.

President Zia termed his 'political plan' of 12 August 1983 as the 'manifesto of his government' during the interim period till the elected civilian governments, both federal and provincial, were installed in March 1985. Under his manifesto, Zia planned to take steps towards the following priorities, saying:

1 On top of the list is the task to carry forward the process of Islamization, and to consolidate the measures already taken in this behalf to a degree that no future government can reverse them.

2 To improve the economy of the country and to rid it of the evil of usury.

3 To improve the law and order situation, to protect the life and property of the people, and to preserve the sanctity of the Chadar and Char-Deewari (the honour of women and the safety and sanctity of the household).

4 To purge society of maladministration and corruption.

5 Among the vital obligations of the government is to ensure that the dispensation of justice to the people is both inexpensive and easy, because Islam lays great stress on the prevention of tyranny and injustice and the provision of justice. In this behalf, some steps have already been taken. More Islamic laws, now under consideration, will be enforced and to that end I will be making a brief announcement on 14 August 1983, *Insha Allah*.

6 To associate more and more people in the affairs of the state; the Majlis-e-Shoora will, by the grace of God, remain intact for this purpose.

7 To make the education system fully conform to Islamic values and to wipe out illiteracy from the country; to that end, education based on Islamic values will be widely promoted; *maktab* schools will be opened to spread elementary education; full attention will be devoted to the promotion of adult education and the education of women, and measures will be taken to promote technical and scientific education.

8 To accelerate the pace of development programmes so that the maximum possible area may be provided with the amenities of the modern age in the minimum possible time.

9 To develop Pakistan into a real Islamic welfare state, where the poor, the indigent, the orphans and the widows are taken care of, the needy have their needs fulfilled, grievances of petitioners are promptly attended to, and a maximum number of people are provided with the maximum of facilities and amenities.[19]

The General Elections

The final step towards restoration of democracy was to hold a general election. In an address to the nation on 12 January 1985, the president announced that general elections in the country would be held on an adult franchise, one-man-one-vote basis in February 1985. In his lengthy address, Zia not only gave the dates of the general elections but also gave the objectives of the proposed elections, the ways in which elections would be held; composition of legislatures, both federal and provincial; qualifications and disqualifications for those seeking membership of the legislature and the 'general rules' governing the election campaign. In fact, it was almost a document on the proposed general elections. At the very beginning, Zia stressed the fact that the coming elections are being held in order to establish an Islamic system of government and an Islamic political system . . . 'The cardinal principles of the Islamic order is to ensure the maximum welfare of the people – an order where the principal objective is socio-economic equality and a just administrative structure.'[20]

In accordance with his objectives for the proposed elections, Zia then gave the following guidelines relating to the conduct of elections:

1 The general elections will be held on a non-party basis and on an adult suffrage basis. I repeat the elections will be on a non-party basis but there will be adult suffrage, God willing.
2 The system of a separate electorate will be followed for Muslim and non-Muslim representatives.
3 The national and provincial assemblies to be formed as a result of these elections will enjoy full powers in all respects within their respective frameworks.
4 Elections to the national and provincial assemblies will be conducted under the supervision of the Pakistan election commission in accordance with recognized procedures.
5 The armed forces will assist the civil administration in the maintenance of law and order during the elections.
6 The coming elections will be held in a free, impartial and fair manner. This is our resolve and we have taken measures to ensure that.
7 All candidates contesting the elections will be equal in the eyes

of the government. The government, *Insha Allah*, will remain totally neutral.

8 In deference to Islamic values, some changes have been effected in the procedure for nomination and nomination papers, some of the important ingredients of which are as follows:

   a Registration of nomination papers has been simplified.

   b Nomination for the national or provincial assembly of an eligible candidate from his constituency must be done by at least fifty voters of that constituency whose names are on the voters' list. The nominated candidate, while accepting the nomination, will declare under oath that he believes in the Pakistan ideology.[21]

President Zia made some changes in the constitution of the national assembly and the provincial assemblies, as well as of the senate. The changes were as follows:

NATIONAL ASSEMBLY

a The present strength of seven seats from Baluchistan in the national assembly has been increased by four to raise the total to eleven.

b The representation of Sind in the national assembly has been increased by three seats, out of which two have gone to Karachi and one to Sukkur.

c The number of reserved seats for women in the national assembly has been increased by one hundred per cent. In other words, the strength has been increased from ten at present to twenty.

d The number of reserved seats for minorities in the national assembly has, likewise, been increased and distributed thus:

For our Christian brothers	4 seats
For our Hindu brothers	4 seats
Quadianis, who also call themselves Ahmadees	1 seat
Other minorities, i.e. Parsis, Buddhists, Sikhs, non-Muslims and those belonging to scheduled castes	1 seat

In this way the total number of seats in the national assembly will be 237.

SENATE

At present the number of members of the senate stands at 63 as follows:

Seats at the rate of 14 seats for each province	56
Seats for the federally administered tribal areas	5
Seats for the federal area of Islamabad	2
Total:	63

Twenty seats have been added to these seats to be equally distributed among the four provinces. These additional seats will be reserved in each province for the ulema, technocrats and professionals.

PROVINCIAL ASSEMBLIES

Seats reserved for women and minorities have also been increased in the provincial assemblies. The seats reserved for women have been increased from ten to twenty, whereas under the separate electorate system minorities will contest for 23 seats instead of 15.[22]

Significantly, Zia gave a long list of qualifications and disqualifications for those seeking membership of legislatures. There were such qualifications and disqualifications in the previous order and act – The House of Parliament and Provincial (Election) Order 1977 and Political Parties Act 1962. Zia elaborated them as follows:

1 A candidate for the national or provincial assembly should be a practising Muslim, and he should not have a reputation of deviating from the injunctions of Islam.
2 He must be adequately conversant with Islamic teachings. He should be a dutiful person, who abstains from major sins.
3 He should not have been convicted of any moral crime or perjury.
4 He should not have opposed national solidarity or the ideology of Pakistan subsequent to the establishment of Pakistan.

   However, non-Muslim members are exempt from the first two conditions laid down above, but it will be imperative for them to have a good reputation in respect of their moral character and conduct.
5 Those who have been penalized after having been found guilty of crimes like smuggling, hoarding, profiteering, bribery or

adulteration of their merchandise will also stand disqualified for these elections even though the prison terms of their sentence may be only six months or even less.

6 For a candidate it is an essential condition that he be sane.

7 That he be upright and virtuous and not be morally depraved.

8 That he be honest and trustworthy.

Some amendments have also been made in the Political Parties Act 1962 governing the eligibility or ineligibility of candidates. According to article 8 of the amended act those who had previously been disqualified for five years will now have their period of disqualification extended up to 12 years. And through another amendment in the same article all such persons stand disqualified for a period of seven years as may have served, subsequent to 1 December 1971, as office-bearers or executive committee members at the provincial or federal level of any political party which did not get itself registered with the election commission by 11 October 1979. Also disqualified for seven years are those who may have served between 1 December 1971 and 5 July 1977 as federal or provincial ministers, ministers of state or advisors, save those who may be or may have been members of the federal council, i.e. Majlis-e-Shoora, or those who may be or may have been members of the federal cabinet or members of the provincial councils or provincial cabinets. Aside from this the president will have the power to exempt any ineligible from ineligibility on a *suo moto* basis or on receipt of a petition to that effect from such a person.[23]

Finally, Zia gave some ground rules governing the election campaign. They were as follows:

1 There will be a total ban on political processions.

2 Political meetings in the open will be prohibited.

3 Door to door canvassing for purposes of electioneering will be allowed.

4 Printing of posters and placing of advertisements will also be allowed.

5 Political meetings indoors or within the four walls of a premises will be allowed.

6 The use of loud-speakers for any public meeting, public gathering or for canvassing will not be permitted.[24]

Elections to the national assemblies were held on 25 February 1985 and to the provincial assemblies on 28 February. The percentage of votes cast in national assembly elections came to 52.93 per cent and in the provincial assemblies 56.82 per cent.

Pakistani voters in large numbers rejected an opposition call for a boycott of the national assembly elections, but at the same time rejected five of President Zia's cabinet ministers and several others associated with his martial law regime. Zia himself had carefully prepared his position for this eventuality by saying in advance that he would not see a vote against his ministers as a vote against his government. He said at a press conference on 24 February 1985 that 'ministers are running as individuals and, though I pray for them, if any of them loses it will be a reflection of the government's impartiality and fairness.'[25] This was a point taken up by Western diplomatic observers after the vote was counted. One of the Western diplomats in Islamabad, while commenting on the results of the election, said, 'People voted and their votes were counted fairly. Whatever his failures in other respects, Zia certainly proved that his elections were no fraud and that Pakistan is prepared to give his transition plans for democracy a chance.'[26]

Zia had said before the voting that he would consider a 40 per cent poll a success against the opposition boycott. The good voter turn out as reported by the election commission was corroborated by independent observers, diplomats and foreign journalists; 'Credible elections', observed a Western diplomat in Islamabad, 'have certainly paved the way for liberalization and a return to democracy.'[27] Most observers agreed that the failure of the opposition to successfully boycott the polls, coupled with the possibility of a new parliamentary opposition, might lead to the collapse of the established opposition leadership. A more widely held view was that the military leadership also would have to be more flexible in dealing with the representatives elected under its own grand rules.[28]

The senate was elected by the elected provincial assemblies in March 1985. The first session of the national assembly was held on 20 March 1985.

After the results of the general elections were announced, President Zia began his crucial moves to form elected civilian governments both at the federal and provincial levels. As already stated, the elections were held on a non-party basis and the process of selecting a prime minister and provincial chief ministers, who had to have the confidence of federal and provincial legislatures respectively, was highly complicated in the absence of a party system. How to determine who had the support of the majorities in federal and provincial legislatures? Zia also had to revive the 1973 constitution, of course, with the amendments he had made under his authority as the chief martial law administrator (CMLA) and as the president under the martial law regime, before the installation of the civilian government at the federal and provincial levels. The hard task of quiet diplomacy began. Members of the assemblies who were elected on a non-party basis tried to form loose groupings to fill the vacuum left by the ban on political party activity. Zia personally met most of the elected members, either individually or in groups. Similarly, the provincial governors met the elected members of four provincial assemblies.

It appeared from all available indications that many of Zia's amendments to the 1973 constitution as announced in 'the Revival of the Constitution of 1973 order 1985' (president's order no. 14 of 1985) were not liked by the elected members of the national assembly. There was no disagreement over the new and additional articles to the 1973 constitution dealing with the strengthening of the Islamic character of the constitution, but there was resentment and disapproval over the increased powers of the president under Zia's amendments as well as against any indirect role of the army in the political system by the provision of the setting up of a national 'security council' in which the chiefs of staff of the three armed services (army, navy and air force) would be members. Though elected on a non-party basis, the members of the national assembly were eager to avoid any undue concentration of powers of the president who was still the CMLA, and to prevent the parliament from turning into a 'rubber-stamp parliament.'[29]

President Zia's amendments to the 1973 constitution were spelled out formally in his 'Revival of the Constitution of 1973 order 1985' issued on 17 March 1985, just three days before the first session of the national assembly on 20 March 1985. The main amendments brought by Zia related to the balance of powers between the president and the prime minister. We have already referred to Zia's comments on the powers and role of the president; he described the position of the president as 'ludicrous, meaningless and downright comic.'[30] So it was obvious that Zia would like to see the powers and role of the president enhanced. Similarly, Zia also wanted to give some form of indirect role to the armed forces in his amended 1973 constitution by incorporating a new article – 152A – which provided:

1 There shall be a national security council to make recommendations relating to the issue of a proclamation of emergency under article 232, the security of Pakistan and any other matter of national importance that may be referred to it by the president in consultation with the prime minister.

2 The national security council shall consist of the president, the prime minister, the chairman of the senate, chairman, joint chiefs of staff committee, the chiefs of staff of the Pakistan navy and the Pakistan air force and the chief ministers of the four provinces.[31]

The composition of the proposed national security council showed that out of its eleven members only four were proposed to be from the members of the armed forces. But the very fact of any association of army personnel in any organs of the constitution was not acceptable to the elected members of the national assembly. Mr Iqbal Ahmad Khan, the then law minister, who introduced the 8th amendment bill in the national assembly, told the present author that the concept of a national security council with army personnel was totally unacceptable to the members of the national assembly. He further added that President Zia, in a spirit of compromise and reconciliation, accepted gracefully the concensus of the national assembly and agreed to withdraw the proposal for the national security council.

As regards the enhanced powers of the president as proposed by Zia, there were differences of opinion in the national assembly. Zia might have been successful in getting his proposals relating to the powers of the president approved by the regular amending procedure under the 1973 constitution – by two thirds of the total members of the parliament. But Zia was still anxious to secure the unanimous passage of the 8th amendment bill, so as to avoid disunity and controversy in the country. Pakistan had had enough constitutional controversy, and Zia wanted to put an end to the debates over constitutional issues.

We shall examine, in detail, differences between Zia's constitutional proposals relating to the role of the president, and the final provisions relating to the same, as unanimously passed by the national assembly on 17 October 1985, in our section on the 'Executive' under the present constitution of Pakistan. Here it is sufficient to note that Zia showed great statesmanship, flexibility and a spirit of compromise to secure the unanimous support of the national assembly for the constitutional amendments.

In the meantime, civilian governments were installed, both at the federal and provincial level. Zia nominated a political leader from Sind, Mohammad Khan Junejo, as the prime minister. Junejo was a comparatively little known political figure. Junejo, 52, is a moderate politican who began his political career as railways' minister in the former West Pakistan provincial government in 1964 during the era of Ayub's 'controlled democracy'. He was a member of Zia's federal cabinet for a brief period (1978–79). So he had some experience of being a civilian minister in a military regime. He was sworn in as prime minister on 23 March 1985. His election was primarily due to the fact that he came from Sind, the seat of political unrest and agitation, and he had the support of the powerful spiritual Sindhi leader, Pir Pagara. Pagara was leader of the Muslim League, a party whose support Zia very much needed in the national assembly. Junejo got a unanimous vote of confidence from the national assembly within twenty-four hours. But though the assembly gave approval to Zia's selection of prime minister, it asserted its independence by refusing to elect a nominee of Zia, also backed by Pagara, Khwaja Muhammad Safder, who was chairman of Zia's nominated Majlis-e-Shoora (1982–85), as speaker of the house. The assembly elected a newcomer to the assembly, Mr Fakar Imam. His wife, Mrs Abida Hussain – the only woman to win direct election to the national assembly – commented on her husband's victory over Zia's nominee by saying that, 'It highlighted the differences between the nominated assembly (federal council) and an elected one.'[32]

Immediately after his appointment as the prime minister, Junejo applied himself vigorously to the task of getting the constitutional amendments to the 1973 constitution approved by the national assembly. The 8th amendment was introduced to the national assembly on 30 September 1985, and was unanimously approved by the house on 16 October 1985. The amendment bill was approved by the senate on 31 October 1985. On the occasion of the unanimous passage of the 8th amendment bill, which was described as a 'vital step towards democracy', President Zia, in his address to the national assembly on 17 October 1985, told the members of the assembly: 'You have amended my amendments [we have already pointed out that the assembly did not like some of Zia's proposed amendments]: but by approving them [the 8th amendment bill] you have endorsed my stance that the constitution of 1973 needed some changes . . . by creating a balance in the powers to be exercised by the president and the prime minister, dictatorship is sought to be buried deep and for ever; on this great achievement, I congratulate you all . . . that the seed of democracy which we planted two years earlier has germinated; it is now bearing fruit.'[33]

Martial Law Lifted and the Constitution Fully Restored

Though the civil governments, both at the federal and provincial levels, were installed by March 1985, Pakistan continued to be governed under martial law till the constitutional problems were settled. It was a delicate position for the civilian prime minister, responsible to the parliament to continue to work while the country was still under martial law. There were persistent demands, both inside and outside parliament, to lift martial law. The prime minister was quietly trying to get martial law lifted. In his address on 14 August 1985 (Independence Day), the prime minister declared that martial law would be lifted before the end of the year, 1985.

Martial law was finally lifted on 30 December 1985, ending the third and the longest martial law regime in Pakistan. President Zia made a lengthy speech to the parliament on the occasion of lifting martial law and the restoration of democracy. He gave a resumé of the circumstances under which the Pakistan army under his leadership had to intervene politically in July 1977; he also referred to various measures and reforms undertaken by his martial law regime for the socio-economic development of the country, for the strengthening of the country's defensive capabilities, thereby increasing Pakistan national security and defence, and above all, his process of Islamization (Nifaz-i-Islam). Zia claimed, 'For the first time in Pakistan, indeed in the continent of Asia, democracy is taking birth from the womb of martial law. Martial law and democracy have been the antithesis of each other. It is said, fire and water do not mix. However, we have managed to evolve a scheme that has combined the two to enable the country to attain its democratic institutions (the assemblies, the senate, civilian governments), they are the hope of our future, they promise the dawn of a new era and herald a new beginning.'[34] In his conclusion, Zia advised the members of the national assembly, 'To learn from history; strengthen democratic institutions; do not repeat the mistakes of the past, avoid conflict and confrontation . . . based on my own experience, I can tell you that this is the only way to avoid the imposition of another martial law in the future.'[35] Even after the lifting of martial law, Pakistan's armed forces will continue to be an important factor in the country's politics. The return to civilian rule entails the gradual withdrawal of military personnel from civilian positions, and the termination of military courts which enjoyed extensive jurisdiction during the past eight and a half years with virtually no appeal. But General Zia-ul-Haq remains president under an amended version of the 1973 constitution which allows him to hold dual responsibility as president and chief of the army staff (COAS).

The offices of governor in Pakistan's four provinces held under martial law by serving lieutenant-generals, were divided equally among civilian politicians and retired officers. The incumbent in Sind, Lt-Gen Jahandad Khan, retained the office after shedding his uniform. Critics maintained that the military had established its presence in all fields through like-minded civilians or retired soldiers and its influence would be all pervasive even after the lifting of martial law.

'Military men have ruled Pakistan for 22 of the 38 years of independence, and Zia's martial law has been the single longest spell of military rule,' an opposition politician remarked, adding, 'The armed forces may not have a formalized role in social affairs like in Turkey or Indonesia, but their authority cannot be denied.'[36]

Military sources insist, however, that the armed forces are serious about returning to their barracks and concentrating on defence functions. There were no more than 300 military officers performing martial law duties, all of whom returned to their previous posts or retired as the case might be. As a senior officer explained: 'The armed forces did not take over police functions under martial law, they only guided policy which was in turn implemented by the normal machinery of government. Soldiers were called to assist in policy implementation only when necessary, much as they are invited to the aid of a civil power. With the end of martial law, the policy-making role of the military officers will end. The army in this country does not intervene in politics until the politicians have made a mess of things, and order has broken down to an extent where it is necessary to restore it through martial law.'[37]

NOTES

1   *Political Plan Announced*, address of President Zia at the Seventh Session of the Federal Council on 12 August 1983, published Islamabad, Ministry of Information and Broadcasting, Government of Pakistan, August 1983, p. 20.

2   *Vital Step Towards Democracy*, address to National Assembly by President Zia on 17 October 1985, published Islamabad, Ministry of Information and Broadcasting, Government of Pakistan, October 1985, p. 7.

3   *The Provisional Constitution Order 1981*, CMLA order no. 1 of 1981.

4   See the text of the Federal Council (Majlis-e-Shoora) Order 1981, President Order No. 15 of 1981, printed by the Manager, Printing Corporation of Pakistan Press, Islamabad, 1981.
5   Based on interviews with President Zia and with the then Law Minister.
6   *Political Plan Announced*, op. cit., p. 3.
7   Ibid, p. 4.
8   Ibid, pp. 6–7.
9   Ibid, pp. 15–16.
10 Ibid, pp. 26–28.
11 *Pakistan, 1986*, op. cit., p. 59.
12 'Zia's carrot and stick', *Far Eastern Economic Review*, 25 August 1983.
13 *Political Plan Announced*, op. cit., p. 33.
14 See the *Referendum Order, 1984*, Islamabad, Ministry of Law and Parliamentary Affairs, Government of Pakistan, 12 December 1984, p. 2.
15 Ibid, p. 3.
16 Ibid, p. 4.
17 Cited in *Far Eastern Review*, 25 January 1985.
18 Cited in ibid.
19 *Political Plan Announced*, op. cit., pp. 35–37.
20 *General Elections*, announcement of dates, address to Nation by President Mohammad Zia-ul-Haq at Rawalpindi on 12 January 1983, published Islamabad, Ministry of Information and Broadcasting, Government of Pakistan, 1985, pp. 3–7.
21 Ibid, pp. 8–9.
22 Ibid, pp. 9–11.
23 Ibid, pp. 11–13.
24 Ibid, p. 13.
25 *Pakistan Times*, Islamabad, 25 February 1985.
26 Cited in *Far Eastern Economic Review*, 7 March 1985.
27 Ibid.
28 Ibid.
29 *Far Eastern Economic Review*, 4 April 1985.
30 *Constitutional Amendments Announced*, op. cit., p. 16.
31 *Revival of the Constitution of 1973 Order, 1985*, president's order no. 14 of 1985, published Islamabad, Ministry of Justice and Parliamentary Affairs, Government of Pakistan, 17 March 1985, p. 212.
32 Cited in *Far Eastern Economic Review*, 4 April 1985.
33 *Vital Step Towards Democracy*, op. cit., pp. 10, 14 and 16.
34 *Martial Law Lifted: Constitution Fully Restored*, address to Majlis-e-Shoora (Parliament) by President Mohammad Zia-ul-Haq on 30 December 1985, published Islamabad, Ministry of Information and Broadcasting, Government of Pakistan, n.d., pp. 16–17.
35 Ibid, p. 25.
36 *Far Eastern Economic Review*, 9 January 1986.
37 Ibid.

Chapter III
The State and Religion
in Islam
The Islamic State in Pakistan

The raison d'être of the emergence of Pakistan was the Indian Muslims' desire to preserve and foster Islamic values. It is maintained that implicit in the demand for Pakistan was the demand for an Islamic state. Some speeches by important leaders like Mohammad Ali Jinnah and Liaquat Ali Khan who were striving for Pakistan lend themselves to this interpretation. In a sense Pakistan has been Islamic from its inception, indeed it owes its birth to the fact that the Islamic feeling of the people wanted to express itself in the form of a state. The movement for Pakistan would never have acquired such impetus had it not been for the politically potent Muslim ideal of a religious community. Why does Islam have to be organized as a socio-political order? If Islam had been a religion of the individual, the Indian Muslims would not have felt the need of a separate state of their own, because an individual can commune with his creator in private even in a state where the majority of the population are non-Muslim; the Muslims might have remained as a permanent and stagnant minority. But Islam is a religion of society, and in order to bring the full effect of the principles of Islam to a human society there must be a fully sovereign Islamic community, having the sanctions of a state to implement Islamic laws.[1]

According to modern Western political theories, politics and religion belong to different spheres of human life. Politics comes within the sphere of reason while religion within that of faith and revelation. After a long period of struggle between the church and the state on the issue of the relationship between spiritual and secular authorities during the medieval period in Europe, the Western Christian world had developed a doctrine of 'two swords' – separating politics and religion. In the early days of Roman

Christianity, the emperor had been recognized as head of both state and church. In the eleventh century the rival powers of the emperor and the pope came to a headlong clash which lasted for two centuries. Out of the early phase of this struggle between church and state the pope ultimately emerged victorious as the unquestioned head of Western Christendom, while the Roman [sc. Byzantium] empire fell into fragments and free cities. But the contest which the Roman emperors had failed to win was taken up later by the kings of the rising national states. The great schism which began with the emergence of national states with powerful kings in countries like England, France and Spain weakened the position of the pope. The struggle between the church and the state was the dominant issue of Western medieval political thought. At the end of the medieval period, it was generally agreed that society had two governments: the authority of the pope in things of the spirit, and the authority of kings in things of the world. This led to 'the doctrine of two swords'. Each power was to rule in its own sphere and neither was to interfere in the affairs of the other.[2]

During the Protestant Reformation, Martin Luther elaborated the base of secular authority, the concept of two kingdoms and the extent of secular authority by saying: 'It must be noted that the two classes of Adam's children – the one in God's kingdom under Christ, the other in the kingdom of the world, the state – have two kinds of law. Every kingdom must have its own laws and regulations.' Christ himself, Luther concluded, made this nice distinction and summed it all up briefly when he said: 'Give unto Caesar the things that are Caesar's and unto God the things that are God's.'[3]

President Zia referred to the Christian concept of two spheres of power in his address to the national assembly on 17 October 1985 when the assembly approved the 8th amendment bill to the 1973 constitution. Zia quoted Allama Syed Suleman Nadvi who examined the relationship between *deen* (religion) and state in Islam in his classic work *Seerat*. Nadvi made the following relevant remarks about the relationship between state and religion in modern Western countries and in Islam:

> There are two types of states in the world. Those in which the state and religion are utterly separated and it has been stated, 'Give unto the king what belongs to him and give unto God what is His.'
>
> In this formula, God and king (state) have been regarded as two distinct separate entities. The commands of one are not applicable

to the other. The states in Europe are all founded on this principle. And on this basis, spiritual and temporal matters have been compartmentalized.

Zia added:

> I say it with regret that there are several voices in our country as well who want separation of religion and the state. You may have gone through statements from several persons to this effect.
>
> The second type of the state is the one in which religion has not been separated. In this state there is no king. In it there is only one supreme authority and unchallenged ruler. He is the supreme dispenser and omnipotent Allah. In this state sovereignty belongs to Allah. His commands are obeyed by all. The worldly rulers and powers that be are to be obeyed only when their orders are in conformity with divine commands and are derived from them or at least are not repugnant to them. Our Holy Prophet (peace be upon him) was the last Da'i, Messenger and Prophet of this 'deen' and he in the state he founded was its first 'amir', ruler and sovereign. Obeying his orders was obeying the divine commands. God says in the Holy Quran, 'He who obeys the Prophet obeys God.'[4]

Zia advised the members of the national assembly to give serious thought to the relationship between state and religion in Islam.

What is the meaning and spirit of Islam? We may refer to a significant statement of an able Islamic thinker of the contemporary Indo-Pak subcontinent, Maulana Abul A'la Mawdudi, whose writings seem to have had great impact on Zia's process of Islamization in Pakistan and his concept of an Islamic state. Mawdudi writes:

> Islam is an Arabic word. It is derived from two root-words: one *salm*, meaning peace, and the other *silm*, meaning submission. Islam stands for 'a commitment to surrender one's will to the Will of God' and thus to be at peace with the Creator and with all that has been created by Him. It is through submission to the Will of God that peace is brought about. Harmonization of man's will with the Will of God leads to the harmonization of different spheres of life under an all-embracing ideal. Departmentalization of life into different water-tight compartments, religious and secular, sacred and profane, spiritual and material, is ruled out. There is unity of life and unity of the source of guidance. As God

is One and Indivisible, so is life and our human personality. Each aspect of life is inseparable from the other. Religious and secular are not two autonomous categories; they represent two sides of the same coin. Each and every act becomes related to God and His guidance. Every human activity is given a transcendent dimension; it becomes sacred and meaningful and goal centred.

Islam is a worldview and an outlook on life. It is based on the recognition of the unity of the Creator and of our submission to His will. Everything originates from the One God, and everyone is ultimately responsible to Him. Thus the unity of the Creator has as its corollary the Oneness of His creation. 'Islam', he adds, embodies 'a framework for the conduct of the whole of human life'.[5]

The renowned Western scholar on Islam, Professor Wilfred C Smith, explained the relationship between state and religion in Islam when in the early 1950s the great debate was going on about the role of Islam in constitution making in Pakistan. He stated:

Islam is a religion, and like other religions, is transcendent, ineffable; no form can continue or exhaust it. Like other religions it has been expressed in many forms – artistic, intellectual, mystic, but more than some others, social. In fact, Islam is characterised among the religions by the particular emphasis which it has from the beginning given to the social order. The prophet Mohammad not only preached ethics, he organized a State. Indeed, Islamic history is calculated to begin not on the year when the Prophet was born (after the fashion of the Christian era), nor when he began to receive Divine revelations, but when the Muslim Community came to power in a State of its own. The year 1 AH marks the establishment of Islam as a religio–political sovereignty in al-Madinah. That State was organized in accordance with God's revelation; it prospered and expanded and Islam as a process in human history was launched on its career. That career has continued until to-day, with many human ups and downs, many variations of fortunes and of form, many vicissitudes, both of achievement and of aspiration, but never very far from being central has been its concern with itself as an organized community. There are many illustrations of this fact; one is the superlative importance in Islam of the Law.[6]

Islam has been a social gospel from the beginning. Major sectarian differences in Islam have had to do with divergences not primarily over dogma but over questions as to how the community should be organized. While the Protestants seceded from the Catholic Church on a point of doctrine, the Shiah seceded from the majority community on a dispute regarding political leadership; Islam is by tradition and by central genius a practical religion, a religion of ethics, including social ethics, and of organized, legalized ethics.

As Sir Muhammad Zafrullah Khan, Pakistan's first foreign minister in the constituent assembly, said:

> The conception that religion and politics occupy distinct spheres which should not be permitted to overlap is born of failure to grasp the full significance of religion. What is religion and what is its function? Religion is the way of life that should enable each individual to attain the highest possible development of his spiritual, moral, physical and intellectual faculties. Its function is to establish and maintain the most harmonious relationship between man and his Maker on the one hand, and between man and man in all aspects of their relationship on the other. Politics is only one aspect of the relationship between man and man. Those who seek to draw a distinction between the sphere of religion and the sphere of politics as being mutually exclusive put too narrow a construction upon the functions of religion. To them religion signifies, at its highest, purely individual spiritual communion with the Creator, and normally only the performance of certain formal and ceremonial acts of what they call worship. This is not the Islamic conception of religion.[7]

In fact, Islam embraces within its legitimate sphere not only those acts and performances to which the followers of many other religions confine the application of the word 'worship', but aspects of individual, communal, national and international activity. It lays down and prescribes the underlying principles of international relationships, of the laws of war and peace, of statecraft, of social relationships and the like. According to Islam the regulation of all aspects of one's life in accordance with these principles is continuous worship of God. As a distinguished Muslim scholar, Dr I H Qureshi, put it: 'To us religion is not like a Sunday suit which can be put on when we enter a place of worship and put off when we are dealing with day to day life.'[8]

Islam is not so much a set of dogmas and rituals as a way of life, with its own distinctive social, cultural and political order. It is a complete way of life. Since the creation of Pakistan in 1947 a number of scholarly works have been published on the relation between state and religion in Islam. This type of research and publication has received further impetus since President Zia came to power in 1977. Zia is never tired of stressing the need for the establishment of a genuinely Islamic political order in Pakistan. He has, true to Islamic principles, consistently consulted scholars, intellectuals and jurists both Muslim and Western to find out the true spirit and significance of Islam in relation to a socio-political system. He recommended the present author on various occasions to refer to the growing literature on Islam, particularly in relation to the concept of an Islamic state. Zia gave the present author a number of scholarly works on Islam, in particular he recommended two books: Muhammad Fazlur-Rahman Ansari's *The Quranic Foundations and Structure of Muslim Society*, in two volumes, and Dr Muhammad Asad's *The Principles of State and Government in Islam*. Another important source of present day Pakistani thinking on the relationship between state and religion in Islam is *A History of Muslim Philosophy*, volumes 1 and 2, edited by M M Sharif. During his two recent interviews with President Zia on 7 August 1987 and 13 April 1988, the present author witnessed Zia's unlimited zeal and enthusiasm to study and consult works on Islam in order to fulfil his goal of completing and consolidating the process of Islamization in Pakistan so that the country might establish a true Islamic state.

Muhammad Asad raises the question whether 'mixing of religion with politics is a genuine postulate of Islam or not?' His answer, based on his study of the original sources of Islamic Law, the Quran and Sunnah, is that Islamic teachings 'not only circumscribe man's relation to God but also lay down a definite scheme of social behaviour to be adopted as a result of that relation.' He adds that what is needed is a precise body of laws which would outline, however broadly, the sphere of human life in all its aspects – spiritual, physical, individual, social, economic and political. It follows, therefore, that the organization of an Islamic state or states is an indispensable condition of Islamic life in the true sense of the word.[9]

Dr Fazlur-Rahman Ansari begins his discussion on 'fundamental principles' governing Muslim society and the Islamic state by quoting from the Holy Quran, which makes it an obligation of the Muslim community (*millat*) to look after and promote the spiritual, moral and general welfare of the individual. Collective effort for establishing what is right and eradicating what is wrong for the individual, and for the creation of a condition wherein truth, perseverance in truth and mutual compassion and well-doing prevail for the benefit of the individual has been directly affirmed and emphasized in the Quran: Do what is right and forbid what is wrong. He further adds, again by quoting verses from the Quran, that side by side with that, the concept of collectivism is the very fibre of Islam. These Quranic injunctions, according to Dr Ansari, 'necessitate the establishment of the Islamic state . . . the collective effort for the moral perfection and happiness of the individual cannot gain its ends truly and comprehensively unless it transforms itself into a free theo-democratic state whose functions should be to enforce the Islamic way of life in its totality and to act as a condition for the natural flowering of the ideals of Islam. Hence the establishment of the Islamic state, whenever and wherever possible, forms, according to the Holy Quran, the duty of the millat (the Muslim community) not only towards Islam but also towards the individual.' Dr Ansari concludes by stating ' . . . that it is an unavoidable duty, in case of ability, is borne out by the fact that the Holy Prophet (peace be on him) established the state at Madina at the very first opportunity . . . fulfilment of Islam as a way of life is not possible without the establishment of the Islamic state.'[10]

From all the views expressed by the leading ulema (religious teachers) as well as by Muslim intelligentsia and scholars, it is quite evident that the Muslims of Pakistan (including former East Pakistan, now Bangladesh – the Bangladesh constitution abolished secularism, as originally introduced by its founder, Mujib, in 1973 and declared Islam the state religion of Bangladesh in 1988) sincerely believe that politics and religion cannot be separated in Islam. In order to preserve Islamic values and ideals, it is essential that Pakistan should be an Islamic state. By and large, the consensus has been that Pakistanis would like to see their country Islamic. The principal political parties of Pakistan are agreed upon this. It was agreed that the foundation of an Islamic state in Pakistan would truly reflect the aspirations and ideals of the people of Pakistan. Framers of the various constitutions in Pakistan since 1947 – the constitutions of 1956, 1962 and 1973 – incorporated some Islamic provisions to designate the country as an Islamic state. Ayub, in his 1962 constitution, dropped the word 'Islamic'; the 1962 constitution described the country as 'the Republic of Pakistan', but soon Ayub, thanks to widespread public demands and pressure, had to redesignate the country as 'the Islamic Republic of Pakistan'. The 1960–61 constitution commission, headed by a former chief justice of Pakistan, Shahabuddin, which preceded the adoption of the 1962 constitution, also discussed the fundamental problems of the relationship between state and religion in Islam. It reaffirmed the view that 'Islam permeates the life of a Muslim and does not allow politics to be kept apart from ethics as is the case with a secular constitution.'[11]

The commission stated that Islam is not merely incessant prayers and meditations, but actual social life lived in accordance with the ideal; that is why asceticism and mystical quietism have been discredited and the Quran emphasizes the deed rather than the idea. It is summed up in theism and virtuous life, the state being primarily an instrument to protect and promote good life. Emphasis throughout the Quran is laid on action for the obvious reason that a mere enunciation of belief unaccompanied by action in accordance with that belief, besides being hypocritical, does not contribute to one's progress either as an individual or as a member of society.[12] The problem of the relation between state and religion produced an immense volume of discussion and talk in Pakistan during the first era of constitution-making (1947–56). Constitution-making involved many deep issues of Islamic self-definition and other aspects of the relationship between state and religion. The constitution commission, once more, reviewed the whole problem and reaffirmed what the framers of the constitution, particularly at the time of the adoption of the objectives resolution in 1949, had enunciated. The commission declared that we have thus an ideology which enables us to establish a model welfare state, and history shows that such a state had been established in the early days of Islam. If the modern generation doubts the efficacy of Islam, it is due to their lack of appreciation of the universal applicability of the Quranic teaching and a lack of knowledge of Islamic history, and the remedy lies in acquainting oneself with the principles of Islam and with Islamic history, and not in discarding religion. Those who talk glibly of secularism in Pakistan overlook the fact that by a mere change of expression one's conduct does not change; if there is any chance of reforming ourselves it lies only in drawing inspiration from Islam.[13]

Our discussion on the issue of state and religion in Pakistan would remain incomplete if we did not refer to some dissenting views expressed by a small group of the Western-educated urban elite who differ from the Islamic state ideology. Their model is a secular, democratic, Westernized state; they would probably accept Turkey as an example. Their belief is that if Pakistan accepts an Islamic constitution, the mullah will control the state; they hold that the Shariah cannot be adequate for a modern complex society. Their argument is that states whose laws are based on religion become incapable, after a short period of time, of satisfying the needs of the country and the nation. They point out that religions express unchanging precepts, while life goes ahead, and needs change rapidly. Religious laws, in their opinion, are no more than words void of sense, and forms without value; changelessness is a dogmatic religious necessity. They further argue that laws which derive their inspiration from religions fetter societies and constitute invincible factors which prevent progress. The purpose of laws is not to maintain old customs or beliefs which have their source in religion but rather to assure the economic and social progress of the nation. When religion has sought to rule human societies it has been the arbitrary instrument of sovereigns, despots and strong men. In short, they believe that religious precepts cannot be brought to conform to the needs of civilization. It may be added here that like some extreme ulema they look upon the Shariah as static and incapable of any further development. They do not agree with the liberal advocates of an Islamic state that the Shariah may be given a dynamic interpretation. They say it is a mistake to adhere to concepts which are outworn and irrelevant to present conditions of life. They expect that religiosity, the emotion on which Pakistan was based, will soon disappear and wish for a Kemal Atatürk in Pakistan to found a secular state.[14]

This group, it would appear, seems to have failed to recognize that if the polity of Pakistan is to be based upon a firm foundation, there is no motive force but that of Islam which can act as the basis. A polity which is not based upon some higher ideals of righteousness and justice may founder against many a rock; it seems, therefore, that the constituent assemblies of Pakistan were right in setting the ideal of Islam as the main objective to be achieved in the constitution. What is needed is that the ideal should be given a rational and dynamic interpretation.

Quaid-e-Azam's Views on the Islamic State

Another point of controversy over the problem of state and religion in Islam is related to the correct views held on this subject by Quaid-e-Azam Mohammad Ali Jinnah. Did he and his colleagues, during the movement for Pakistan in the 1940s, want to make the promised separate state for Indian Muslims an Islamic state? The controversy was acute in the early 1950s when the first constituent assembly was engaged in framing Pakistan's first constitution (1956). The controversy over Jinnah's views on the Islamic state is still alive, and we, therefore, would like to examine it in its true perspective and historical background.

While it is true that the leaders of the Pakistan movement appealed primarily to the inherent sentiment of the people, they did not define the nature of the Islamic state in Pakistan. The reasons are obvious. It might have created dissension and division when unity was most needed to achieve Pakistan. This, however, only postponed the controversy. The opponents of an Islamic state maintain that while the leaders relied on Islamic ideals in the struggle to achieve Pakistan, they gave no definite picture of an Islamic constitution for Pakistan. Their contention is that the leaders needed religious sentiment to win over the support of the illiterate Muslim masses, but they had no desire to frame an Islamic constitution for Pakistan when it would actually be established. Particularly, the attitude of the Quaid-e-Azam, Mohammad Ali Jinnah himself, who was the leader of the movement for Pakistan and is universally recognized as its founder, has become a subject of controversy. The opponents of the Islamic state claim that the Quaid-e-Azam's ideal was a modern national secular state. This claim has received added importance in view of its acceptance in the Report of the Court of Enquiry for the Panjab disturbances of 1953.

This enquiry was presided over by a former chief justice of the federal court, Mr M Munir. Quoting from some speeches of Jinnah, the report makes the conclusion the Quaid-e-Azam said that the new state would be a modern democratic state with sovereignty resting in the people, and the members of the new nation would have equal rights of citizenship regardless of their religion, caste or creed.[15] The Quaid-e-Azam's speech of 11 August 1947 to the constituent assembly of Pakistan has led some people to argue that he was not favourable to the idea of an Islamic state. But a careful analysis of the same speech and his other utterances before and after partition convinces one that he had no objection to a state based on the broad principles of Islam. Let us examine his views more closely, as his opinions are still held in high respect and exercise a powerful influence on any issue facing Pakistan. Jinnah, in his speech of 11 August, said:

If you work in co-operation, forgetting the past, burying the hatchet, you are bound to succeed, if you change your past and work together in a spirit that everyone of you, no matter to what community he belongs, is first, . . . second and last a citizen of this State with equal rights, privileges and obligations, there will be no end to the progress you will make . . . we are starting with this fundamental principle that we are all citizens and equal citizens of one State. You may belong to any religion or caste or creed – that has nothing to do with the business of the State . . . I think we should keep that in front as our ideal and you will find that in course of time Hindus would cease to be Hindus and Muslims would cease to be Muslims, not in the religious sense because that is the personal faith of each individual but in the political sense as citizens of the State.[16]

What is the spirit of this speech? It was made at a time when the whole Indian sub-continent was swayed with communal frenzy; millions of people, both Muslims and Hindus, were victims of communal riots. The Quaid-e-Azam was stressing communal harmony and peace for the progress of the new nation. He again and again stressed in this memorable speech that there would be no distinction made between Hindus and Muslims on the grounds of religion, caste or creed, but he never said that Islamic principles should not be the guiding factor in the constitution of Pakistan. In fact, he made no reference to the future constitution; he was speaking only against recent communal bitterness between Hindus and Muslims, and said that Hindus would have equality as citizens. Even here he appealed to Islamic ideology. He said that the tolerance and good will that Emperor Akbar showed to the non-Muslims was not of recent origin; they dated back thirteen centuries when the Prophet laid down these principles. The Quaid-e-Azam expressed his views on the character of the future constitution in another important speech. In a broadcast talk to the people of the United States in February 1948, he declared:

The Constitution of Pakistan has yet to be framed by the Pakistan Constituent Assembly. I do not know what the ultimate shape of this constitution is going to be but I am sure that it will be a democratic type, embodying the essential principles of Islam; Islam and its idealism have taught us democracy; it has taught equality of man, justice and fair play to everybody. We are inheritors of these glorious traditions, and are fully alive to our responsibilities and obligations as framers of the future Constitution of Pakistan.

But he also emphatically denied that Pakistan would be run by the ulema.

In any case Pakistan is not going to be a theocratic state to be ruled by priests with a divine mission. We have many non-Muslims, Hindus, Christians and Parsis, but they are all Pakistanis. They will enjoy the same rights and privileges as any other citizens, and will play their rightful part in the affairs of Pakistan.[17]

Jinnah's views on the Islamic state are further corroborated by several historical events and documents, and statements. President Zia referred to one more observation of Quaid-e-Azam. Addressing the Karachi Bar Association on 25 January 1948, on the occasion of the 12 Rabi-ul-Awwal, Quaid-e-Azam said:

I fail to understand why some people indulge in the mischievous propaganda whether or not the constitution will be in accordance with the Islamic Shariah. Islam today is as much a practicable religion as it was thirteen hundred years ago. It is a standard bearer of democracy. It is Islam which guarantees justice, fair play and equal rights to everyone. And the whole world will see that we will frame our constitution in accordance with it.[18]

What do these various utterances of the founder of Pakistan indicate? It seems to us that he was anxious to give Islamic ideology a dynamic interpretation, and to him, making Pakistan an Islamic state meant basing it upon Islamic principles, particularly the principles of equality, brotherhood and social justice. He found these principles of Islam not incompatible with democratic ideals. What he tried to imply is that Pakistan should not be Islamic and democratic, possessing these qualities as two distinct and separate attributes, but that it should be through the democratic process, Islamic. Democracy becomes an aspect of its Islamic-ness, a part of the definition of the Islamic state.

The demand for an Islamic state, therefore, has its roots in the Pakistan movement itself and if Pakistani Muslims are asked what kind of country they wish Pakistan to be, the majority of them are likely to answer 'Islamic'. There is fairly general accord on this.

Divergent Concepts of an Islamic State in Pakistan

While it has been generally agreed that the constitution of Pakistan should be an Islamic one, there are wide differences about the exact definition and characteristics of an Islamic state for Pakistan. On the one side, there are some extremist ulema (religious teachers) who want what they term a fully-fledged Islamic state. On the other hand, there are Muslim intelligentsia as well as enlightened ulema who want to give Islamic ideology a dynamic interpretation. Islamic ideology, according to this group, enables Muslims to establish a model welfare state, and history shows that such a state was established in the early days of Islam. Pakistan's second governor-general who also became the country's second prime minister, Khawaja Nazimuddin, a devoted Muslim, said in the first constituent assembly: 'The principles enunciated by Islam have to be interpreted in terms of democratic constitutional practice of the twentieth century . . . so that we could bring about a synthesis not only of the fundamental teachings of our faith and requirements of progressive democracy but also of the requirements of the twentieth century and best elements in our own tradition and history.'[19] Nazimuddin's views as expressed in this statement were similar to those of Jinnah as already pointed out.

Before we discuss the opposing views of extremist ulema and those of the Pakistani intelligentsia and liberal ulema, we ought to examine the concept of an Islamic state as laid down in the Holy Quran and Sunnah. We should also refer to Muslim jurists and philosophers' views on the subject before the creation of Pakistan in 1947.

THE QURANIC SOURCES

What are the principles laid down in the Quran relating to the constitution of the Islamic state? According to one school of thought there are only two or three clear principles relating to constitutional matters in the Quran: the first is that Muslims should obey God, His Prophet and those who from amongst themselves are put in authority over them. It means that a Muslim's first duty is to God and he should do nothing which comes into conflict with that duty. He must not obey an un-Islamic order of the government. In other words, an Islamic government can never ask its people to carry out an un-Islamic policy. Obedience to those who are in power is stressed, but rebellion is permitted in cases of gross tyranny and when the authority issues an order against the dictates of Islam. The second principle is that Muslims should co-operate in righteousness and justice, which probably means that the basis of human action should be moral and not merely political; there should be no divorce between fundamental morality and political activity. This is applicable to states and individuals alike. The third principle is that government has to be organized on a basis which makes it possible for decisions to be the result of mutual consultation. Muslims are expected to order their affairs by mutual consultation, and it is claimed that it is inherent in the idea of consultation that a majority view should prevail. This is, therefore, regarded as perfectly compatible with the democratic principle of majority rule.[20]

These constitutional principles, Pakistanis believe, are not difficult to incorporate in a modern constitution, and a polity based on these principles need not necessarily be out of tune with a democratic constitution.

But other Muslim scholars like Dr Fazlur-Rahman Ansari, Dr Asad and learned ulema like Sayyid Abul A'la Mawdudi hold the view that the Quran provides a number of guidelines regarding the constitution of the Islamic state. The present author, while planning to write this book dealing with, among other topics, the process of Islamization in Pakistan under President Zia, has done extensive research on the Quranic concept of the Islamic state. As a result of that extensive research and study, he is inclined to agree that there are more than just two or three constitutional principles in the Quran. If one wants to analyse the system of government from the standpoint of Islam, those principles have to be studied. Dr Ansari in his two volumes of the *Quranic Foundations and Structure of Muslim Society* has given those principles by quoting the relevant verses from the Quran. We shall reproduce some of those verses from the original sources.

The Holy Quran
The Quranic constitution of the state rests on the following principles:

1 Sovereignty
Sovereignty belongs to God.

إِنِ الْحُكْمُ إِلَّا لِلّٰهِ أَمَرَ أَلَّا تَعْبُدُوا إِلَّا إِيَّاهُ ذٰلِكَ الدِّينُ الْقَيِّمُ وَلٰكِنَّ أَكْثَرَ النَّاسِ لَا يَعْلَمُونَ.

'. . Authority and control belong to Allah only He hath commanded that ye serve none save Him: that is the right religion, but most human beings understand not.'

(XII:40)

اَلاَ لَهُ الحُكْمُ وَهوَ أَسْرَعُ الحَاسِبِيْنَ.

'Is not His the Command? And He is the swiftest in taking account.'

(VI:62)

'To Him belongeth the kingdom of the heavens and the earth.'

(XLIII:85)

لَهُ مُلْكُ السَّمْوٰتِ وَالأَرضِ

'He does not share His Command with any person whatsoever.'

(XVIII:26)

وَلاَ يُشْرِكُ فِي حُكْمِه اَحَدَاً.

2 The Right to Legislate

a The right to legislate belongs basically to God.
In the Holy Quran we read:

اِنَّا اَنزَلنَاۤ اِلَيكَ الكِتٰبَ بِالحَقِّ لِتَحكُمَ بَينَ النَّاسِ بِمَا اَرٰنكَ اللّٰهُ.

'Lo! We (God) have revealed unto thee (O Muhammad) the Scripture with truth, that thou mayest judge between mankind by that (law) which Allah hath shown.'

b Having been given the divine law it is not permitted for the Muslims to adopt, when they have their own state, any law which is repugnant to it. The following verses emphasize this fact very vehemently:

وَمَن لَمْ يَحْكُمْ بِمَا اَنزَلَ اللّٰهُ فَأُولٰئِكَ هُمُ الكٰفِرُونَ.

'If any do fail to judge and command by (the light of) what Allah hath revealed, they are Unbelievers.'

(V:47)

c It should be noted that the Holy Quran prohibits only the violation of 'what Allah hath revealed'. But it does not lay down, either in the verses just quoted or anywhere else, that

Muslims are forbidden from following any laws which Allah has not revealed, thus leaving it open to frame new laws for meeting the exigencies of new situations. Of course, all such laws should be in conformity with divine guidance, as the Holy Book says:

اَفَحُكْمَ الْجَاهِلِيَّةِ يَبْغُونَ، وَمَنْ اَحْسَنُ مِنَ اللّهِ حُكْماً لِقَوْمٍ يُؤْقِنُونَ.

Thus, a controlled and limited, but positive, freedom has been given to the Muslims in respect of legislation.

3 Status of Government Authority

Human beings are vicegerents of God; hence, governmental authority can be held by them only as a delegated function and as a trust under the sovereignty of God.

4 Objectives of the Islamic State

The objectives of the Islamic state are:

   a To maintain internal order and ward off external aggression.
   b To establish absolute justice for all citizens. The Holy Quran says:

اِنَّ اللّهَ يَأْمُرُكُم اَنْ تُؤَدُّوا الاَ منيتِ الى اَهْلِهَا، واِذَا حَكَمْتُم بَيْنَ النَّاسِ اَنْ تَحكُمُوا بِالعَدلِ، اِنَّ اللّهَ نِعِمَّا يَعِظُكُم بِه، اِنَّ اللّهَ كَانَ سَمِيعاً بَصِيراً.

'Allah doth command you to render back your Trusts to those to whom they are due; and when ye judge between man and man (whether Muslims or non–Muslims), that ye judge with justice: Lo! comely is the teaching which he giveth you! Lo! Allah is He Who heareth and seeth all things.'

(IV:58)

يَاَيُّهَا الَّذِينَ امَنُوا كُونُوا قَوَّمِينَ بِالقِسطِ شُهَدَآءَ لِلّهِ وَلَوْ عَلَى اَنفُسِكُم اَوِ الوَالِدَينِ وَالاَقَرِبِينَ، اِن يَّكُنْ غَنِيّاً اَو فَقِيراً فَاللّهُ اولَى بِهِمَا فَلاَ تَتَّبِعُوا الهَوٰى اَن تَعدِلُوا، وَاِن تَلوٓا اَو تُعرِضُوا فَاِنَّ اللّهَ كَانَ بِمَا تَعمَلُونَ خَبِيراً.

'Oh ye who believe! stand out firmly for justice, as witnesses to Allah, even as against yourselves, or your parents, or your kin, and whether it be (against) rich or poor: For Allah can best

protect both. Follow not the lusts of your hearts, lest ye
swerve, and if ye distort (justice) or decline to do justice, verily
Allah is well acquainted with all that ye do.'

(IV:135)

c To do all that lies in its power and to employ all means and
media, including *tableegh*, for the establishment of 'all that is
right' (*al-ma'ruf*) and the elimination of 'all that is wrong' (*al-munkar*).

d To organize institutions for spiritual and social welfare.

In respect of (c) and (d) above, the Holy Quran says:

اَلَّذِيْنَ اِنْ مَكَّنَّهُمْ فِي الأَرْضِ اَقَامُوا الصَّلٰوة وَاٰتَوُا الزَّكٰوة وَاَمَرُوْا
بِالمَعْرُوفِ وَنَهَوْا عَنِ المُنكَرِ وَلِلّٰهِ عَاقِبَةُ الأُمُورِ.

'(Muslims are) those who, if we bestow on them (authority) in
the land, establish regular prayer (pursue spiritual welfare) and
give regular charity (pursue economic welfare), enjoin (all)
that which is right and forbid (all) that which is wrong (pursue
moral and political welfare). And unto Allah is the end of (all)
affairs.'

(XXII:41)

Again:

لاَ خَيْرَ فِي كَثِيرٍ مِن نَجْوٰيهِم اِلا مَنْ اَمَرَ بِصَدَقَةٍ اَو مَعْرُوفٍ اَو اِصلاحٍ
بَيْنَ النَّاسِ، وَمَنْ يَّفْعَلْ ذٰلِكَ ابْتِغَاء مَرْضَاتِ اللّٰهِ فَسَوفَ نُؤْتِيهِ اَجراً
عَظِيماً.

'In most of their secret conferences there is no good: but if one
commandeth a deed of economic well-doing or justice or *islah*
(i.e., establishment of peace, happiness and order) among
human beings: to him who does this, seeking the good pleasure
of Allah, We shall soon give a reward of the highest value.'

(IV:114)

Moreover, from the social and economic point of view, the
function of the Islamic state is to transform the Muslim
community into a community of middle-roaders – of the
middle-class standard – with elimination of the evils of poverty
on the one hand, and the evils of riches on the other.

Islam steers the middle course between capitalism and

communism and bears witness to the evil of their extremism – an evil from which they themselves are trying to recede gradually, thus proving the truth of Islam.

e To endeavour actively to make Islam the supreme ideological force on the world-front.

5 Democratic Rights of the People

People are to be free and in possession of democratic rights.

People in the Islamic state are to be free from subjection to any human being, because their government is the government of law and they are subjects of God alone.

We have been told:

$$\text{اِنِ الْحَكْمُ اِلا لِلهِ اَمَرَ اَلاَ تَعْبُدُوا اِلا اِيَّاهُ، ذٰلِكَ الدِينُ القَيِّمُ وَلٰكِنّ اَكْثَرَ}$$
$$\text{الناسِ لاَ يَعلَمُونَ.}$$

'The authority and control belong to Allah only. He hath commanded that ye serve none save Him. That is the right religion but most human beings understand not.'

(XII:40)

Then the Holy Quran lays down the following principle in respect of the collective life of Muslims:

$$\text{وَاَمْرُهُمْ شُوْرٰى بَيَنَهُمْ.}$$

' . . . Who (conduct) their affairs (or, government) by mutual consultation . . . '

(XLII:38)

It is evident that the administration of the state on the basis of mutual consultation is impossible and unthinkable without the citizens enjoying freedom and full democratic rights.

Moreover, it is the essential condition and consequence of the establishment of absolute justice enjoined vehemently by the Holy Quran that the people should be in possession of freedom and equality of opportunity – in other words, full democratic rights – and this actually has been realized in the Islamic state.

6 Qualifications, Status and Functions of the Head of the Islamic State (*Amir al-Mo'minin*)

a He must be a Muslim, endowed with a high standard of piety, knowledge, wisdom and physical qualities, including bravery. That he must be a Muslim is borne out by the words 'from among you' in the following Quranic verse:

يَآيُّهَا الَّذِينَ امَنُوٓا اَطِيعُوا اللّٰهَ وَاَطِيعوا الرَّسُولَ وأُولِى الأَمرِ مِنكُمْ.

'O ye who believe! obey Allah and obey the Messenger and those charged with authority from among you.'

(IV:59)

The head of an ideological state can reasonably be only he who believes in and represents that ideology.

As regards the high standard of piety, the Holy Quran lays down the law:

اِن اَكرَمَكُم عِندَ اللهِ اَتقٰكمُ.

'. . . Verily, the most honoured of you with Allah is (he who is) the most pious of you . . .'

(XLIX:13)

Knowledge, wisdom and physical merits have been affirmed.

b His status is that of (i) the vicegerent of God (ii) the successor to the Holy Prophet Muhammad (peace be on him) (iii) the representative of the people who delegate their authority to him:

i He is the vicegerent of God; as it has been said about David (peace be on him):

يٰدَاودُ اِنَّا جَعَلنٰكَ خَلِيفَةٍ فِى الأَرضِ.

'O David, We did indeed make thee a vicegerent on earth . . .'

(XXXVIII:26)

ii He is the successor to the Holy Prophet Muhammad (peace be on him).

The Holy Prophet being the founder and the first head of the Islamic state, every other head of the Islamic state who comes after him is naturally his successor.

(This is his historical status, or status in relation to the Holy Prophet, peace be on him.)

iii He is the representative of the people, who, as vicegerents of God, delegate their authority, out of organizational and administrative necessity, to him.

The administration of the Islamic state being based on mutual consultation, as seen in the foregoing, no one can impose himself as a despotic ruler on the Muslims. Rather, he is to be elected by them; and, as such, he is to be their representative.

(This is his political status, or status in relation to the people.)

c   His functions are:

   i   As vicegerent of God, his natural function is to live for God, to carry out divine commands and to surrender his ego completely to divine pleasure.

   ii   As successor to the Holy Prophet (peace be on him), his natural function is to imitate the Holy Prophet as a Muslim and as head of the state, as best as he can.

   iii   As representative of the people, his natural function is to be the servant of the people and not their master.

   Hence he should lead a life of austerity and self-negation. It has been said about good Muslims that they sacrifice their own interests and comforts for the sake of other Muslims. The head of the Islamic state is, therefore, duty-bound, more than any other Muslim, to base his life on self-sacrifice.

   Thus, his life must be exemplary for the people in respect of the Islamic way of life.

d   His relationship with his people.

   i   Parliament

   He should rule the state in consultation with the people. Thus, there should be a parliament.

   According to the Holy Quran, the Holy Prophet (peace be on him) was commanded by God, in spite of his unique position as God's Messenger, to administer the state in consultation with the people, who were his followers. The command reads:

$$\text{وَشَاوِرُهُم فِي الأَمرِ.}$$

'. . . And consult with them upon the conduct of affairs.'

(III:59)

Thus, as successor to the Holy Prophet (peace be on him), the head of the Islamic state cannot assume the position of an autocrat or a dictator, and cannot disturb the democratic rights of the people.

ii People's right to differ

The citizens of the Islamic state have the right to differ with the head of the state; and when such a situtation arises, the dispute is to be referred to the Holy Quran and the Prophetic Guidance (Sunnah) for arbitration.

The right to differ is directly contained in the right to give opinion, while the principle for settlement of differences has been given in the following verse:

فَإِنْ تَنَازَعْتُمْ فِي شَيْءٍ فَرُدُّوهُ إِلَى اللّٰهِ والرَّسُولِ إِنْ كُنْتُمْ تُؤْمِنُونَ بِاللّٰهِ وَالْيَوْمِ الْآخِرِ، ذٰلِكَ خَيْرٌ وَّأَحْسَنُ تَأْوِيلاً.

'If ye differ in anything among yourselves, refer it to Allah and His Messenger, if ye do believe in Allah and the Last Day: That is best, and most suitable for final determination.'

(IV:59)

iii Supremacy of the law

The above brings out that the head of the Islamic state is not above the law, his function being not to administer the state arbitrarily and at will, but positively, on the basis of truth and justice as given in the divine law, as the following verse establishes:

فَاحْكُمْ بَيْنَ النَّاسِ بِالْحَقِّ وَلاَ تَتَّبِعِ الْهَوٰى فَيُضِلَّكَ عَنْ سَبِيلِ اللّٰهِ.

' . . . So judge between mankind with truth, and follow not caprice and lust of the heart, lest it cause thee to err from the path of Allah (i.e., do not subordinate the welfare of the people to thy personal inclinations and interests, because that would lead thee away from absolute obedience to the Divine Law and upholding it as supreme).'

(XXXVIII:26)

However, as long as he administers in conformity with the guidance given by God and His Messenger Muhammad (peace be on him), he should be implicitly obeyed by all, as it has been commanded:

يَاأَيُّهَا الَّذِينَ امَنُوٓا أَطِيعُوا اللّٰهَ وَأَطِيعُوا الرَّسُولَ وأُولِي الْأَمْرِ مِنْكُم.

'Oh ye who believe! Obey Allah, and obey the Messenger

and those charged with authority among you.'

(IV:59)

7 Separation of the Executive and Judiciary

If as we have noted, the head of the Islamic state is subordinate to the law given by God and His Messenger (peace be on him), the principle of the supremacy of law is established. Now, the only way to ensure the supremacy of law is the keeping of the judiciary independent of the executive and the total avoidance by the head of the state of tampering with the functioning of the judiciary.

As a duty of the Islamic state, 'establishment of regular prayer' and 'enjoining what is right and forbidding what is wrong' in spiritual affairs mean:

a the construction and maintenance of mosques
b appointment and maintenance of the requisite staff for the proper functioning of the mosques
c organization of spiritual education at the highest level as well as at the level of the general masses, and making it compulsory for every Muslim citizen of the state to acquire that education
d enforcement of laws whereby the above is ensured
e curbing and eliminating all those forces, customs and institutions which are opposed to, or are capable of hindering, the proper functioning of Islamic spiritual values.

(1) Duty of ensuring the spiritual welfare of the people

The Holy Quran proclaims 'exhortation to Truth' as one of the essential conditions of human success (CIII:3). Hence, it is the duty of the Islamic state as the vicegerent of God, successor to the Holy Prophet (God's blessings be on him), and representative of the people, to uphold, propagate and ensure the functioning of truth, and consequently, the spiritual values – which form the basic content of truth in the lives of Muslims.

The Holy Quran says:

اَلَّذِينَ اِنْ مَّكَّنَّهُمْ فِي الأَرْضِ اَقَامُوا الصَّلٰوةَ وَاٰتَوُا الزَّكٰوةَ وَاَمَرُوْا بِالْمَعْرُوْفِ وَنَهَوْا عَنِ الْمُنْكَرِ، ولِلّٰهِ عَاقِبَةُ الأُمُوْرِ.

'(Muslims are) those who, if We establish them (in authority and power) in the land, establish regular prayer and give regular charity, enjoin the right and forbid the wrong: With Allah rests the end (and decision) of (all) affairs.'

(XXII:41)

(2) Duty of ensuring the moral welfare of the people

The verse, i.e. XXII:41, lays down 'enjoining what is right and forbidding what is wrong' as one of the functions of the Islamic state. Viewing this function in the perspective of morals, the fact stands out as self-evident that it is the duty of the Islamic state:

i   to organize and institute the moral education of the people, and to do all that is necessary in that respect

ii to take all positive steps, including the enactment and enforcement of laws, for ensuring the proper practice of Islamic morals with a view to preserve and promote moral welfare

iii to adopt all measures necessary, including the enactment and enforcement of laws, for combatting all tendencies, acts and forces, that are detrimental to the cause of moral welfare, and for punishing the actual offenders.

(3) Duty relating to the intellectual development of the people

When we study the attitude of the Holy Quran regarding the intellectual development of human beings, we find that

i   it classifies humanity distinctly into two groups: the possessors of knowledge and the ignorant, and emphasizes clearly the superiority

$$\text{هَل يَستَوِى الَّذِينَ يَعلَمُونَ وَالَّذِينَ لاَ يَعلَمُونَ، اِنَّمَا يَتَذَكَّر أُولُوا الأَلبَابِ.}$$

'Are the possessors of knowledge equal with those who possess not knowledge? It is the possessors of understanding that are mindful.'

(XXXIX:9)

ii But it goes beyond that, because, while emphasizing most vehemently the importance of intellectual development in human life, it makes the quest of knowledge a duty of paramount importance for an individual.

To the problem with which we are concerned here – has the Islamic state any duty towards the citizens in respect of their intellectual development? – the plain answer is 'yes', as the following observations bear out:

i   According to the Holy Quran, God educated Adam, the progenitor of the human race:

وَعَلَّمَ اذَمَ الأَسمَآءَ كُلَّهَا

'And He imparted to Adam the knowledge of the nature of all things.'

(II:31)

Then, the Holy Quran lays down the law that divine blessings are meant to be transmitted to others:

وَأَحسِنْ كَمَا أَحسَنَ اللّهُ اِلَيّكَ.

' . . . and do thou good (to others) as Allah has been good to thee.'

(XXVIII:77)

Thus, the knowledge imparted by God to Adam was meant to be transmitted to mankind, generation after generation, and to be developed further and further by them.

Now, who can organize this difficult and great pursuit better than the possessor of the powers of collective vicegerency of God?

Thus, it is the duty of the Islamic state to organize universal education for the intellectual development of its citizens.

ii The Holy Quran has taught the prayer:

رَبِ زِدنِي عِلماً.

' . . . O my Lord! advance me in knowledge.'

(XX:114)

This shows that it is God who advances human beings in knowledge. He does so, however, through human beings, of which the institution of prophethood is the proof.

All the prophets, from Adam to Muhammad (Allah bless them all), were the vicegerents of God par excellence and, as such, the teachers of mankind.

Every state is also the vicegerent of God, the Islamic state being supremely so, because besides its status as 'state', it is also the inheritor of the blessings conferred on mankind by God through His Messengers.

This vicegerency makes it incumbent on the Islamic state to undertake the development of knowledge to higher and higher levels, and to organize and enforce the education of all its citizens with a view to their intellectual advancement, with all the resources at its command.

iii The Holy Quran refers to the establishment of justice and a balanced life among human beings as the objective of divine guidance and, consequently, as the objective of the Islamic state:

لَقَدْ أَرْسَلْنَا رُسُلَنَا بِالْبَيِّنَاتِ وَأَنْزَلْنَا مَعَهُمُ الْكِتَبَ وَالْمِيزَانَ لِيَقُومَ النَّاسُ بِالْقِسْطِ.

'We sent aforetime Our Messengers with Clear Signs and sent down with them the Book and the Balance (of Right and Wrong), that men may stand forth in justice . . .'

This objective cannot, however, be achieved without a universal dissemination among the people of the knowledge of the Islamic way of life as a compulsory measure.

The Islamic way of life is, in its turn, built upon divine guidance, which is the highest knowledge, and as such necessitates the acquisition of all knowledge for its proper understanding.

Thus, free, compulsory and universal education, based on divine guidance, having the promotion of the Islamic way of life as its objective and being widest in its scope, stands out as one of the foremost duties of the Islamic state.

iv The Holy Quran commands Muslims to build up their power to the utmost and in all respects (VIII:60). The objective is only achievable, among other things, through:

a universal and basic religious and general education of the people

b the highest theological, philosophical, scientific and technological education of those who possess the proper aptitude

thereby building up a community of intellectuals which should endeavour ceaselessly to attain the highest level in every field of knowledge.

All that education should, of course, be inspired by the ideal of making truth and justice reign supreme in the world, whereby alone the mission of Islam is fulfilled.

The crux of the above discussion is that in respect of intellectual development, it is the duty of the Islamic state:

a to organize, establish and enforce free compulsory basic universal education

b to devise ways and means whereby all branches of

knowledge are cultivated at the highest level

c to harness all intellectual endeavour in the cause of the advancement of truth and justice.

(4) Duties relating to the political and social welfare of the people

  i Establishment of happiness, peace and order for ensuring healthy existence and development of the individuals, is enjoined.

The Holy Quran says:

فَاتَّقُوا اللّٰهَ وَاَصْلِحُوا ذَاتَ بَيْنِكُمْ.

'. . . So fear Allah and pursue *islah* (i.e., happiness, peace and order) between yourselves.'

(VIII:1)

  ii Administering justice without discrimination and without any extraneous consideration, for the preservation of life, honour and property of the individuals, is enjoined.

The Holy Quran says:

يَاَيُّهَا الَّذِينَ اٰمَنُوا كُوْنُوا قَوّٰمِينَ بِالْقِسْطِ شُهَدَاۤءَ لِلّٰهِ وَلَوْ عَلٰى اَنْفُسِكُمْ اَوِ الْوَالِدَيْنِ وَالْاَقْرَبِينَ، اِنْ يَّكُنْ غَنِيّاً اَوْ فَقِيراً فَاللّٰهُ اولٰى بِهِمَا فَلَا تَتَّبِعُوا الْهَوٰى اَنْ تَعْدِلُوا، وَاِنْ تَلْوٰۤا اَوْ تُعْرِضُوا فَاِنَّ اللّٰهَ كَانَ بِمَا تَعْمَلُوْنَ خَبِيراً.

'Oh ye who believe! stand out firmly for justice, as witnesses to Allah, even as against yourselves, or your parents, or your kin, and whether it be (against) rich or poor; for Allah can best protect both. Following not the lusts of your hearts, lest ye swerve, and if ye distort (justice) or decline to do justice verily Allah is well acquainted with all that ye do.'

(IV:135)

Again:

يَاَيُّهَا الَّذِينَ اٰمَنُوا كُوْنُوا قَوّٰمِينَ لِلّٰهِ شُهَدَاۤءَ بِالْقِسْطِ، وَلاَ يَجْرِمَنَّكُمْ شَنَاٰنُ قَوْمٍ عَلٰى اَلاَّ تَعْدِلُوا، اِعْدِلُوا، هُوَ اَقْرَبُ لِلتَّقْوٰى، وَاتَّقُوا اللّٰهَ، اَنَّ اللّٰهَ خَبِيرٌ بِمَا تَعْمَلُوْنَ.

'Oh ye who believe! be maintainers of your pact with Allah,

as witnesses to fair dealing, and let not the hatred of others to you make you swerve to wrong and depart from justice. Be just: that is nearest to Piety: and fear Allah. For Allah is well acquainted with all that ye do.'

(V:9)

iii Ensuring the democratic rights of people, enjoined:

إِنَّ اللّٰهَ يَأْمُرُكُم اَن تُؤَدّوا الاَ مِنتِ اِلى اَهلِهَا.

'Allah doth command you to render back your Trusts (i.e., all obligations towards God and fellow-beings) to those to whom they are due . . .'

(IV:58)

(5) Duties relating to the economic welfare of the people

i Harmonizing different interests to end exploitation and the creation of a classless society, is enjoined.

In this respect:

a The Holy Quran establishes the brotherhood of Muslims:

إِنَّمَا المُؤْمِنُونَ اِخوَة فَاَصلِحوا بَينَ اَخَوَيكُم وَاتَّقوا اللّٰهَ لَعَلَّكُم تُرحَمُونَ.

'The Believers are but a single Brotherhood. Therefore, establish happiness, peace and order among two (contending) members of your Brotherhood, and observe your duty to Allah that haply ye may obtain mercy.'

(XLIX:10)

b The Holy Quran lays down the law for ending exploitation at all levels and in all respects:

لاَ تَظلِمُونَ وَلاَ تُظلَمُونَ.

'Ye shall neither wrong, nor be wronged.'

(II:279)

Again:

إِنَّمَا السَّبِين عَلَى الَّذِينَ يَظلِمُونَ النَّاسَ وَيَبغُونَ فِي الأَرضِ بِغَيرِ الحَقِّ، أُولئكَ لَهُم عَذاب اَلِيم.

103

'The blame is only against those who oppress men with wrong-doing and insolently transgress beyond bounds through the land, denying right and justice: For such there will be a penalty grievous.'

(XLII:42)

c The Holy Quran enjoins active steps, through coercive authority, for ending exploitation:

وَاَن طَآئِفتنِ مِنَ المُؤمِنِينَ اقتَتَلُوا فَاَصلِحُوا بَينَهُمَا، فَان بَغَت اِحدٰهُمَا عَلَى الأُخرٰى فَقَاتِلوا الَتِي تَبغِى حَتٰى تَفِىء اِلَى اَمرِ اللّهِ.

'If two parties among Believers fall into a quarrel, make ye peace between them: but if one of them transgresses beyond bounds against the other then fight ye (all) against the one that transgresses until it complies with the command of Allah . . .'

(XLIX:9)

In its general bearing, it provides also the principle that if a group of Muslims tries to exploit another group, it is the duty of the Islamic state to restrain the exploiters by force.

Prohibition of usury and interest, whereby the rich exploit the poor, is a part of Quranic legislation in this regard.

ii Ensuring the economic characteristics of Muslim society in terms of its being the 'balanced community' by eliminating the evils of poverty as well as the evils of riches is enjoined.

The means which the Holy Quran prescribes for adoption by the Islamic state are:

a It propounds the principle that all human beings have equal right to the means of sustenance found on earth, and that, consequently, the citizens of the Islamic state have equal right to the means of sustenance found in the state:

هُوَ الَّذِي خَلَقَ لَكُمَ مَا فِي الأَرضِ جَمِيعاً.

'He (Allah) it is Who created for you (i.e., for the benefit of all of you), O mankind! all that is on the earth.'

(II:29)

According to this verse, no human being has originally any exclusive and absolute right to anything found on the earth.

'And We have provided therein (i.e., in the earth) means of subsistence – for you and for those for whom ye provide not.'

(XV:20)

Still again:

وَقَدَّرَ فِيهَا اَقْوَاتَهَا فِي اَرْبَعَةِ اَيَّامٍ، سَوَاءً لِلسَّائِلِينَ.

'. . . and (Allah) ordained in due proportion therein (i.e., in the earth) the sustenance thereof (for the purpose of fulfilling the requirements of its inhabitants) in four days: equal for those who seek (to fulfil their needs).'

(XLI:10)

b It lays down the law that value lies in labour:

اَنْ لَيْسَ لِلإِنسَانِ إِلا مَا سَعَىٰ.

'That man can have nothing but what he strives for (through labour).'

(LIII:39)

c It teaches that God rewards man's labour in full. Hence, it is the duty of the Islamic state, as the vicegerent of God, to establish an economic order wherein the labour of every citizen is fully rewarded:

وَاَنَّ سَعْيَهُ سَوْفَ يُرَىٰ، ثُمَّ يُجْزِيهُ الْجَزَاءَ الأَوْفَىٰ.

'And that his (man's) effort will be seen; then he will be repaid for it with fullest payment.'

(LIII:40, 41)

d It sets forth the principle that all human beings are equally honourable in respect of their humanity:
It has been proclaimed:

وَلَقَد كَرَّمْنَا بَنِي اَدَمَ.

'Verily We have honoured the children of Adam.'

(XVII:70)

Hence, it is the duty of the Islamic state, as God's

vicegerent, to organize, ensure and promote honourable living and livelihood for all of its citizens.

e It approves the right to private property:

لِلرِّجَالِ نَصِيبٌ مِمَّا تَرَكَ الوَالِدَانِ وَالأَقْرَبُونَ، وَلِلنِّسَاءِ نَصِيبٌ مِمَّا تَرَكَ الوَالِدَانِ وَالأَقْرَبُونَ مِمَّا قَلَّ مِنْهُ او كَثَرَ، نَصِيباً مَفرُوضاً.

'From what is left by parent and those nearest related there is a share for men (to own) and there is a share for women (to own), whether the property be small or large – a determinate share.'

(IV:7)

Again:

لِلرِّجَالِ نَصِيبٌ مِمَّا اكتَسَبُوا، وَلِلنِّسَاءِ نَصِيبٌ مِمَّا اكتَسَبْنَ.

'. . . To men the benefit of what they earn and to women the benefit of what they earn . . .'

(IV:32)

f It protects the rights of the owner of private property against violations by others:

وَلاَ تَبْخَسُوا النَّاسَ أَشيَاءَهُمْ.

'. . . and wrong not mankind in their goods (i.e., possessions) . . .'

(VII:85)

g It does not, however, permit the institution of private property to promote the evil of concentration of wealth. Rather, among other measures to which references have been made in the foregoing, it lays down the principle for the division of property among inheritors on a wide scale, by taking into consideration all the male and female categories of near relatives and permitting the bequest of one-third of property for the welfare of the non-inheritors, so that the Muslim community may remain essentially a community of middle-roaders from the economic point of view.

The foregoing makes it evident that the Quranic point of view steers clear of both free economy (capitalist) and controlled economy (communist), and prescribes a partially free and partially controlled economy. In that respect:

a   it sanctions the right of private ownership

b   its principle that value lies in labour envisages peasant proprietorship of agricultural land and forms a condemnation of absentee landlordism

c   it advocates wages for the labourer commensurate with honourable living

d   its emphasis on the gifts of nature being meant for all human beings, the right to own mines, water, perennial forests, etc., should belong only to people as a whole, namely to the state

e   its emphasis on the principle that wealth should not be permitted to become concentrated in a few hands makes it incumbent that the economic order should be such as to have no room for monopolists of wealth – the industrial barons and the business lords.[21]

The concept of the Islamic state, as one can gather from an analysis of the various injunctions in the Quran, produced by Dr Ansari, is also supported by other Muslim scholars and leading ulema like Maulana Mawdudi who, in his discussion on 'essential features of the Islamic political system', more or less agrees with the concept of an Islamic state as given by Dr Ansari based on the principles laid down in the Quran itself.[22]

What picture of an Islamic state emerges from the Islamic principles as laid down in the Quran? First, that the sovereignty belongs to God and God alone. But does it mean a revival of the old theory of the 'Divine Right of Kings'? The answer is clearly negative because the sovereignty of God is not delegated to any individual or any group like the ulema (the religious teachers). The sovereignty is to be exercised by the people and no one else. The representatives of the people, chosen through election, will exercise sovereignty as the agents of God. The sovereignty of God in Islam does not imply any idea of theocracy as it is understood in Western political thought. Islam does not recognize any priesthood who alone can exercise authority or interpret the injunctions of God. It is the people and their elected representatives, their elected head of the state, who will exercise powers as given by God. So, there is no conflict between the Islamic concept of the sovereignty of God and the idea of popular sovereignty which is the fundamental ingredient of democracy.

The two other essential features of a democracy, rule of law and equality of all citizens, are also stressed in the Quranic concept of an Islamic state, similarly the fundamental right of citizens, including the right to resist an arbitrary ruler who may be unjust or becomes a tyrant, is fully recognized. Even the highest authority in an Islamic state is not above the law. Independence of judiciary and separation of powers between the executive and judiciary are clearly laid down. Equal emphasis is given to social justice and for a fair and equitable economic order – these are widely regarded as essential ingredients of a modern democratic state; there is no scope for any dictatorship in Islam.

Is there any scope for a legislature in an Islamic state? Some fundamentalists argue that since the Shariah (Islamic law) contains provisions governing the whole field of human activity, there is no scope in an Islamic state for a legislature to make any laws. But we find injunctions in the Quran, and the Shariah gives general principles and leaves large scope for legislation on other matters where there are no specific provisions in the Shariah. The Pakistani intelligentsia like Professor I H Qureshi raises the question, should we accept the Shariah as it stands today without any reinterpretation or reorientation? He answers, 'It has been recognized in all Muslim countries that in many respects the mutable part of the Shariah requires considerable overhauling and the immutable parts (i.e. the Quran and the Hadith) need a new interpretation.' Who will do this work of 'overhauling' and 'new interpretation' of Islamic laws? Not the ulema.

It is obvious that the only place where discussion can take place in connection with the reinterpretation and reorientation of the Shariah, is the legislature, because as supreme representatives of the people, the legislature alone can speak for them and accept on their behalf what seems rational and proper out of a mass of argument and commentary putting forward different points of view.[23]

This dynamic concept of the Shariah as expressed by Professor Qureshi was also supported by the leading Muslim jurists and philosophers in India before partition. Sir Mohammad Iqbal, who is regarded as the originator of the idea of a separate state of Pakistan, in his book, *The Reconstruction of Religious Thought in Islam*, stressed the dynamic nature of Islamic law; he pointed out that the assimilative spirit of Islam is more manifest in the sphere of law than in anything else. While commenting on the Quran as the source of Islamic law, he observed that the Quran is, however, not a legal code. Its main purpose is to awaken in man the higher consciousness of his relation with God and the universe. No doubt the Quran does lay down a few general principles and laws of a legal nature. But, it is perfectly clear that far from leaving no scope for human thought and legislative activity, the intensive breadth of these principles virtually acts as an awakener of human thought. The early Muslim jurists, taking the Quran as its groundwork, evolved a number of legal systems. The ulema claim finality for the popular schools of Muslim law. But this attitude of the ulema is not correct. Since things have changed and the world of Islam is today confronted with, and affected by, new forces set free by the development of human thought in all of its directions, this attitude should be discarded, and the claim of the present generation of Muslim liberals to reinterpret the foundational legal principles in the light of their own experience and the altered conditions of modern life is perfectly justified.[24] Thus Ameer Ali, in his *The Spirit of Islam*, discusses this problem in his chapter on the political spirit of Islam. This learned author says that Islam gave to the people a code which, however archaic in its simplicity, was capable of the greatest development in accordance with the progress of material civilization. It conferred on the state a flexible constitution, based on a just appreciation of human rights and duty. It limited taxation; it made men equal in the eyes of the law; it consecrated the principles of self-government. It established a control over the sovereign power by rendering the Islamic executive authority subordinate to the law – a law based upon religious sanctions and moral obligations.[25]

What is clear from these utterances is that the Pakistani intelligentsia regard the Shariah not as something static and fixed once and for all. Wilfred Smith rightly says that they see the Shariah not as a static system, but as a dynamic development; a process in which the historical stages of the past are available for study and guidance, but in which the proper present and future developments are matters of creative extrapolation. This interpretation would accent continuity and revision.[26] So, according to this interpretation of Islamic law, there is definite scope for a legislature in an Islamic republic. The legal sovereign should be the Muslim law, but its definition should be in the hands of the legislature, representing the people, which would decide how to apply the principles of Islam to the needs of the community in varying circumstances. The political sovereign should be the people who elect and dismiss their legislature and government.

Some of the extremists among the ulema, however, disagree with the concept of an Islamic state as we have presented it in the preceding pages, based on the views of learned Muslim scholars and jurists as well as Western scholars like Professor W C Smith, who has carefully followed the debates and discussion on an Islamic state in

Pakistan in the 1950s. This extremist section of the ulema fails to distinguish between the principle and the method of expression of the principle. They are not content with the principles of Islam alone, but wish to adopt in an Islamic state in Pakistan every action and institution which was set up in seventh century Arabia. They hold the view that the form of government in Pakistan, if it is to comply with the principles of Islam, will not be democratic. This small section of the ulema fail to see the inherent impossibility of reproducing in one age the activities and constructions of another. They give too narrow an interpretation of Islamic principles. They look upon Islam as a dead, unprogressive and static collection of injunctions and prohibitions. They fail to comprehend that Islam cannot be content merely with precedents and traditions, but needs a new interpretation at every stage of its development. In order to apply Islamic principles in modern society, it must be given a dynamic interpretation; Islam does not discard precedents and traditions but lays emphasis upon the progressive unfolding of the creative instincts of mankind. The difficulty with the extremists is that they consider as their own preserve the interpretation of the principles of Islam, and while interpreting, they cannot make the proper distinction between a principle and its method of expression. The khalifa, for instance, was elected but the mode of election was altogether different from modern election. The principle of election was there but the method was different: some of the ulema would describe an election as un-Islamic if it does not agree with the particular method which was suitable in seventh century Arabia; they are not satisfied unless every particular and detail which existed in the early days of Islam has been adopted.[27]

Now one may raise the question that if the Quranic concept of the Islamic state and a modern democratic state are basically the same, why do the Pakistanis insist on what may be termed as Islamic democracy rather than simply democracy. In order to appreciate this fact we have to go deeper and explain the raison d'être of the Pakistani demand for an Islamic state or Islamic democracy. Muslims draw their inspirations for a good life and good society from their faith, Islam, which, at the cost of repetition, is not just a mode of worship but provides for the Muslim a whole code of life. When Muslims want to establish a society which is fair, free and just to everybody, irrespective of race, colour, language, sex and religion, and create equality in all spheres of life – political, economic and social – they sincerely believe that the Quranic principles relating to an Islamic state are the best and the only guide for them to establish such a good society. This is the main justification for insisting upon Islamic democracy rather than just democracy as it is understood in a modern secular state. We shall conclude our discussion on the Islamic state by referring to Professor W C Smith's comments on this demand of Muslims for 'Islamic democracy'. He seems to have appreciated the significance and true meaning of Muslims' desire to have it rather than simply 'democracy'. The phrase 'Islamic democracy', Professor Smith states, has puzzled many who wondered how it may be different from other democracies or where in classical Islamic history it is to be found. But as he points out, 'Islamic democracy' gains its significance from the fact that democracy has both a political and an ethical element. It cannot exist without the concurrence of both a governmental form and a popular ideal. The ethical aspect is a no less important ingredient; it must have content, and must have some solid basis for continuing support. A democrat must believe not only in the democratic structure of the state; he must also believe in the fundamental significance and value of the other persons in his society. For the West, Professor Smith relates, this faith, the ethical element, comes from two main sources: the Greek tradition and the Judaeo-Christian. In the case of Pakistan, that ethical element is Islam. Moreover, for a Westerner on certain matters, judgments of value, even though their content be Christian, would be cast in a form derived from the Greco-Roman tradition. Westerners – to some extent Muslims educated in Western ways – are accustomed, for example, to considering political questions by means of concepts, categories and modes of thought stemming from the Greek root of Western civilization. For a Muslim his whole civilizational heritage is, if not religious, set in Islamic forms. Herein lies the true significance of the phrase 'Islamic democracy'. Professor Smith further points out that the demand that Pakistan should be an Islamic state is a way of saying that Pakistan should build for itself a good society – not merely an independent or a strong or a wealthy or a modern society. All these things it should be perhaps, but it should also be a good society. He concludes that a Muslim's apprehension of goodness is coloured by his environment, the pressures and complexities and limitations of his particular time and place, and by his own capacity, his moral acumen and the sensitivity of his spirit. It is coloured also, and more uniquely, by the fact that he is a Muslim.[28]

NOTES

1 Nasir Ahmad Sheikh, *Some Aspects of the Constitution and Economics of Islam*, Woking, Surrey, England, 1957, p. 16

2 For details see Raymond G Gettell, *History of Political Thought*, New York, 1924, chapters 5 and 6.

3 William Ebenstein, *Great Political Thinkers; Plato to the Present*, New York, 1960, chapter 12, pp. 310 and 313.

4 *Vital Steps Towards Democracy*, op. cit., pp. 23–24.

5 Abul A'La Mawdudi, *Towards Understanding Islam*, translated and edited by Khurshid Ahmad, London, 1981, pp. 10–11.

6 See Wilfred C Smith, *Pakistan As An Islamic Democracy*, Lahore, 1951.

7 *Pakistan (first) Constituent Assembly Debates*, 1949, vol. 5, no. 5, pp. 66–67.

8 Ibid, p. 96.

9 Muhammad Asad, *The Principles of State and Government in Islam*, first published California, 1961; new edition, Gibraltar, 1980, pp. 2–4.

10 Muhammad Fazlur-Rahman Ansari, *The Quranic Foundation and the Structure of Muslim Society*, Karachi, 1977, vol. 2, pp. 342–344.

11 *Report of the Constitution Commission*, op. cit., p. 120.

12 Ibid, p. 121.

13 Ibid, p. 121.

14 Based on personal interviews; see also the author's *Constitutional Developments in Pakistan*, op. cit., pp. 71–72.

15 *The Report of the Court of Inquiry*, Punjab Disturbances of 1953, Lahore 1954, pp. 206–207.

16 *Pakistan (first) Constituent Assembly Debates*, vol. 1, no. 2, pp. 19–20.

17 See *Quaid-e-Azam's broadcast to the USA*, 14 February 1948, in *Dawn*, Karachi, 15 February, 1948.

18 Cited in *Political Plan Announced*, op. cit., pp. 9–10.

19 *Pakistan (first) Constituent Assembly Debates*, vol. 2, no. 2, pp. 57–58.

20 I H Qureshi, 'Future Constitution of Pakistan', *Proceedings of the First All-Pakistan Political Science Conference*, Lahore, 1950, pp. 4–5.

21 *The Quranic Foundations and Structure of Muslim Society*, op. cit., vol. 3, pp. 344–57 and 360–80.

22 For details of Maulana Sayid Abul A'la Mawdudi's views on the Islamic State see (1) *The Islamic Way of Life*, edited by Khurshid Ahmad and Khurram Murad, London, 1986 (2) *Islamic Perspectives – Studies in Honour of Sayid Abul A'La Mawdudi*, edited by Khurshid Ahmad and Zarfar Ishaq Ansari, London, 1979.

23 I H Qureshi, *The Conception of Sovereignty and Executive Government*, Proceeding of the Second All-Pakistan Political Science Conference, Karachi, 1952.

24 Sir Mohammad Iqbal, *The Reconstruction of Religious Thought in Islam*, London, 1934, pp. 150–60.

25 S Ameer Ali, *The Spirit of Islam*, London, 1935, p. 277.

26 W C Smith, *Pakistan as an Islamic State*, preliminary draft, Montreal 1951, p. 25.

27 For details of this rigid and narrow concept of an Islamic state held by some extremists, see *Pakistan, The Report of the Court of Inquiry*, op. cit., pp. 210–212.

28 W C Smith, op. cit., pp. 30–35.

Chapter IV
Nifaz-i-Nizam-i-Islam
The Process of Islamization

From the very inception of his military rule, President Zia-ul-Haq has put stress on giving his country a 'real Islamic state and the Islamic system of working'. In his various speeches between 12 August 1983 and 30 December 1985 when martial law was finally lifted, Zia never missed a single opportunity to stress his positive plan for the Islamization of the political and social system in Pakistan. The most novel and outstanding feature of the present-day constitution in Pakistan is the important role of Islam in the country's political order. In fact, the problem of the relationship between state and religion has always been, as already stated, a major issue in the lengthy process of constitution-making in Pakistan: 1947–56, 1961–62, 1972–73 and 1983–85. But with Zia, the issue became the most important aspect of his proposals for constitutional reforms in Pakistan.

In the three constitutions – 1956, 1962 and 1973 – adopted in Pakistan since its inception in 1947, there were some Islamic provisions to designate the country as an 'Islamic state'. But in the constitutions of 1956, 1962 and 1973, the Islamic provisions were more in the nature of an ideal or ideology; there was no real substance to make the political order a real Islamic one. The first big step towards the concept of an Islamic state in Pakistan was taken when the first constituent assembly of Pakistan passed a resolution on the 'aims and objects of the constitution', popularly known as the 'objectives resolution', in March 1949. The outstanding feature of the objectives resolution was that it sought to base the constitution of Pakistan on the ideals of Islam. The resolution recognized the sovereignty of God and declared that all authority must be subservient to God. It also laid emphasis on the principles of democracy, freedom, equality, tolerance and social justice, but qualified them by saying that these principles should be observed in the constitution as they have been *enunciated in Islam*. The 1949 objectives resolution became the preamble to the Pakistan constitution of 1956, 1962 and 1973. But the preamble was never made part of the constitution; it was not enforceable by the courts. It was more in the nature of a goal or ideology on which the constitution aimed to be based.

There were other Islamic provisions in the 1956, 1962 and 1973 constitutions such as that no law should be passed in Pakistan which would be repugnant to the teaching of Islam as laid down in the Holy Quran and Sunnah; that existing laws should be brought into conformity with such injunctions. Pakistan was designated as the Islamic Republic of Pakistan; the head of the state should be a Muslim; there were also provisions for an Islamic research organization and an 'Advisory Council of Islamic Ideology'; a number of 'directive principles of state policy' were also provided in which stress was laid on steps which should enable the Muslims of Pakistan, individually and collectively, to order their lives in accordance with the Holy Quran and Sunnah. In the 1973 constitution, Islam was also made the state religion of the country. But with President Zia the process of Nifaz-i-Nizam-i-Islam is an article of faith. The new Islamic provisions, and the measures already taken to implement them, make Pakistan a meaningful Islamic state. It is no longer in the realm of an aim or objective. The new concept and definition of the Islamic state as a result of Zia's constitutional amendments (8th amendment of December 1985) have given rise to a new and comprehensive concept of an Islamic constitution in Pakistan.

According to Zia, Nifaz-i-Nizam-i-Islam and the restoration of democracy were the two principle objectives of his constitutional reforms. Even before the civilian government was restored in 1985, Zia took a number of far-reaching measures towards the process of Islamization of the country's political system; there were also lengthy and scholarly discussions on the role of Islam in the country's socio-political system. A number of reports dealing with the relationship between state and religion have been published such as the 'report of the special committee of the federal council on the form and system of government in Pakistan', from an 'Islamic point of view', known as the Fida Commission Report, 1983; 'Constitutional Recommendations for the Islamic system of government' by the council of Islamic ideology, 1983 and the 'Ansari Commission Report on the form of Government', 1983. These reports and the debates in the Pakistan parliament (Majlis-e-Shoora) on the 8th amendment to the 1973 constitution, provide valuable guides to the understanding of the new trends in the relationship between state and religion in Pakistan. When Zia first announced his political plan for the restoration of democracy in Pakistan on 12 August 1983 he said that whatever system we adopt it must fully conform to Islamic principles, and must, at the same time, fulfil present-day requirements. He thinks that there is no contradiction between the two because Islam is a progressive and an enlightened religion. When God, Zia says, revealed the Holy Quran for the guidance of mankind, it was not for any particular period but for all times to come. The Quran provides only the guiding principles and leaves out many things. Where the Quran, Zia points out, is silent, Muslims have the option of resorting to *Ijtihad* (individual judgement and consensus). Zia talks about adjusting a particular case to the requirements of a particular situation at a given place.[1]

This suggests giving Islam a dynamic and flexible interpretation similar to the previous three constitutions in Pakistan. But Zia's latest constitutional reforms go far beyond the measures taken by his predecessors in Pakistan.

Islamic Provisions in the (Original) 1973 Constitution

Before we discuss President Zia's process of Islamization through various ordinances and amendments to the 1973 constitution, let us first examine the Islamic provisions in the 1973 constitution as passed by the national assembly of Pakistan on 10 April 1973.

The identification with Islam begins, as in the 1956 and 1962 constitutions, with the preamble. The relevant sections of the preamble are as follows:

> Sovereignty of the entire universe belongs to Almighty Allah alone and the authority exercisable by the people is a sacred trust.

Unlike the preamble of the 1956 and 1962 constitutions, there was no reference to Jinnah's views on the Islamic state.

> Principles of democracy, freedom, equality, tolerance and social justice, as enunciated by Islam, should be fully observed in Pakistan. The Muslims of Pakistan should be enabled individually

and collectively to order their lives in accordance with the teachings and requirements of Islam.

The preamble to the 1973 constitution, as far as the Islamic character of the constitution is concerned, is almost identical with the preamble to the 1956 and 1962 constitutions; authority, to be exercised by the people of Pakistan within the limits prescribed by Him (Allah), is a sacred trust.

The most outstanding and novel feature of the preamble, as was the case with the objectives resolution of 1949, is that it seeks to base the constitution of Pakistan on the ideals of Islam. The preamble makes a frank and unequivocal recognition of the sovereignty of God and declares that all authority must be subservient to God. As pointed out by the first prime minister, Liaquat Ali Khan, at the time of the adoption of the 1949 objectives resolution, 'All authority is a sacred trust entrusted to us by God for the purpose of being exercised in the services of men, so that it does not become an agency for tyranny and selfishness.'[2] While the preamble emphasizes the sovereignty of God, it also declares that the state should exercise its power and authority through the representatives chosen by the people. It can, therefore, be argued that the preamble is not a resuscitation of the theory of the divine right of kings. In accordance with the spirit of Islam, the preamble fully recognizes that the people would exercise the authority. It does not give any special privilege or exclusive power to any particular class or priesthood. Islam does not, as already stated, recognize either a priesthood or any sacerdotal authority. Such an idea is absolutely foreign to Islam.

The preamble to the constitution is not unique in its reference to the sovereignty of God. We find a similar reference in the constitution of Ireland (Eire) 1937: 'In the name of the most Holy Trinity from whom all authority and to whom as our final end, all actions both of men and state must be referred . . .' (preamble). Then again, 'all powers of government legislature, executive and judicial, derive under God, from the people . . .'

We have already explained that the concept of the sovereignty of God is not incompatible with the theory of popular sovereignty. The preamble makes the frank declaration that there is no power but from God. In this sense we may say that the constitution of Pakistan is theocratic. But the term theocracy in Islam does not have the usual connotations. There are no special agents of God recognized, and hence theocracy in the ordinary sense has no place in Islamic statecraft. The right to rule is not necessarily associated with a special form of government; either one or another may be assumed, provided that it be such as to ensure the general welfare. Moreover, it may be argued that the sovereignty of God ensures that civil authority must not be subservient to the advantage of one or a few, for it is established for the good of all; or if those who are in authority should rule unjustly or if they should err through arrogance or pride; if their measure should be injurious to the people, then let it be known that hereafter an account must be rendered to God. In such a confirmation of the state, there is nothing that may be incompatible or out of tune with the spirit and tradition of democracy. On the contrary, when there is an emphasis on the moral aspects of the civil and political authority, it may help to ensure that laws aim to the common good, and are determined by truth and justice, and that authority is restrained from deviating from what is just and overstepping the limits of power. Hence, we conclude that reference to the sovereignty of God is not incompatible with any idea of popular sovereignty. This was made clear by Liaquat Ali Khan and others who took part in the debates on the objectives resolution in 1949.

The preamble, like the objectives resolution, lays emphasis on the principles of democracy, freedom, equality, tolerance and social justice, but qualifies them by saying that these principles should be observed in the constitution as they had been enunciated by Islam. Why these qualifications? Here again we may quote Liaquat Ali Khan: 'It has been necessary to qualify this term because they are generally used in a loose sense, for instance, the Western powers and Soviet Russia alike claim that their system is based upon democracy and yet it is common knowledge that their politics are inherently different. It has, therefore, been found necessary to define these terms further in order to give them a well-understood meaning . . . When we use the word democracy in the Islamic sense, it pervades all aspects of our lives, it relates to our system of government and to our society with equal validity.'[3]

Democracy becomes an aspect of Islamicness, a part of the definition of the Islamic state. That was the spirit in which the words 'as enunciated by Islam' were incorporated into the objectives resolution of 1949, and we hope the same would be the objective of the incorporation of these words in the new preamble as there is no room for an authoritarian system in a truly Islamic constitution.

Islamic provisions are contained, as in the 1956 and 1962 constitutions, in the 'principles of state policy' which, however like the preamble, are not enforceable in the law courts, but are expected to serve as a guide to the state authorities in the formulation of policies. According to the directive principles as laid down in the new constitution, 'the Muslims of Pakistan should be enabled individually and collectively to order their lives in accordance with the fundamental principles and basic concepts of Islam, and should be provided with the facilities whereby they may be able to understand the meaning of life according to those principles and concepts.' Much would depend on the interpretation of the words, 'fundamental principles and basic concepts of Islam.' To meet the requirements of a modern complex society, these principles and concepts have to be given a progressive and dynamic interpretation, otherwise such a clause will prove to be an excellent tool in the hands of reactionary elements. Fortunately, Islam is a dynamic force and capable of rational interpretation.

Further it is laid down in the principles of policy that (i) teaching of the Quran and Islam to the Muslims of Pakistan should be made compulsory; (ii) unity and observation of Islamic moral standards should be promoted among the Muslims of Pakistan; (iii) proper organization of zakat, waqfs and mosques should be ensured. Another article on 'principles of policy' (article 38) provides that the bonds of unity among the Muslim countries should be preserved and strengthened. A similar provision was also made in the 1956 and 1962 constitutions, but this should not be interpreted as pan-Islamism, as the same article enjoins Pakistan to foster friendly relations among all nations, Muslim and non-Muslim. Pakistan, however, since its inception has always stressed 'the natural and religious link, the common culture and identity of economic outlook' (Liaquat), between herself and other Muslim countries and persistently supported the causes of Muslim countries.

Like the constitution of Iran and Saudi Arabia, there is a new provision making Islam the state religion in Pakistan.

The head of the state, the president, is to be, as in the 1956 and 1962 constitutions, a Muslim. The argument for reserving the presidency for a Muslim is that Pakistan was founded on the basis of Islamic philosophy and it is, therefore, logical that the president should be from amongst those who believe in that philosophy. The president is not only the chief executive but also the symbolic head of the state, which is based on an ideology, and it is, therefore, claimed that he should be a believer in the philosophy that created Pakistan.

With the exception of this one clause, there is no discrimination against any citizen on the grounds of religion, colour, race or nationality. Moreover, adequate and generous provisions have been made in the constitution to safeguard the interests of the non-Muslim minorities – the legitimate rights and interests of the minorities. The principles of state policy further declare that the members of the minorities should be given due opportunity to enter the services of Pakistan. Hence there is no basis for apprehension that the Islamic provisions in the constitution will regulate the non-Muslim citizens to an inferior status. We may describe here the status of religious minorities in an Islamic state like Pakistan.

Religious Minorities in an Islamic State

Pakistan was claimed as a homeland for Indian Muslims on the principle of the right of self-determination. When Pakistan actually emerged as a free nation on 14 August 1947, it was not exclusively Muslim in population but contained several millions of non-Muslim citizens. Many had doubts whether there would be room for any non-Muslims in a state that had come into being pre-eminently because the Muslims had sought a homeland wherein they could lead a life of their own based on a common religion and a common ideology. Yet Pakistan had a substantial minority population. According to the first census of 1951, minorities constituted 14.1 per cent of the entire population of undivided Pakistan before 1971. They consisted mainly of Hindus, Christians, Parsis and Buddhists. The bulk of the Hindus, who constituted the biggest minority group, lived in East Pakistan (now Bangladesh), where they constituted 23.2 per cent of its population. In one district, namely the Chittagong Hills tract, the non-Muslims even formed the majority of the population.

The Hindus occupied a very important position in the economic life of East Pakistan, and were an integral and vital part of it. The greatest number of landlords in East Pakistan were Hindus. All but one or two of the textile mills of the provinces were owned and managed by them; they dominated the bar and occupied very important places in the educational services of East Pakistan and they had substantial shares in commerce and industry. They had a number of political parties of their own such as the Pakistan National Congress and the Scheduled Castes Federation; there were Hindu cultural organizations as well. There were numerous religious sects among the Hindus; the most important division in Hindu society is between caste Hindus (the upper class) and the scheduled castes (the depressed classes).

Next to the Hindus, the Buddhists were the most important minority community in undivided Pakistan; they also lived in East Pakistan. The total number of Pakistani Buddhists was 319,000; the tribal Buddhists, who constituted the majority of these, enjoyed a fair measure of administrative autonomy. They have three tribes – the Chakma, Mong and Bomong, each having a chief of its own who administers tribal affairs with little outside interference.

Christians and Parsis are two other important minority groups in 'new' Pakistan today. They play an important role in the economic and cultural life of the country. Parsi businessmen have always performed an important part in the country's commerce and business. The activity of Christians in the educational life of the country is substantial. The Muslims of Pakistan are deeply conscious of the valuable contribution which their non-Muslim compatriots have made, and continue to make, towards enriching the national life, socially, economically and culturally.

What the rights and safeguards for these non-Muslim minority groups in Pakistan should be, is a question which engaged the attention of the framers of the constitution from the very beginning of their work. The first constituent assembly of Pakistan came into existance on 10 August 1947, and within two days of its establishment, it set up a committee to advise it on the fundamental rights of citizens of Pakistan, and on matters relating to the minorities. Jinnah in his inaugural speech in the constituent assembly laid down the policy of the new state towards its minorities. He declared:

> You may belong to any religion or caste or creed, there is no discrimination between one community and another, no discrimination between one caste or creed and another. We are starting with this fundamental principle that we are all citizens and equals of one state.[4]

It was a very good beginning and an excellent ideal. The declaration of the founder of the state had a most welcome reception among the minorities. The minority leaders in defending their claims in the constituent assembly and elsewhere have referred to this memorable speech on many an occasion. It was regarded as the Magna Carta of the minorities in Pakistan. But a single declaration or one speech cannot solve such a complex problem; the application of general principles to specific problems is always beset with difficulties. The problem of minorities, particularly of religious or racial minorities, is one of the most perplexing problems of modern democracy. What is the use, asked Hare and Mill, of broadening and extending the franchise unless all the parties have representation in the legislature? Did not the minorities run the risk of being swamped, and was not there the possibility of representative democracy turning into an unqualified and intolerable tyranny of the majority? In a democracy all basic questions affecting the governance of that country are usually decided by an appeal to the majority principle. But it is an equally important principle of democratic institutions that minorities must be duly safeguarded; their culture, their legitimate rights should not be open to attack or assault by the majority. This question has engaged the attention of statesmen for a long time. Its traces are found in the early history of Islam; in Europe one finds them in the peace of Augsburg, 1555; the pact of Warsaw, 1573; the edict of Nantes, 1598; and the treaty of Westphalia, 1648. After the conclusion of the Great War of 1914–18, numerous new states were set up as a result of the break up of the Austro-Hungarian, German and Russian empires. Safeguarding the interests of the minorities in these various succession states was sought through the 'minorities' treaties' whose implementation was placed under the auspices of the League of Nations. About a score of such states (like Poland, Czechoslovakia, Yugoslavia, Latvia, Rumania, etc.) entered into these international agreements for the protection of the racial, linguistic and religious minorities within their respective borders. In undivided India about half a century ago, the Muslim community, who constituted the biggest minority in India, began to demand separate representation and weightage in order to safeguard their rights and interests. Since that time, the necessity to provide such safeguards has been recognized in various constitutional acts for the government of India. The Morley-Minto Reforms (1909), the Montagu-Chelmsford Reforms (1919) and following upon the Simon Commission and the Round Table Conferences, the Government of India 1935, had to take the question of the minorities into consideration, and provide safeguards. The Muslims, however, felt that their religious, economic, cultural and political rights were not adequately protected, and eventually they lost their faith in constitutional safeguards and decided upon separation. In this sense, Pakistan itself is the creation of a minority problem.

In Pakistan the problem of non-Muslim religious minorities was further complicated by the demand for an Islamic state. The 1949 objectives resolution, as adopted by the first constituent assembly, proposed a constitution wherein the 'principles of democracy, freedom, equality, tolerance and social justice as enunciated by Islam' should be fully observed.

The question, however, continued to be debated: what should be the rights and duties of a non-Muslim in Pakistan who does not believe in an Islamic ideology? Muslim scholars and ulema engaged themselves in determining the position of non-Muslims in an Islamic state. What is the attitude of Islam towards minorities? Islam stands for the equality of all races and colours: all are alike in its great brotherhood; all can aspire to any position or vocation. Islam also inculcates respect and toleration for other religions; this spirit was embodied in the charter which was granted to the Jews by the Prophet Muhammad after his arrival in Medina and in the notable message sent to the Christians of Najran and neighbouring territories after Islam had fully established itself in the Arabian Peninsula. The latter document pledged the security of the lives, religion and property of the Christians: 'There should be no interference with (the practice of) their faith or observances, nor any change in their rights or privileges'. There have been occasional lapses in the observance of these principles; but the principles themselves have never been modified. As Professor Arnold pointed out: 'The theory of the Muslim faith enjoins toleration and freedom of religious life for all those followers of other faiths who pay tribute in return for protection, and though the pages of Muhammadan history are stained with the blood of many cruel persecutions, on the whole, unbelievers have enjoyed under Muhammadan rule a measure of toleration the like of which is not to be found in Europe until quite modern times . . . the very existence of so many Christian sects and communities in countries that have been for centuries under Muhammadan rule is an abiding testimony to the toleration they have enjoyed and shows that the persecutions that they have from time to time endured at the hands of bigots and fanatics have been excited by some special and local circumstances rather than inspired by a settled principle of intolerance.'[5]

The critics of the Islamic state, on the other hand, maintain that whatever may be the theory of tolerance in Islam, history contradicts it. Even in the best days of the Islamic state, non-Muslims suffered in spite of the Prophet's assurance. In support of the thesis that non-Muslim subjects of Islamic states labour under severe disabilities, reference is made to the narrow views of canonists and lawyers of Islam. In an Islamic state, the critics point out, the best status that the non-Muslim can have is that of Dhimmis (people living in alliance with and under the protection of Islam in a Muslim land). It is argued that Dhimmis have protection for their lives, families and property, but they have a definitely inferior status. They are not full-fledged citizens but enjoy the status of protected wards. They are to be accorded toleration and protection, but are outside the full community of the state. They must pay a special tax in return for protection. They are allowed to retain their own religious organizations, personal status, places of worship and religious trust.

Non-Muslim citizens in Pakistan naturally expressed apprehension with regard to their position in the proposed Islamic constitution of Pakistan. They were given some grounds for their apprehension by certain ulema. According to some of the extremists of Pakistan, the position of non-Muslims in the Islamic state of Pakistan should be that of Dhimmis, and they would not be full citizens of Pakistan because they would not be given the same right as Muslims. They would have no voice in the making of the law, no right to administer the law and no right to hold public office.[6] According to one prominent member of the ulema who was also a member of the constituent assembly, 'they (non-Muslims) cannot be entrusted with the responsibility of framing the general policy of the state or dealing with matters vital to its safety and integrity.'[7] This statement was misunderstood, because what the speaker meant was that Muslims in an Islamic state cannot permit the substance of sovereignty to slip from their hands. However, the government, the framers of the constitution, and the Muslim intelligentsia have never accepted the views of the extremists who do not fully understand the manner in which the basic political concepts of Islam should be applied in the world today. The notion of an Islamic state has not led to any suggestion that the constitution should bestow any special privilege or exclusive power upon the ulema. Intellectual Pakistanis think that the ulema may offer interpretations of Islam, but it lies within the province of the people to accept or reject them. Pakistan is elaborating a new approach to this problem.

What is the position of non-Muslims in the modern concept of an Islamic state as interpreted in Pakistan today? The founder of the state had already formulated the principle of equality of citizens irrespective of caste, creed and religion. We find in the objectives resolution of 1949, which laid down the foundation of an Islamic state in Pakistan, that 'adequate provision shall be made for the minorities freely to profess and practise their religions and develop their cultures, and adequate provision shall be made to safeguard the legitimate interests of minorities'. Further the minorities, like other Muslim citizens, of Pakistan are guaranteed fundamental rights including the equality of status, of opportunity before the law, of social, economic and political justice, and of freedom of thought, expression, belief, faith, worship and association. Certain conclusions encouraging liberals may be drawn from the debate on the 1949 objectives resolution. Although it was intended that Muslims should be subject to the economic and social obligations prescribed by their religion, there would be no distinction between Muslims and non-Muslims in their rights of citizenship. The privileges and status of non-Muslims, according to the objectives resolution, would not be in any way less than those of Muslims. The concept of a lower status for non-Muslim citizens was most emphatically repudiated.

It may be added here that before the partition of India, some distinguished Hindu scholars admired the broad and liberal principles of Islam and believed that a state based on these principles need not be out of tune with democracy. Dr Radha Kamal Mukerjee, an eminent Indian sociologist and ardent member of the extremist Hindu Sabha, in his *Democracies of the East* writes:

The communal-democratic system of politics, founded upon the basis of theocracy in the Islamic Commonwealth, is one of the most remarkable phenomena of political evolution, not less significant than the development of the Athenian democracy and the Roman Republic . . . The democratic spirit of the Islamic Law corresponded with the Semitic idea of a republican state and with a large measure of freedom and independence that were still reserved for local bodies, tribal councils, and communal assemblies. The history of the Caliphate proves that election by the people or nomination by the sovereign was regarded as the only valid title to sovereignty. Sacredness was attached to the oath of allegiance and homage to the sovereign-elect. During the Caliphate of Omar, all business was conducted on rightly ordered constitutional lines. The laws of the Republic and rights of the citizens, Muslims and non-Muslims, were proclaimed by the messengers in the provinces and towns by Abu Bakar and Omar and in these perhaps the most significant feature was the concept of law ruling through the utterances of justice and the noteworthy separation between judicial and executive authority.

He examined in detail the administrative system of the early khalifas and reached the conclusion:

> All testify to the remarkable development of the democratic spirit of the Islamic administration . . . In Muslim India (i.e. Pakistan) the development towards modern constitutionalism was made easier by building on the original and essential democracy of the time-honoured Majlis and Punchayat; the renewal of the Mussalman Commonwealth on this basis will be a new experiment in communalistic policy which will be more satisfying than the importation of western democratic institutions and methods.[8]

Wilfred Smith has analysed the problem of non-Muslim minorities in the Islamic constitution of Pakistan in a brilliant way. He says:

> It is fundamental to remember that the rights accorded to any minority or other non-powerful group in any state depend on the ideal of those in power . . . A state may be democratic in form but unless it is democratic also in ideal, unless the majority of its citizens are actively loyal to the transcendent principles of democracy, recognizing the ideal validity of every man's status as a man, then the arithmetic minority has, through the democratic form, no right at all . . . Many outsiders and several Pakistani Christians and Hindus . . . have stated or supposed that these minorities would be better off if Pakistan was simply a 'Democratic' instead of an Islamic State. This is irresponsibly glib. For if Muslims do in fact treat non-Muslims unjustly then a democratic framework (without the Greco-Roman and religious tradition of democracy to vitalize it) would merely give them as a majority the constitutional authority for doing so without let or hindrance.[9]

Turning back to the Islamic provisions of 1973, we find that article 1 of the 1973 constitution designates Pakistan as 'the Islamic Republic of Pakistan'. There was similar provision in the 1956 constitution; in the 1962 one, Ayub initially dropped the word 'Islamic' but as pointed out earlier, Ayub had to redesignate the state as the 'Islamic Republic of Pakistan' because of public pressures and demands. Left to himself, Bhutto would also probably have dropped the word 'Islamic'. He was highly Western educated and Western orientated in his personal life. But Bhutto knew the strong sentiment and feelings of the Pakistanis in favour of an 'Islamic state'. So Bhutto did not make the mistake that Ayub did in 1962. It may be added that Bhutto was an influential member of Ayub's cabinet and played a significant role in making the 1962 constitution as a member of the cabinet sub-committee which gave final shape to the 1962 constitution.

The most important Islamic provision in the 1973 constitution (as was the case in the 1956 constitution) is article 227 which lays down: 'All existing laws shall be brought in conformity with the injunctions of Islam as laid down in the Holy Quran and Sunnah . . . and no law shall be enacted which is repugnant to such injunctions.' This article does not apply to personal laws of non-Muslim citizens or their status as citizens. Article 228 provides the procedure for enforcing the provisions of article 227 – the procedure is as follows.

A council of Islamic ideology would be constituted within a period of ninety days from the commencing day of the constitution, i.e. 12 April 1973. The council shall be appointed by the president. In selecting the members of the council, the president shall take into account, the person's understanding and appreciation of Islam and understanding of the economic, political, legal or administrative problems of Pakistan. The president, when appointing the members of the council, shall ensure that so far as practicable, various schools of thought are represented in the council; that no less than two members are or have been judges of the supreme court or of a high court; that no less than four of the members have been engaged for a period of not less than fifteen years in Islamic research or instruction, and that at least one member is a woman. The members shall hold office for a period of three years. The president, however, may remove a member from office if a resolution is passed by a majority of the total membership of the council.

The functions of the council shall be to make recommendations to the government, both national and provincial as to the steps and means which would enable and encourage the Muslims of Pakistan to order their lives in accordance with the principles and concepts of Islam. The most important function of the council is to advise the national assembly, a provincial assembly, the president or a provincial governor on any question as to whether a proposed law 'is or is not repugnant to the injunctions of Islam'. Another important function of the council is to make recommendations as to the measures for bringing existing laws into conformity with the injunctions of Islam and the stages by which such measures should be brought into effect. The council shall also compile, in a suitable form for the guidance of legislatures, both national and provincial assemblies, 'such injunctions of Islam as can be given legislative effect'. When a question is referred either by national assembly or by provincial assembly or by the president or by the governor of a province to the council for advice, it shall inform, within fifteen days, the relevant authority, the period within which the council shall be able to furnish their advice. If the legislatures, national and provincial, or the president, or the governor of a province as the case may be, consider that in the public interest, the proposed law should be made without waiting for the advice, the law may be made before the advice is furnished, but if the council subsequently advises that the law is repugnant to the injunctions of Islam, the national assembly, or the provincial assembly or the president or the provincial governor as the case may be, shall reconsider the law so made. The significant point is that the legislatures, or the president or the governor as the case may be, will only reconsider a law passed against the advice of the council but it does not say what will happen if even after the reconsideration, the law remains unchanged or not repelled. There is no provision that the advice of the council will be binding on the legislatures or the executive authorities; no veto power for the council is envisioned. It is the legislature, which, as the elected representatives of the people, shall decide, in the final stage, whether a proposed law is or is not repugnant to Islam; whether any of the existing laws is against the injunctions of Islam. This is in accordance with the spirit of Islam. When Pakistan's first constitution was in the process of being adopted in 1956, the then law minister, I I Chundrigar, said 'It should be for the people to decide what was, according to their lights, in conformity with the injunctions of Islam. No special set of people, howsoever learned they might be, could be given the prerogative of deciding what was contrary to or in conformity with the injunctions of Islam.'[10]

This is a matter which everyone should decide according to his conscience and therefore it is proper that the elected members of the national assembly should decide for themselves as to whether the provisions of any particular legislation are in conformity with the injunctions of Islam or not. The then prime minister, Choudhry Mohammad Ali, justified the new procedure on the grounds that:

> Our objective is the development of Islamic culture and the Islamic spirit as it operates in our society, our laws and, in fact, in the entire sphere of collective human relationships. We may have

127

differences as to the interpretation of the injunctions of Islam or the legal system of Islam . . . but Islam enjoins upon us not compulsion but discussion and consultation together in our National Parliament and to arrive at conclusions . . . I see nothing wrong in that process . . . It is the duty of all right minded citizens to try to reach agreement on how the essential principles of Islam are to work in our society, in our body politic, in our laws and in all concerning that society.[11]

There was provision for a council of Islamic ideology under Ayub's 1962 constitution, but its role and functions were lesser than those of the council under the 1973 constitution. In Pakistan the idea of such a special body to examine if any proposed law is or is not repugnant to Islam was first proposed in the 1952 draft constitution, presented by the country's second prime minister, Khawaja Nazimuddin. But it was not accepted by the second constituent assembly when the first constitution was finally adopted after nine years of frustration and effort in 1956.

As long as the Islamic council, or any special body like the 'Board of Ulema' as proposed in 1952, is not given any veto power over the actions of the legislature there is nothing wrong in having advice for the legislature from an expert body such as the Council of Islamic Ideology. When such a council was provided under the 1962 constitution, the then law minister, Justice Munir, claimed that the provision for a council represents the first instance in modern history where an effort is being made to bring Islam in contact with modern political, legal, ethical, social and economic conditions and to present new and unanticipated problems for solution to a jurisprudence (Shariah) which has for almost one thousand years been in a static condition.[12]

Under the 1973 constitution there was no provision for any 'Islamic Research Institute' as was the case in the 1956 and 1962 constitutions. The need for such research in Pakistan could hardly be overemphasized. The Islamic ideology needs proper understanding and appreciation if it is to act as a potent factor in the development of a better society. A large-scale programme of study and research is needed before the Islamic values as bearing upon current social, cultural and economic problems can be comprehended. The constitution commission of 1960–61 stressed the need for research and study on Islam.

There was no dearth of Islamic provisions in the 1973 constitution as introduced by Z A Bhutto. His law minister, A H Pirzada, even claimed that 'a serious effort has been made to take out the Islamic provisions [of the constitution] from the cold storage of the principles of policy . . . and bring them into substantial parts of the constitution.' He added that the Islamic provisions of the 1973 constitution would transform the basic injunction and tenets of Islam into law and give legislative effect.[13]

But until President Zia came to power in 1977, the Islamic injunctions and tenets continued to remain in 'cold storage' as was the case under the 1956 and 1962 constitutions. Let us now turn to the process of Islamization under Zia (1977–88).

The Process of Islamization under President Zia

Although the constitution of 1973 and every constitution that preceded it provided, as already pointed out in the preceding pages, elaborate Islamic provisions that the existing laws of Pakistan should be brought into conformity with the injunctions of Islam and that no law should be passed in Pakistan which would be repugnant to the Quran and Sunnah, yet no worthwhile steps were taken in the implementation of the Islamic provisions of the constitution. It was only after President Zia came to power on 5 July 1977 that significant steps were taken towards Islamization in Pakistan – Nifaz-i-Nizam-i-Islam. We have referred to Zia's reforms to introduce Islamic taxes like zakat and ushr and an Islamic system eliminating riba (interest) and replacing it with a basis of participation in profit and loss of a bank. We shall now discuss various other measures taken by Zia from 1977 to 1985 towards Islamization in Pakistan culminating in promulgating an ordinance on 15 June 1988 declaring the Shariah (Islamic law) as the 'supreme law of the country' with immediate effect. While promulgating the ordinance, Zia told his countrymen that from the day he took over the reins of the government on 5 July 1977, he had always been 'insisting from every forum, every platform and on every occasion that justification of the creation of Pakistan was *Nifaz-i-Shariah*' (rule by Islamic law). He added, '[Nifaz-i-Shariah] is not only the basis of our existence but also is a guarantee for our survival.' He concluded by saying: '*Insha Allah* [by the grace of God], the time is not far off when Pakistan will become in the true sense a cradle of Islam, the craze of un-Islamic values will peter out; the atmosphere of suspense and misgivings will wither away, anti-Islam forces will become weaker and ascendency of *Shariat-i-Mohammadi* will permeate every nook and corner of the dear motherland.'[14]

The advisory council of Islamic ideology working under the 1962 constitution and the council of Islamic ideology set up under the 1973 constitution, before the present regime took over in July 1977, made a number of recommendations for Islamization of laws and society, but the government perhaps lacked sincerity of purpose and hence no headway in the achievement of the objectives for which Pakistan came into being could be made. When General Muhammad Zia-ul-Haq took over he showed keen interest in the workings of the council to accelerate the process of Islamization and assured the full co-operation of his government. In the appointment of the members of the council when constituted in September 1977 and reconstituted in May 1981, special care was taken that it consisted of proper and capable persons worthy of accomplishing the job of the process of Islamization within the framework of article 230 of the 1973 constitution. Through a constitutional amendment made, vide PO no. 16 of 1980, the number of members of the council has been increased from 15 to 20. Further, in order to increase the efficiency of the working of the council, it has been conferred with autonomy within permissable limits in the discharge of its constitutional obligations.

HUDOOD LAWS (ISLAMIC PENAL CODE)

The president of Pakistan, on the recommendations of the council of Islamic ideology, also promulgated five ordinances on 10 February 1979 amending the existing Pakistan penal code relating to certain offences affecting moveable property of people and the moral and social order of the society, so as to bring it in conformity with the Holy Quran and the Sunnah. By these ordinances the existing laws relating to the offences of theft, robbery and dacoity, adultery, false accusation of adultery and wine drinking were replaced by the Islamic provisions of Hudood. Drinking of wine (i.e. all alcoholic drinks) was, for instance, not a crime under the Pakistan Penal Code. In 1977, however, the drinking and selling of wine by Muslims was banned in Pakistan and the sentence of imprisonment for six months or a fine of Rs.5,000, or both, was provided under Hudood Laws.[15]

QAZI COURTS

For further effective implementation of Islamic laws with Islamic procedure, steps are under way to establish courts of qazis with jurisdiction over an area comprising the limits of one *thana* (jurisdiction of a police station) or two. This would provide speedy and inexpensive justice on one's doorstep. Similarly, at tehsil headquarters, *izafi zila qazis*, equivalent to additional district and sessions judges, and at district level, zila qazis, equivalent to district and sessions judges, will be set up.

TRAINING IN ADMINISTRATING ISLAMIC LAWS

The International Islamic University, Islamabad, has made arrangements for imparting training in the enforcement and administration of Hudood and other Islamic laws to the sessions judges and additional sessions judges and the prosecuting officers. On average 35 judicial officers are being trained during each term.

We have already discussed zakat and ushr. We may here add its impact on the taxation system of the country.

With a view to giving relief to tax-payers, it has been provided in the Zakat and Ushr Ordinance 18 of 1980 that, notwithstanding anything contained in any other law in force for the time being:

a i under the Income-tax Ordinance 1979, his taxable income shall be reduced by the amount paid by him to a zakat fund during the previous year relevant to that assessment year

  ii under the Wealth-tax Act 1983, his assets in respect of which zakat or contribution in lieu thereof, has been deducted at source during the year relevant to that assessment year shall be excluded form his taxable wealth

b land-revenue and development cess shall not be levied on land on the produce of which ushr or contribution in lieu thereof has been charged on a compulsory basis.

It is, in fact, a step, though minor, towards Islamizing the taxation system in Pakistan.

An international economic seminar, held at Islamabad during 6–11 January 1981, observed, regarding the report of the council of Islamic ideology on the elimination of interest from the economy, in its communiqué issued on the last day of its session that:

The seminar complimented the Government of Pakistan and the Council of Islamic Ideology for the intensive work done to find ways and means of eliminating *Riba*. It regarded the Report of the Council of Islamic Ideology on the elimination of interest as a historic document and a pioneering effort which would be of great use to other Muslim countries in their efforts to transform their banking system in accordance with Islam. It was recommended that to ensure its widest possible readership it should be translated into Arabic and other languages.

In response to the above recommendation, the International Centre for Research in Islamic Economics, King Abdul Aziz University, Jeddah, has translated the said report of the council into Arabic in April 1982.[17]

THE ESTABLISHMENT OF A SHARIAH FACULTY/ ISLAMIC UNIVERSITY

The advisory council of Islamic ideology felt the necessity of producing intellectuals in the country who are not only well-versed in the knowledge of modern jurisprudence and laws, but are scholars of Muslim jurispudence and also of the sources and details of the past and contemporary Muslim law. The council, therefore, recommended that the government should direct the universities of the country to revise their syllabi of law for meeting the ideological requirements of the nation, and for this purpose, stress the importance of immediate initiation of specialized studies and research in Muslim law at postgraduate level and granting liberal scholarships to attract talent to this field of utmost national importance.

President Zia inaugurated on 8 October 1979 the Shariah Faculty at the Quaid-e-Azam University, Islamabad, where special arrangements were made for instruction in Shariah law at postgraduate level. A select group of students has been admitted to the course of LLM (master of Law) degree. This will serve as a base for the reorientation of Islamic learning especially in *Fiqh*, and to cater to the needs of the Shariah court. In November 1980, an Islamic university was established into which the Shariah faculty has been transferred and incorporated. It may not be out of place to mention here that the King Abdul Aziz University of Saudi Arabia extended its full support and co-operation in the establishment of this Shariah

Faculty and the Islamic University. The Al-Azhar of Egypt also helped the university, which was headed by an Egyptian scholar as its vice-chancellor, in several respects.

As a result of these socio-economic and legal reforms, President Zia took significant steps towards Islamization in Pakistan. According to Justice T W Rahman, Pakistanis 'will feel a visible change in socio-economic, educational and political sphere of life of the Muslim society in Pakistan.'[18]

VARIOUS COMMISSIONS ON THE ISLAMIC SYSTEM AND THEIR REPORTS

Before formulating his 'political plan' on 12 August 1983 for the transfer of power to an elected civilian government, Zia gave considerable thought as to how a genuine Islamic system could be established in Pakistan. His twin objectives were to restore democracy and to set up an Islamic order in Pakistan. To achieve his goal of establishing an Islamic order in Pakistan, he consulted a large group of Muslim scholars, jurists and ulema to work out guidelines for an Islamic system in Pakistan. In order to legalize his various socio-economic legal measures towards Islamization taken during the martial law period in Pakistan, he had to formulate measures to be incorporated in the 1973 constitution by introducing appropriate amendments to that constitution. In addition to his consultation with experts on Islam, he set up three important commissions to recommend measures for the realization of a socio-political order in Pakistan based on the broad principles and ideology of Islam. The reports of these commissions are extremely valuable in understanding the current thinking on an Islamic order in Pakistan. These reports will be of great interest to those who wish to know the nature of the new concept of an Islamic state in Pakistan. We shall, therefore, give our readers resumés of these reports.

The Report of the Council of Islamic Ideology: 'Constitutional Recommendations for the Islamic System of Government'

The basic principles of Islam and fundamentals of an Islamic state, its form and duties were, according to the findings of the council of Islamic ideology, the following:

Basic Principles

1 a The Muslims of the world are one ummah.

   b The basic source of all legislations are the Quran and Sunnah.

   c The president, his ministers, advisers, government officials and the members of the Majlis-e-Shoora are accountable for their actions to the people in accordance with the injunctions of the Shariah.

   d Mutual co-operation, help and compassion shall be the fundamental principles of social life.

   e *Amr bil-maroof* (enjoining good conduct) and *nahye ani munkar* (forbidding misconduct) is *farz-i-kifayah* (public duty) for every citizen and *farz-i-ain* (obligatory) for the state.

   f The family, as the basic unit of an Islamic society, shall be provided with protection and help. Special care with necessary monetary assistance for mother and child shall also be guaranteed by the state. Religion and morals are the basic elements which play the most vital role in the unity and welfare of the family.

   g Public health is the responsibility of the state, and the government shall be duty-bound to provide the citizens with necessary medical facilities and protect them from diseases.

   h Acquiring knowledge is the duty of every man and woman; providing educational facilities for the people shall be the responsibility of the state.

   i Religious education and training shall be the essential part of public education at every stage.

   j The government shall make proper arrangements in the present educational institutions for the teaching of the Quran *nazria* (view point) and *hifz* (memory) and shall establish new institutions for the purpose. The government shall also be responsible for ensuring the correct printing and widespread publishing of the Quran.

   k Free mixing of men and women shall be prohibited, and the public shall be bound to observe *hijab* (prevention of free mixing of men and women) as required by the Shariah.

   l The government shall take all necessary steps to develop the sense of abstention from immodesty (*be-hijabi*) in public.

   m The Islamic calendar shall be introduced in the country.

   n All powers shall be exercised in the public interest, and special guarantees for the protection of religion, intellect, life, property and honour shall be provided to every citizen.

   o The economic system of the state shall be based, in accordance with the Shariah, on the principles of freedom, justice and equality, and the government shall be duty bound to implement it through effective planning.

p   Freedom of trade, industry and profession shall be guaranteed within the limits of the Shariah. Elimination of hoarding, black-marketeering and all other prohibited business shall be the responsibility of the government. Property acquired by lawful means shall be protected.

q   For the up-lift of the economic condition of society the government shall, in accordance with the Shariah, plan such projects as lay equal emphasis on material and spiritual progress.

r   Interest bearing transactions shall be prohibited totally in all public and private dealings.

s   Public revenues shall be raised on the basis of zakat, ushr, *khums* (one fifth) and *fai* (booty): the government, however, shall, within the limits of Shariah, be authorized to levy such other taxes as are necessary.

FUNDAMENTALS OF AN ISLAMIC STATE: ITS FORM AND DUTIES

Definition of Islamic State

2   A state wherein the Muslims enjoy ruling power, submitting themselves to the sovereignty of Allah, and as vicegerents of Allah, enforce and practise the injunctions of the Quran and Sunnah, and wherein the Islamic laws are held supreme to all the other laws, is an Islamic state.

Laws Repugnant to the Quran and Sunnah to be Void

3   a   All laws of the state shall be in conformity with the injunctions of the Quran and Sunnah.

   b   Any law, or any custom or usage having the force of law, in so far as it is repugnant to the injunctions of the Quran and Sunnah, shall to the extent of such repugnancy be void.

Duties of the Islamic State

4   a   It shall be the duty of the Islamic state to make people follow and uphold the injunctions of the Quran and Sunnah and to eradicate objectionable practices. The revival and establishment of the supremacy of Islamic *sha'air* (values) shall

also be the responsibility of the state. The state shall make arrangements for recognized Muslim sects to get Islamic education in accordance with the teachings of their respective schools of thought.

b The Islamic state shall be duty bound to strengthen the brotherly ties among the Muslims of the world. It shall also work for the safety of unity and solidarity of *Millat-i-Islamia* by eliminating all racial, linguistic and territorial feelings or other distinctions based on *asbiyat-e-jahiliyya* (i.e. prejudices).

c The state shall be responsible for providing basic human necessities like food, clothing, residential accommodation to those who are rendered unable to earn their livelihood due to illness or any other reason or are temporarily jobless, regardless of their race and religion.

d It shall be obligatory on the state to make and enforce a law under which a person who is not a Muslim shall neither pose as a Muslim nor adopt or use *sha'air-i-Islam* (Islamic symbols), and in case of violation he shall be liable to punishment.

Rights of Citizens

5 a The citizens of the state shall have, within the limits of the law, all such rights as are conferred on them by the Islamic Shariah, such as security of life, property, honour, and freedom of religion and belief, freedom of person, speech, movement, association and profession, and equality of opportunity and the right to benefit from all welfare institutions.

b No citizen shall be deprived of any aforesaid rights and freedoms at any time, except in accordance with Islamic law, and no citizen shall be arrested and punished under the charge without being provided with an opportunity of being heard and defended in a court of law.

c The recognized Islamic sects shall have full freedom of religion within the limits of law and shall have the right to impart religious education to their followers in accordance with their respective schools of thought. They shall propagate their ideas freely and their personal matters shall be decided by the law of their own schools of thought. The government shall make arrangements that personal matters of a sect be decided by a qazi belonging to that sect.

d Non–Muslim citizens of the state shall, within the limits of law, have full freedom of religion, worship, culture and religious education. They also shall have full rights to decide their personal matters in accordance with their religious law or custom or usage.

e The contracts made with non–Muslim citizens of the state, within the limits of the Shariah, shall be valid and binding. The non–Musim citizens of the state shall have all the civil rights mentioned in clause (a).

Form of Government

6 a In the light of the precedent set by the Holy Prophet and the four guided Caliphs, one comes to the conclusion that the unitary form of government is preferable and nearer to the Islamic concept of state.

b Similarly in the light of the precedent set by the Holy Prophet and the four guided Caliphs, the obvious conclusion is that the presidential system of government is nearer to the Islamic concept.[19]

Special Committee of the Federal Council (Majlis-e-Shoora)

A special committee of the federal council (Majlis-e-Shoora), the nominated federal legislature, was set up to recommend 'form and system of the Government in Pakistan from the Islamic point of view'. Their findings on an Islamic state for Pakistan were as follows:

Islamic State

Islamic state means a state governed in accordance with the tenets of Islam or, more appropriately, a state where the divine order, as contained in the Holy Quran and Sunnah, reigns supreme and government, in its various spheres, is conducted with a view to executing the will of Allah, as laid down in the Shariah. The significant implication of an Islamic state and, for that matter, of any ideological state like Pakistan, is that all the places from where the policies of government emanate must necessarily be in the charge of such persons only, who not only believe in the fundamental principles underlying that particular ideology, but also conform to the minimum standards of conduct necessary to ensure a sincere execution of the code, promulgated under that particular ideology. Any political framework, which fits into the above broadly defined statehood, could be said to have an Islamic character.

Functions and Duties of an Islamic State

The main idea behind the establishment of an Islamic state is to enforce *amr-bil-maroof* (to enjoin what is good) and *nahye-ani-munkar* (to prohibit what is wrong) in accordance with the Holy Quran and Sunnah as already enshrined in the objectives resolution of 1949. The purpose of an Islamic state is to foster harmony and brotherhood in the Muslim ummah. The state should establish security and peace, ward off internal disorder and external aggression, and organize for Muslims the institution of prayer and the collection of zakat. Such a state should afford equal opportunity to people, irrespective of caste, creed, colour or race, and ensure irrevocable fundamental rights, like protection of life, property and reputation, freedom to profess religion, freedom of assembly and speech, and freedom of trade, business or profession, equality of citizens, safeguards against discrimination, protection against detention and arrest without proper trial. It should also take adequate measures to ensure the procurement of the necessities of life such as employment, food, health care, education and social security, etc., and dispensation of expeditious and inexpensive justice to all without fear, favour and discrimination.

The committee gave its fullest possible consideration to the form and system of government from the Islamic point of view. The members of the committee, which also included some of the well-known ulema, expressed the view that Islam had neither prescribed nor did it insist on any specific form of government, political system or framework. It had left it for the state to run the administration according to the political framework, which suited the peculiar conditions, aspirations and genius of the people, provided that it fitted into the broad definition of an Islamic state mentioned above.

It may be added that, during the discussions, some members expressed the view that the presidential form of government was nearer to Islam. At the same time, they conceded that a parliamentary form of government was not averse to Islamic injunctions.

After duly considering the constitutional history of Pakistan, the committee came to the conclusion that the parliamentary form of government, which was in accordance with Islam, would be more appropriate for Pakistan.

The 1973 Constitution

As the 1973 constitution was based on a parliamentary form of government and was also made with a general consensus, the committee decided that the said constitution should form the basis of its deliberations and the political framework provided therein should be adopted with the mininum number of essential changes in its provisions. Before, however, dealing with such changes, it was considered necessary to examine an even more important aspect of the constitution, namely its Islamic character, since there is a total commitment by the government and the people of Pakistan to bringing about Islamization in the country. The committee, therefore, proceeded first to examine the 1973 constitution to see how it fitted the above objective. The committee felt no hesitation in arriving at the conclusion that the 1973 constitution represented an Islamic character and ensured the preservation and promotion of Islamic order in the country. However, despite the above provisions, in the opinion of the committee, certain articles in the constitution required suitable amendments to achieve the self-same object:

1 Fundamental Rights
   Fundamental rights, though guaranteed in the constitution, can be suspended in certain situations. Islam does not permit the suspension of fundamental rights in any manner whatsoever. Therefore, adequate provisions may be made in the constitution to ensure that the executive authority does not suspend fundamental rights, guaranteed by the constitution.

2 Independence of the Judiciary
   According to the Shariah, the judiciary of an Islamic state must be independent of executive control. Though provision has been made in the constitution to this effect, this has not come about yet as it was intended. The committee recommends that, to make Pakistan reflect an Islamic state, it would be imperative for the judiciary to be independent of all executive control, and adequate provisions may be made in the constitution for this purpose. The committee also felt that the fetters and limitations, if any, imposed on the judiciary for their functioning should, as far as practicable, be removed. Consistent with the above recommendations, it was genuinely felt that, in view of the elevated position which members of the judiciary should occupy in an Islamic set-up, only such persons should be appointed to the benches of courts who are known to be pious and God-fearing, have adequate knowledge of the Shariah and are imbued with Islamic values, integrity and rectitude. Provisions to the above effect may also be made in the constitution. The committee noticed that certain provisions in the constitution grant immunity to certain

dignitaries from the process of law. Such a provision did not fit into the scheme of things in Islam, wherein everyone is equal before the law and no one is above it. Accordingly, a provision may be made in the constitution to eliminate such a discrimination.

Qualifications of the President (Article 41)

Since Pakistan is professedly an Islamic state, the committee considers it necessary that the president of Pakistan should be a practising Muslim with adequate knowledge of the Holy Quran and Sunnah. Accordingly, it recommends that, in clause (2) of article 41, the following words be added at the end of the clause after the words 'National Assembly', namely:

> *And he should be a practising Muslim with adequate knowledge of the Holy Quran and Sunnah.*

Powers of Pardon by the President (Article 45)

The committee thought that the provisions of article 45 did not conform to the tenets of Islam because, under the Islamic Shariah, courts of justice were to be absolutely immune from the control of the executive. Therefore, the sentences passed by them were only for execution. As the granting of pardon or reprieve to the accused, duly convicted by the court of law, did not conform to this principle, the committee recommends that the provision of article 45 may be substituted by the following:

> The president shall have power to refer a case, decided by a court or tribunal or other authority, to the supreme court, for a review of the merits of the final decision. The decision made by the supreme court, on review, shall be final.

Political Parties

Some members of the committee expressed the view that the concept of political parties is foreign to Islam, because there was no party system in its early period. Islam is a dynamic religion, which has a universal appeal and is adaptable to all times and conditions. There is no clear-cut injunction in the Shariah that political parties or a political system, based thereon, are un-Islamic. Islam believes in democracy and the development of democratic institutions and traditions through which it seeks to secure the welfare and well-being of the people. Without a political forum and political parties, no government, believing in democracy, can properly function. Islam being a democratic religion, the system of political parties fits into its scheme of things.

Accordingly, the committee felt that, in an Islamic state, political parties should be allowed to function in order to protect the rights of the people and to ensure checks and balances against the excesses and high-handedness of the government in power. Pakistan has had a chequered political history. It lost the Quaid-e-Azam soon after independence. This was followed by the assassination of Khan Liaquat Ali Khan, the first prime minister of the country. A crisis of leadership then ensued, stalling the growth and development of political institutions in the country on a national level. Consequently, political power passed on to the bureaucrats, who wielded such power arbitrarily and whimsically. The political vacuum thus created was filled by a mushroom growth of regional political parties and regional leadership, which gave the people no national political programme or manifesto. These regional parties and leaders further weakened the political fabric of the country by entering into political alliances for selfish and negative political objectives, to project their regional leaderships. These parties and leaders hardly enjoyed a country-wide popular support or credibility and thus rendered no creditable service to country-wide popular support. Moreover, corruption, bribery and lack of political acumen, integrity and honesty were evils which became associated with politics in the country, as a result of which members elected on the platform of one political party changed their affiliations and loyalties, crossed the floor in the House and joined other political parties at will. This created further instability and uncertainty in the body politic of the country.

Pakistan is an ideological state based on Islam. To purge the political system of the country of the evils mentioned above, the committee recommended that suitable legal measures may be adopted to create a healthy climate, under which political parties with a national base can get established in the country. Restrictions may also be imposed on the registration of political parties, crossing of the floor and changing of affiliation by the elected members of political parties. The steps recommended by the committee in this regard are as follows:

1 the provisions of the Political Parties Act of 1962, regarding the registration of a political party, be strictly followed and the following further provisions be made therein:

a political parties be organized on an all-Pakistan basis and the manifesto of a political party must state clearly that it believes in the integrity and indivisibility of the country

b it should support the enforcement of Nizam-i-Islam in the country

c it should adhere to the concept of indivisible Pakistani nationhood

d its office-bearers should be educated, pious and God-fearing and be elected by the members periodically in a party election, to be held at least once in five years on the basis of fresh enrolment of members in that political party

e only such a political party which has its branches in all the four provinces of the country should be qualified to participate in the elections

f the minorities' communities should have the right to form political parties to safeguard their rights and interests, but no political party organized by them should be allowed to act or work against the ideology of Pakistan or the enforcement of Nizam-i-Islam.[20]

The report of the sub-committee of the federal council has made some other recommendations on elections, on additional qualifications and disqualifications of members of the legislations both federal and provincial and on a few other matters but they are not of any special significance.

The Ansari Commission

Another important committee was set up with Maulana Zafar Ahmad Ansari as chairman and eighteen other prominent jurists, scholars, intellectuals and experts on Islam. The commission, known as the 'Ansari Commission', submitted its report on the form of government for Pakistan. The summary of the Ansari Commission's recommendations were as follows:

The Consultative System of Government in Islam

The commission strongly recommended the adoption of a consultative system of government in the Islamic Republic of Pakistan rather than any system of government operating in Britain, the USA, France or any other country. This should not prevent us, however, from benefiting as much from our own experiences as from those of others in working out the details of the proposed system.

The Amir-e-Mumlakat (Head of the State)

According to the Islamic consultative system, the head of the state shall also be the head of the government and he will be called Amir-e-Mumlakat. His qualifications, powers, duties and the mode of his election and removal are summarized below:

The qualifications and criteria for the office of Amir-e-Mumlakat shall be the following:

a   That he should be a Muslim and a male.

b   That he should have been at least for a period of ten years a citizen of Pakistan and a resident thereof.

c   That he should not be less than 40 years of age.

d   The he should be physically and intellectually capable of performing satisfactorily the duties of the amir.

e   That he should have adequate knowledge of Islamic teachings.

f   That he should practise the obligatory duties laid down by Islam and abstain from the major sins.

g   That he should not have, since the establishment of Pakistan, opposed the ideology or integrity of Pakistan.

h   That he should be qualified to be elected a member of the Shoora.

The following shall be the duties of the amir:

a   The amir shall be responsible for the administration of the state and shall perform all the duties that devolve on him as the constitutional and administrative head of the state.

b   The amir shall be, ex-officio, the commander-in-chief of the armed forces of Pakistan.

The powers of the Amir-e-Mumlakat shall be the following:

a   The amir shall be empowered to appoint, at his discretion, ministers as needed in order to carry on the administration, but these ministers should ordinarily be nominated from amongst the elected members of the Shoora.

b   When the Majlis-e-Shoora is not in session, the Amir-e-Mumlakat shall have the power to promulgate, with a view to safeguarding vital national interests, an ordinance in cases of emergency. However, such an ordinance shall be placed before the Majlis-e-Shoora for endorsement or amendment within three months from the date of its promulgation. After the expiry of three months since the promulgation of the ordinance, it shall cease to have any legal force, and the amir shall have no power to promulgate any ordinance of a like nature and intent within three months of its expiry.

In the exercise of his power the amir shall be bound by the following limitations:

a That the amir shall exercise all his powers within the limitations and according to the conditions provided for in the Holy Quran and the Sunnah.
b The amir shall have no power to suspend the constitution, either wholly or in part.
c The amir shall have no power to dissolve the Majlis-e-Shoora in any circumstance whatsoever.
d In respect of his rights and duties as a citizen, the amir shall be on a par with other Muslims and shall not be above the law.

Majlis-e-Shoora

The central Majlis-e-Shoora shall consist of two houses; the Upper House and the Lower House.

The Lower House of the central Majlis-e-Shoora shall be elected by constituencies throughout the country on the basis of equal representation for each province. The latest census figures shall be the basis for the fixation of the number of seats of the Lower House of the central Majlis-e-Shoora as well as the provincial Majlis-e-Shoora.

A Muslim member of the Majlis-e-Shoora should have the following qualifications:

a He should be of good character and not commonly known as one who violates Islamic injunctions
b He should have adequate knowledge of Islamic teachings and he should practise obligatory duties (prescribed by Islam) as well as abstain from major sins
c He should be a graduate from a university or from a recognized religious institution of learning or should be certified by a duly constituted body of educationists to be of equivalent level
d He should not be less than 25 years of age
e He should not have been convicted of a crime involving moral turpitude or of giving false evidence
f He should be a citizen of Pakistan and his name should appear in the electoral roll
g He should not have, after the establishment of Pakistan, worked against the integrity of the country or opposed the ideology of Pakistan.

The non-Muslim members of the Shoora shall be exempt from the conditions (a) and (b) above but it will be necessary for them to have a good moral reputation.

For women candidates the following additional qualifications shall be required besides those referred to above:

a They should be not less than 50 years of age

b If the husband is alive, they should have his written permission.

Women having the above qualifications shall be eligible for election from any general constituency. Moreover, for the next ten years five per cent of the general seats of the house shall be exclusively reserved for women candidates.

A council shall be constituted for nominating women candidates to these reserved seats. This council shall propose the names of the women according to the qualifications mentioned above, proposing twice the number of women for the reserved seats. The Amir-e-Mumlakat shall then nominate for these reserved seats the required number from among the names proposed.

Non-Muslims shall be elected to seats reserved for them according to the system of separate electorates. These seats in the Shoora shall be in proportion to their population. If any non-Muslim minority is insignificant in number, it shall be given representation in conjunction with another such minority.

Basic Principles of State Policy
Under the heading 'the Basic Principles of Policy', articles 3, 34 and 40 of the 1973 constitution shall be amended in the light of the injunctions of Islam.

The basic principles incorporated in the draft constitution of 1954 shall be incorporated in the constitution in order to make the 'Basic Principles of Policy' more comprehensive.

Khatt-e-Naskh, which is the script of the Quran, as well as of the regional languages of Pakistan, namely, Pushto, Sindhi, Baluchi, etc., shall be adopted for use till at least the primary stage of education in all the provinces of Pakistan.

To oversee the implementation of the Basic Principles of State Policy, a special committee consisting of members of the federal Majlis-e-Shoora shall be constituted to review the performance of the government in this behalf at the end of each year and call to account persons concerned in cases where the principles have been violated.

Islamic Provisions and Islamic Institutions
The 1949 objectives resolution shall be included in the text as an operative portion of the constitution instead of as a mere preamble so that it may become enforceable through the courts and may provide a guarantee that all the laws of the land, including the constitutional laws, shall be governed by the injunctions of the Quran and the Sunnah, and the principles laid down in that resolution and only that

147

interpretation of the provisions of the constitution and law shall be valid which accord with the principles of the objectives resolution, and all the laws that are in conflict with these principles shall be deemed to be void. The commission is of the opinion that the inclusion of the resolution should be done without any further delay.

The Islamic Research Institute should be made a constitutional body as it was under the 1956 and 1962 constitutions.

As proposed in the draft constitution of 1954, an independent institution should be constituted for do's and don'ts according to the tenets of Islam.

National Security Council

To meet unavoidable emergent situations, the commission consider it expedient that the constitution should provide for the formation of a national security council which shall have the power to proclaim a state of emergency and shall also have all powers necessary to take suitable steps accordingly.

The national security council shall be composed of the following:

i	The Amir-e-Mumlakat	1
ii	The chairmen of the two houses of the Majlis-e-Shoora	2
iii	The chief justices of the supreme court and the federal Shariah court	2
iv	The ministers-in-charge of defence, foreign affairs, law, interior and information	5
v	The wafaqi muhtasib	1
vi	The chairman of the council of Islamic ideology	1
vii	The heads of the three armed forces	3

It shall be necessary to obtain the approval of the Majlis-e-Shoora for the proclamation of the emergency within 30 days of its enforcement, failing which, the proclamation shall cease to have any legal force.[21]

An analysis of the reports and recommendations of the three commissions, set up by President Zia, shows that Pakistan under Zia has been elaborating a more comprehensive and broader concept of the Islamic state than that of the first and second constituent assemblies in Pakistan (1947–56). The only exception was the report of the board of *Talimat-i-Islamiah*, set up by the first constituent assembly in 1951 which gave a rather rigid definition of an Islamic state.[22] Its concept of an Islamic state was, however, not accepted by the framers of the 1956 constitution. Ayub's constitution commission of 1960–61 also gave recommendations for an Islamic form of government in Pakistan.[23] Zia's three commissions have made far-reaching recommendations for the Islamic form of government in Pakistan. They are in tune with the process of Islamization, already undertaken by Zia under martial law. But some of their recommendations were not accepted by the national assembly, elected under Zia's martial law. It is encouraging to note that neither President Zia himself nor the three commissions accepted any narrow concept of the Islamic state as demanded by some extremists among the ulema. They have not, for instance, ruled out any role for a legislature in an Islamic state, nor excluded women's rights of voting; on the contrary, Zia and his various commissions have stressed the need for a legislature, independence of the judiciary, fundamental rights of all citizens, man and woman, Muslims and non-Muslims. The concept of the sovereignty of God was unanimously stressed, but God's authority would be exercised by the elected representatives of the people and by a head of the state, to be elected by the people in accordance with the broad principles of Islam. Where the Islamic law, the Shariah, is silent, the people, through their chosen head of the state and their legislature will enact laws which should not, however, be repugnant to basic principles as laid down in the Quran. Zia gave his own concept of an Islamic state as follows:

1 From the Islamic point of view sovereignty belongs to God Almighty; and those in authority exercise their powers as a trust from God Almighty.
2 Islam provides some broad guiding principles about the form of government but does not prescribe any specific form.
3 There is no concept of papacy or theocracy in Islam.
4 An Islamic state is a welfare state; among its responsiblity is to take care of all its citizens, particularly the poor and the needy.
5 In my opinion, in an Islamic state the concept of an independent and powerful judiciary is there but according to Islam the judiciary is also required to be answerable.
6 There is rule of law in an Islamic state and all its citizens, including the president, are equal in the eyes of law.
7 In accordance with the dictates of the present-day world any method of elections can be adopted, the only condition being that a person contesting elections must be honest and endowed with outstanding qualities; he should also be a practising Muslim and a true Pakistani.

In other words, Islam does not bind us to any particular form of elections or form of government. The only bar is that when a government comes to power through any of these methods its distinguishing characteristics must be justice and grace (*ehsan*) in every sphere of human relations. The ruler of the day must be virtuous, just and God-fearing, and in sorting out the affairs of the state, he must seek the counsel of the people because Islam attaches great importance to mutual consultation. Similarly it has to be ensured that those entrusted with high office enjoy unblemished reputations, and their piety and fear of God are beyond reproach.[24]

CONSTITUTIONAL AMENDMENTS TOWARDS ISLAMIZATION

While presenting his amendments to the 1973 constitution, President Zia, in his address to the nation on 2 March 1985, ensured that the various reforms towards the process of Islamization of the country's political, legal, economic and social order be fully protected in the constitution.

While the national assembly did not, as already stated, approve some of Zia's proposals relating to the additional and increased powers of the president, they accepted Zia's proposed amendments relating to the Islamic provisions of the constitution such as the federal Shariah court, zakat and ushr and other similar provisions with the object of strengthening the Islamic character of the constitution. The most significant amendment was to provide under a new article 2A that 'principles and provisions set out in the (1949) Objective Resolution . . . are hereby made a substantive part of the Constitution and shall have effect accordingly.'[25]

The 1949 objectives resolution was adopted in all the previous constitutions – 1956, 1962 and 1973 – in the form of a preamble. It was not a basic part of those previous constitutions and as such not enforceable in law courts. It was merely an ideal to be expected to be taken into account by the law-makers. But as a result of Zia's initiative, it is now an integral part of the present day constitution of Pakistan, enforceable by the law courts.

THE SHARIAH ORDINANCE 15 JUNE 1988

While the national assembly accepted Zia's new Islamic provisions, it did not complete the adoption of the Shariah – there was a 9th amendment bill before the national assembly but the bill introducing the Shariah was put, to quote Zia's words, in 'cold storage'. The civilian government, since the restoration of democracy with the lifting of martial law in December 1985, was not very enthusiastic about the process of Islamization as begun by Zia in 1977. The 9th amendment bill was passed by the senate but the national assembly did not take any initiative to approve the bill introducing the Shariah.

In the meantime, President Zia dissolved the national assembly on 29 May 1988. Among the reasons given for dissolving the national assembly and the provincial assemblies and dismissing the civilian cabinets, both federal and provincial, Zia stressed the delay in furthering the process of Islamization. Finally Zia introduced the Shariah by proclaiming an ordinance on 15 June 1988 declaring the Shariah as 'the supreme law' of the country with immediate effect. The salient features of the Shariah ordinance of 15 June 1988 are as follows:

Experienced and qualified ulema shall be eligible to be appointed as judges of the court.

The president shall, in consultation with the chief justice of Pakistan, the chief justice of the federal Shariah court and the chairman of the council of Islamic ideology appoint *muftis* (experts on Islamic Law).

The state shall make effective arrangements for the teaching of and training in the Shariah and Islamic jurisprudence.

The state shall make effective arrangements for providing education and training in various branches of Islamic law in order to ensure the availability of manpower training in the administration of justice.

The state shall take effective measures to include courses in the Shariah in the syllabi of the law colleges of Pakistan.

The president shall, within 30 days from the commencement of the ordinance, appoint a permanent commission consisting of economists, jurists, ulema, elected representatives, etc.

The commission shall submit its reports from time to time to the federal government.

The commission shall monitor the process of Islamization of the economy and bring cases of non-compliance to the notice of the president.

The state shall take steps to ensure that the educational system of Pakistan is based on Islamic values of learning and teaching.

The president shall within 30 days from the commencement of

this ordinance appoint a Commission consisting of educationalists, jurists, ulema and elected representatives and such other persons as he deems fit, and appoint one of them to be its chairman.

Steps shall be taken by the state so that the mass media promote Islamic values.[26]

There have been some criticisms against Zia for introducing the Shariah by an ordinance rather than by the national assembly. But Zia made it clear that the ordinance would be subject to approval by the new national assembly which, Zia promised, would be elected according to the provisions for having elections within 90 days after any dissolution of a legislature by the president under article 58 (1) of the amended 1973 constitution.

The whole world, in particular, the Western and Muslim order, will be watching with great interest the experiment of an Islamic state, based on Islamic injunctions and law and simultaneously preserving the democratic values and form of a modern state. In the history of Islam, President Zia's far-reaching progress towards Islamization in Pakistan is a matter of great importance and meaning. If it succeeds, a new chapter in the relationship between Islam and democracy will emerge.

NOTES

1 *Political Plan Announced*, op. cit., pp. 20–21.
2 *Pakistan (first) Constituent Assembly Debates*, vol. 5, nos. 1–2.
3 Ibid, p. 3.
4 *Pakistan (first) Constituent Assembly Debates*, vol. 1, no. 2, pp. 19–20.
5 T M Arnold, *Preaching of Islam*, London, 1913, p. 420.
6 *Pakistan, Report of the Court of Inquiry*, op. cit., p. 212.
7 *Pakistan (first) Constituent Assembly Debates*, vol. 5, no. 3, p. 45.
8 R K Mukerjee, *Democracies of the East*, London, 1923, pp. 174–76.
9 W C Smith, *Pakistan As An Islamic State*, op. cit., pp. 41–43. For details on the status of religious minorities in an Islamic state see G W Choudhury, 'Religious Minorities in Pakistan', *Muslim World*, Connecticut, October 1956.
10 *Pakistan (second) Constituent Assembly Debates*, January–February 1956.
11 Ibid.
12 *Dawn*, Karachi, 31 July 1962.
13 *The National Assembly of Pakistan: Constitution-Making Debates*, 19 February 1973, pp. 103–104.
14 *Pakistan Times*, Islamabad, 16 June 1988.
15 For details see Justice Tanzil-ur-Rahman, *Islamization in Pakistan*, Islamabad, Council of Islamic Ideology, Government of Pakistan, May 1984.
16 *Pakistan 1986*, op. cit., pp. 53–55.
17 *Islamisation in Pakistan*, op. cit., pp. 7–9.
18 Ibid, p. 23.
19 *Constitutional Recommendations for the Islamic System of Government*, Islamabad, Council of Islamic Ideology, Government of Pakistan, June 1983.
20 *Report of the Special Committee of the Federal Council on the Form and System of Government in Pakistan from an Islamic Point of View*, Islamabad, Federal Council, Majlis-e-Shoora, Secretariat, July 1983, pp. 4–9 and pp. 13–16.
21 *Ansari Commission's Report on Form of Government*, Islamabad, August 1983, pp. 65–66, pp. 69–70 and pp. 72–74.
22 See *Constitutional Developments in Pakistan*, op. cit., p. 68.
23 See *Report of the Constitution Commission, 1960–61*, op. cit., pp. 19–20.
24 *Political Plan Announced*, op. cit., pp. 19–20.
25 *The Constitution of the Islamic Republic of Pakistan*, as modified up to 30 December 1985, Islamabad, Ministry of Justice and Parliamentary Affairs – Justice Division, Government of Pakistan, n.d., p. 5.
26 For the text of the ordinance and Zia's address to the nation on 15 June 1988, see *Pakistan Times*, Islamabad, 16 June 1988. For the text of the ordinance see *Enforcement of Shariah Ordinance*, 1408 AH, 1988 AD, Islamabad, Aiwan-e-Sadr, President's House, Islamabad, n.d..

Chapter V
Parliamentary vs.
Presidential System

Pakistan began its political career with the British parliamentary system when it gained independence in 1947, just like most of the former British colonies. There was hardly any debate over the system of government. Under the Indian Independence Act 1947, the government of Pakistan, like that of India, was to be conducted in accordance with the Government of India Act 1935 until a new constitution was framed. The 1935 act became the interim constitution of Pakistan. While India was successful in framing a new constitution by 1950, it took Pakistan nine years (1947–56) to frame a new constitution. The 1935 act provided for a parliamentary form of government both at the centre and in the provinces. The parliamentary system was recommended in the various constitutional drafts of 1951, 1952, 1953 and it was finally adopted in the country's first constitution in 1956. There were, however, some who believed that the parliamentary type of government was not suited to Pakistan. Their argument was that in the absence of two strong, stable and responsible political parties, the parliamentary type of government, wherein real executive authority is vested in a cabinet responsible to the legislature, would be unworkable and stable government a forlorn hope. Some of the ulema who wanted a fully fledged Islamic state considered the presidential system nearer to Islam, yet the parliamentary system was opted for in the country's first constitution, 1956.

The working of the parliamentary system in Pakistan was however, far from satisfactory. There was not a single general election in the country during the era of the parliamentary system; parliamentary democracy without elections is a farce. There were seven prime ministers during the era of the parliamentary system but none of them was selected through an election or by a majority vote in the legislature. They were products of the 'palace intrigues' which became the dominating feature of Pakistan politics after the death of its two ablest leaders, Jinnah and Liaquat.

After the abrogation of the 1956 constitution and the rise of military rule under Ayub Khan in 1958, a great debate started about whether the parliamentary system had proved to be a failure in Pakistan. The constitution commission of 1980–81 was entrusted with examining the causes of the alleged failure of the parliamentary system. The commission, after thorough investigation and analysis, came to the conclusion, as already stated, that parliamentary rule in Pakistan was a failure because of a number of factors; the most important ones, according to the commission, were lack of leadership of well-organized and disciplined parties and the general lack of character in the politicians and their undue interference in the administration.

Having made the conclusion that the parliamentary system of government had proved a failure, the commission inquired whether some form of modified parliamentary system could be made suitable for the country. The modifications suggested by the commission were as follows:

a control of parties by restricting their numbers and requiring legislation.

b restriction on the change of party affiliation by imposing obligation to resign and stand for re-election.

c conventions existing in the United Kingdom should be incorporated in the constitution.

d statutory prohibition of interference by the politicians and ministers in day-to-day administration and stringent laws for punishing them for misconduct.

e provisions against interference by the president except during an emergency and the few months preceding the elections when he should have the power to take over.

The commission examined each and every one of these modifications and found it neither possible nor desirable to introduce these modifications by statutes in the constitution itself. For instance, the control of parties by laws might not serve the purpose for which it would be intended. Similarly, statutory prohibitions of ministerial interference in day-to-day administration would create more difficulties than it would solve, nor did the commission favour the idea of incorporating the conventions observed in England into the constitution on the grounds that these conventions were liable to change with a change of circumstances and the incorporation of them in the constitution would create new difficulties. Ultimately the safeguards for the parliamentary system, in fact, for any democratic system, depend on the sense of responsibility of the ministers and the members of the legislature, and mere statutory prohibitions in the constitution, the Commission felt, would not solve the problems facing the country.

The commission recommended a form of government where there is only one person at the head of affairs with an effective restraint exercised on him by an independent legislature, members of which, however, should not be in a position to seriously interfere with the administration by exercising political pressure for their personal ends. The commission concluded that such a system is available in the presidential form of government as it exists in the United States of America. The commission's preference for the presidential system was influenced by the following factors:

1　First, under the presidential system there is only one person at the head of affairs and not two (president and prime minister) and the the collision of personalities which marked Pakistan politics since the deaths of Jinnah and Liaquat would be averted.

2　Secondly, the opportunities and temptation open to an average member of the legislature to exploit his position to advantage are so restricted under the presidential form that persons who in the past treated election to the parliament as an investment would be discouraged from standing for election.

3　Thirdly, in the presidential form there is greater stability which is Pakistan's prime need.

4　Further, under the presidential form, administrators can be selected from among the ablest of men available and not necessarily from among the members of the parliament.

While recommending the presidential form, the commission however, stressed the importance and role of the legislature: if we want to have a democratic form of government, it (the legislature) should be in a sufficiently strong position to act as a check on the executive by the exercise of its extensive power without at the same time affecting the firmness of the administration. Under the scheme proposed by the commission, the legislature would control the public purse, legislate for the country, and could criticize the administration. The commission dismissed the fear that the presidential system would deteriorate into dictatorship as happened in some of the Latin American countries. It, however, pointed out:

> Our recommendation that the presidential form of government may be adopted does not mean that we regard it as a foolproof scheme which would avoid any constitutional break-down in

future. We recommend that form of government because, on a careful consideration of the possibilities and probabilities of the situation and experience we have given during the past few years since independence, we consider that it is a safer form to be adopted in our present circumstances.

The commission's scheme for the presidential system was greatly modelled on the American pattern and proposed a comprehensive system of checks and balances.[1]

Though the 1962 constitution introduced the presidential type in Pakistan for the first time, an attempt was made to introduce a modified version of the presidential system in 1954–55 by the Governor–General Ghulam Mohammad who had no faith in the democratic process, and whose model was not the presidential system but the 'viceregal' system of the British period. The British constitutional expert, Sir Ivor Jennings, was commissioned to draft a system of government for Pakistan in which, to quote his words, the American idea of an executive for four years was grafted onto a British system of representation. Sir Ivor Jenning's draft constitution of 1955 not only tried to draft the American system with the British one but also proposed serious limitations on the powers of the legislature in money matters which is unknown in either the American or British system. Jenning's proposal concerning the financial powers of the legislature over the approval of the budget was that if the national assembly failed to pass an appropriation bill before the beginning of the financial year to which it related, the president might by ordinance continue in operation for that financial year the appropriation act which related to the last preceding financial year, and the ordinance would have full force and effect for the financial year to which it related as if it were an act of parliament. There was, however, a time limit to this power of certification by the president of the central budget by means of ordinance. No ordinance relating to appropriation bills should be promulgated for two consecutive financial years. It was further provided that if the national assemby refused any demand for grant in respect of any financial year, notwithstanding that a demand for grant in respect of the same service was voted in the last financial year, the president might, by ordinance, authorize expenditure from the federal consolidated fund for that service to an amount not exceeding the amount voted in respect of that service in the last preceding financial year.[2]

The urban elite in Pakistan, as in India and Bangladesh, seems to identify a democratic system with the British parliamentary type. The presidential type which is suitable for many reasons for a developing country is usually looked upon with some suspicion, particularly with a military man as president.

Before we go further in our discussion on parliamentary vs. presidential systems, let us give the salient features of the two systems. The essentials of cabinet government as it has developed in Britain and in other parts of the Commonwealth may be summarised as follows:

1 The leader of the party with a majority in the popular branch of the legislature is appointed prime minister by the head of the state.
2 The prime minister reports to the head of the state on the deliberations and decisions of the cabinet.
3 The prime minister selects his ministerial colleagues from those in the legislature who support his programme. The cabinet meets in private under the presidency of the prime minister. The ministers are collectively responsible for the acts and policies of the cabinet; no minister should dissent from cabinet policy; if disagreement is fundamental, he resigns.
4 The cabinet controls and co-ordinates the activities of government departments and determines the policy to be submitted to the legislature.
5 The cabinet is responsible to the legislature and resigns if defeated in the popular branch of the legislature on an issue of major importance.[3]

The fundamentals of the presidential system are as follows:

1 A president is elected independently of the legislature and has a direct mandate from the electors to perform the executive functions of the government.
2 He holds office for a fixed term and cannot be removed from office by an adverse vote in the legislature against any of his policies but only by a special process of impeachment.
3 The legislature is elected independently and holds office for a fixed term.
4 The legislature functions independently of the executive and cannot be dissolved by the executive or the head of state as is the case in the parliamentary system.
5 The legislature is the supreme law-making body of the country and no proposal can become law unless voted by this body.
6 The judiciary is responsible for the interpretation of laws and executive orders in the light of the principles embodied in a written constitution.

As in Britain where the parliamentary system originated and reached its perfection, so the United States of America furnishes a perfect and mature example of the presidential system. Chief of state, chief executive, commander-in-chief, chief diplomat, chief legislature – these functions make up the strictly constitutional burden of the American president. A number of political and social forces in recent years have brought the American presidency to a state of immense power and influence. Its powers are huge, but are of no real effect unless exercised through the constitutional forms and within constitutional limits. No great policy, domestic or foreign, can be maintained effectively by a president without the approval of congress in the form of laws and money and there is no way under the American constitution for a president to force congress to pass a law or spend money against its will. If the members of the congress cannot force the president to resign by a vote of no-confidence neither can he dissolve the congress.

The most reliable single limitation on the American presidency is the independent existence of a proud, jealous, watchful co-ordinate branch.[4] A president limited by the will of congress, says Laski, is always like a sailor on an uncharted sea.[5]

A new variety of presidential system or more accurately a synthesis of parliamentary and presidential system is found in the French constitution of the Fifth Republic. Since December 1958, France has had a largely presidential regime which is complicated by operating in the guise of a parliamentary democracy. In normal times, the president's powers under the Fifth Republic are meant to initiate a 'moral magistracy'. He incarnates the national will; but in times of emergency he assumes 'the character of a constitutional dictator'. Once armed with emergency power the French president can do anything but amend the constitution or dissolve the assembly. He alone judges when the emergency arises and what is to be done. The result is a 'Hanoverian monarch masquerading as a republic president who is also a head of state, guardian of the ark of the covenant, one head of a two-headed executive, mediator within his cabinet and between the government and parliament and in a great crisis, constitutional dictator.'[6] Which of the two systems is more suitable for a developing country like Pakistan? We may begin the discussion by referring to a valuable report: the Report of the Simon Commission which the British government appointed to examine the working of the limited form of parliamentary system in India under the Act of 1919 and to make recommendations for the next 'instalment' of democracy. The Simon Commission was the first step in the lengthy process of the enactment of the Government of India Act 1935.

The commission, submitted its report on 12 May 1930. The report, whatever might be the defects or criticisms of its recommendations, is one of the most valuable documents on the problems and dilemmas of representative institutions in the sub-continent. Like its predecessor in 1919, it discussed the fundamental problems of introducing full responsible government in India and referred to the big obstacles presented to it by the divisions of Indian society, above all the Hindu–Muslim differences. In the light of the experiences gained under the reforms of 1919, the commission discussed the suitability of a parliamentary form of government for India, and its remarks and observations in this context may be cited here as giving a better clue to the understanding of some of the problems which even today the framers of the constitution in Pakistan had to take into consideration while deciding the form of government most suited to its people. Unlike its predecessor, the Simon Commission expressed grave doubts about the suitability of parliamentary democracy for India. It observed, 'The British Parliamentary system has developed in accordance with the day-to-day needs of the people and has been fitted like a well-worn garment to the figure of the wearer, but it does not follow that it will suit everybody. Customs and conventions have retained in it various provisions which, formed for one purpose, are in practice used for another. Many of its detailed contrivances work only because there is the will to make them do so or because there is the general understanding that they will be used in moderation.' The commission rightly pointed out, 'British Parliamentarism in India is a translation and even in the best translation the essential meaning is apt to be lost.' These remarks of the commission may well be kept in mind by those who seem to feel that a carbon copy of the Westminister variety of democracy will solve the problems and dilemmas of the new democracies in Asia. In fact, the commission itself stated, 'The British Constitution is not a panacea which can be used in all times and in all places.' The commission also gave the reminder that although the principles and practice of the British parliamentary system might have been accepted by educated Indians as the best example of democracy, they were to be applied in a country where the condition and the mental habit of the people were very different. 'A mode of Government must, in fact,' the commission observed, 'be the expression of the political instincts of a people. The British system is not an easy one to imitate, for its success depends on a number of factors which cannot be introduced into the provision of a statute. In other countries where a system of shifting groups obtains, the constitutional position of the government is, in fact, quite different from that of the Cabinet in the British system.'[7] The actual working of parliamentary democracy in Pakistan under the interim constitution of 1947 as well as under the 1956 and 1973 constitutions seemed to have provided almost a text-book demonstration of the correctness of the apprehensions and doubts as expressed by the Simon Commission.

Like any other military ruler, Ayub was in favour of a strong and stable executive. He, therefore, advocated a presidential system on the ground that 'We have adopted the presidential system as it is simpler to work, more akin to our genius and history and less liable to lead to instability – a luxury that a developing country like [Pakistan] cannot afford.'[8] What Ayub, however, adopted in the 1962 constitution was not a genuine presidential system. The constitution was not based on the recommendations of the constitution commission which provided for a presidential system with checks and balances as it exists in the United States. But the 1962 constitution, given by Ayub with the help of his civil and military advisors, opted for an all-powerful president. The legislature, unlike the US Congress, was weak and powerless. It was a kind of 'controlled democracy' as advocated by some top Pakistani civil and military officials.

But it is still quite difficult to disagree with Ayub's diagnosis that Pakistan's 'basic requirements are for development, progress and awakening.'[9] As the *Round Table* (London) pointed out 'An underdeveloped country like Pakistan with its agricultural economy and a disturbingly increasing population has to develop at a very rapid pace, not only to provide a better standard of living for her masses but for her very survival. As such what she needs, above all, is a strong, stable and efficient administration.'[10]

The comments were made in the early 1960s. Pakistan has made good progress in economic development since the 1960s, and in parliamentary development under President Zia (1977–85), but Ayub's remarks and the *Round Table*'s comments about the need for a strong, stable and efficient administration are still valid for Pakistan. The author is inclined to prefer a presidential system for Pakistan as is needed for Bangladesh also.

Both Mujib Rahman and Z A Bhutto revolted against Ayub's presidential form of government under the 1962 constitution. Bhutto was, however, one of the chief architects of Ayub's 1962 constitution but when there was anti-Ayub agitation in Pakistan in 1968–69, Bhutto, like a true political opportunist, became the loudest critic of Ayub's political system. Similarly Mujib, while fighting for the demands of Bengalis (the then East Pakistanis), always stressed the parliamentary system, as it was the only form of government under which the Bengalis could expect to have some share in the decision-making process on vital issues; the cabinet, the real executive authority under the parliamentary system, would consist of, at least, half of its members from East Pakistan. Under the political dynamics existing in undivided Pakistan, no East Pakistani could expect to become president. So, Mujib rightly stressed the need for the parliamentary system in Pakistan till 1970–71. In fact, one of the 'points' of his famous 'six points' programme with which he fought for the creation of Bangladesh specially related to the demand for a true parliamentary system.

But subsequent political developments in Bangladesh and in 'new' Pakistan since 1971 proved that neither Bhutto nor Mujib had any genuine regard for parliamentary democracy. Both had opted for the parliamentary system in their constitutions – the 1972 constitution of Bangladesh and the 1973 constitution of Pakistan – after the separation of East Pakistan in 1971. In the case of Mujib, he formally abolished the parliamentary system by introducing the 4th amendment to the 1972 constitution of Bangladesh, he not only introduced the presidential system but he also established a one-party dictatorship by banning the multi-party system. His own party was the sole and single party. A military ruler, Zia-ur-Rahman, restored democracy in Bangladesh by reviving a multi-party system. Existence of more than one party is regarded as one of the fundamental prerequisites of any form of democracy, but the presidential system with military personnel as president has been continuing in Bangladesh.

In the case of Pakistan, Bhutto did not abolish the parliamentary system by any formal amendments to the 1973 constitution, but in practice, as we have already shown, he turned his political system into a 'civilian democracy' under the garb of democracy. All the powers were concentrated in the office of the prime minister and the role of the president was simply pathetic and helpless.

The real problem is that politicians in Pakistan, as in many other parts of the third world, have no regard for tolerance, mutual understanding, the spirit of 'give and take' or any form of compromise which are requirements for the successful working of democracy, be it parliamentary or presidential or any other form.

Democracy has been defined as a political system which provides regular constitutional opportunities for changing governing officials, but if a political system is not characterized by a value allowing the peaceful play of power – the adherence by the 'outs' to decisions made by the 'ins', recognition by the 'ins' of the rights of the 'outs' – there can be no stable democracy.[11]

President Zia's Choices and Dilemmas

When President Zia was seriously engaged in formulating his constitutional reforms for the transition from military rule to a civilian one in Pakistan in 1983, he seemed to have positive preferences for a presidential system. In his speech of 12 August 1983 in which he announced his 'political plan', he indicated his preference for a presidential system. He referred to Quaid-e-Azam Mohammad Ali Jinnah's comments on a presidential vs. parliamentary form of government to the members of the Majlis-e-Shoora (federal council).

Zia quoted extensively the views of Quaid-e-Azam on the form of government in Pakistan from historical documents and Jinnah's personal notebook. We shall produce below the views of Jinnah as his views and commands on any issue of national importance are still of great significance. We have already pointed out the importance of Jinnah's views in Pakistan while discussing the relationship between state and religion in Islam. Jinnah's concept of an Islamic state as already stated was given top priority and utmost importance. Keeping this fact in mind, Zia began his discussion on the form of government by quoting Jinnah's views on the subject:

> While I am on the form of government I will refer you to the views of Quaid-e-Azam on the subject. What I am about to draw your attention to is very important and I think very few people have knowledge of it. The British government has published recently documents relating to the transfer of power. So far twelve big volumes have been published. These documents contain Lord Mountbatten's personal report number 11, in which there is a reference to a letter, dated July 4 1947. Lord Mountbatten writes in this letter that he told Mr Mohammad Ali Jinnah that if he chose to become a constitutional governor general he would have limited powers: whereas as prime minister

he would be able to govern effectively. Quaid-e-Azam gave him a curt reply which was, 'My prime minister will do whatever I ask him to do'. In his own words: 'The state of affairs is such that whatever advice I give in my position others will act upon it.'

Also in the same historical documents, there is another letter of Lord Mountbatten written by him on 10 July 1947, in his capacity as viceroy to the secretary of state in England. Lord Mountbatten says:

I should like to inform you that the draftsmen, who are working on recasting the Government of India Act 1935 so that it may serve as the interim constitution for the new dominion, have been instructed by Mr Jinnah that in connection with the powers of the head of state they should concentrate on Schedule 9 instead of Part II of the India Act.

Lord Mountbatten goes on to say:

You must be fully aware of the implications of the instruction. it means that acting on this instruction the Governor-General will aquire, apart form other things, the following powers:
One: the appointment of members of Government,
Two: fixing their number,
Three: the appointment of Vice-President
Four: rejecting the majority opinion of the government,
Five: to determine the rules of business, and
Six: making schedule 9 as the basis of the exercise of powers would also mean that it would usually be the Governor-General who would be presiding over the meetings of the Cabinet.

These ideas and disclosures are further corroborated by the interim constitution order of 1947 which was drafted under the supervision of Quaid-e-Azam. This interim constitution is quite explicit about the powers of the head of state.
Zia then adds:

It is also said that the position of Quaid-e-Azam was such that he alone could have been vested with such powers and since no one else could come up to his stature such powers could not be vested in any other person. From an historical and factual standpoint this was [the] correct approach. And it was the father of the nation who alone could be entrusted with such powers. But at the same time it makes another aspect of the matter very clear and that is that Quaid-e-Azam, in principle, wanted to see that the office of the head of state should be very effective as well as powerful. A clue to this is also available from the personal note book of Quaid-e-Azam which, luckily, is still available to us in our national archives. The entry has been made in Quaid-e-Azam's own handwriting. The entry is in English and I will read it out to you.

In the first line, Quaid-e-Azam writes in the diary:

'Dangers of Parliamentary Form of Government'.

He points to the dangers of the parliamentary form of government as item number one.

i Parliamentary Form of Government: it has worked satisfactorily so far in England, nowhere else.

Then the next point:

ii Presidential Form of Government – more suited to Pakistan.

Zia points out that these are Quaid-e-Azam's own words inscribed in his diary which we have preserved.

Zia concludes by saying:

In view of the historical importance of this documentary evidence the government has decided to issue it to the press for publication. I believe that after this explicit evidence, in fact, command of Quaid-e-Azam, the controversy about the form of government should come to an end because the form of government of his choice not only meets the requirements of the modern age but is also very close to Islam.[12]

The present author has had on several occasions lengthy and exclusive discussions with President Zia on the form of government. On the basis of those discussions, the author has no doubt that left to himself Zia would have opted for a presidential system. It is also evident from his positive reaction to Jinnah's views on the subject.

Zia has also been most anxious to give Pakistan a truly Islamic system of government. Islam has not given any injunctions about the form of government but a large number of experts on Islam consider a presidential system nearer to an Islamic state. Both the council on Islamic ideology and the commission headed by Maulana Ansari recommended the presidential system as preferable from the Islamic point of view.

But Zia had not forgotten the fact that the all-powerful presidential system introduced by Ayub in the 1962 constitution was still resented by the people. Pakistan continued to be governed under the 1962 constitution with President Yahya Khan up to 1971; though the martial law had abrogated the 1962 constitution in March 1969, the political order under which the Yahya regime operated was still based on the 1962 constitution. The greatest defect of Ayub's political order was the lack of opportunities for the Bengalis to have any share in the decision making process. The vital national issues were decided, in the final analysis, by President Ayub with the help of a small ruling elite composed entirely of a few West Pakistani top bureaucrats and top army generals. The Bengalis could only react, and not act, on all vital national issues whether related to economic or political or defence or security. This total exclusion of the Bengalis from any sharing of powers was one of the basic factors, if not the basic one, for the disintegration of Pakistan in 1971. The loss of East Pakistan and the humilating defeat of Pakistan in the third Indo-Pakistan war in 1971 are still very fresh in the minds of Pakistanis. The Presidential system is regarded as a form of dictatorship because of Ayub's political order. They cannot appreciate, as in certain quarters in Bangladesh as well, that democracy can also flourish under a presidential system as it exists in the United States.

Just as the tyrannical rule of the English monarch, George III, had an impact on the constitution-makers in the United States after their independence in the 18th century, similarly the unfortunate consequences of the all-powerful presidency in the 1962 constitution had an impact at the time of framing a new constitution in Pakistan after the tragic events of 1971. This is why Bhutto had to opt for a parliamentary system though he was, as pointed out earlier, one of the chief architects of Ayub's system. The parliamentary system seems to have become synonymous with democratic governments. So Zia could not replace the parliamentary system with a presidential one. Even Zia's nominated legislature – the federal council (Majlis-e-Shoora) – had in its report 'on the form and system of government in Pakistan from an Islamic point of view' recommended the parliamentary system though it recommended changes in the balance of powers between the president and the prime minister as provided in Bhutto's 1973 constitution.

Another fact was that Zia had already become the president of Pakistan as a result of the referendum held on 19 December 1984 for a period of five years before the 1973 constitution was given its present shape as a result of the passage of the 8th amendment in October 1985. A president who is directly elected by the people cannot be expected to be a mere constitutional figurehead as the Queen in England or as the governor-general in commonwealth countries like Australia or Canada, or as the president in India who is elected by the legislatures, both federal and provincial with the support and approval of the prime ministers. Zia was, therefore, anxious to ensure that the role of the president should be meaningful and should have more powers than those of the president in Bhutto's 1973 constitution in which all the powers were concentrated in the office of the prime minister and the position of the president was, to quote Zia's words, 'ludicrous, meaningless and downright comic'.[13]

President Zia, while proposing the constitutional amendments to the 1973 constitution, asked his countrymen: 'What is the good of a helpless head of state or president who can take no action when he sees that the country is sliding into the quagmire of a serious crisis?' Referring to the 1977 political crisis when the country was heading towards a civil war, Zia told his nation, 'The president is watching this entire development [the 1977 crisis] from the presidency. He is a patriot and wants to save the country; but he is helpless unless the prime minister advises him, he cannot make a slight move . . . In fact, under the 1973 constitution he is not even entitled to know what action is being taken by the cabinet or the prime minister.'[14] On a previous occasion, Zia stated: 'The crux of the matter is that under the constitution there was an enormous imbalance between the powers of the president and the prime minister that led to the further aggravation of the 1977 crisis. The president was so helpless and ineffective that he could not prevent the prime minister, who was wielding dictatorial powers, from pursuing an undemocratic and arbitrary path.'[15] Zia decided to restore the 1973 constitution, but he made it clear that a proper balance must be brought about between the powers of the president and prime minister. Before we discuss Zia's proposal to bring a better distribution of powers between the president and the prime minister, and how far Zia's constitutional proposals were approved by the national assembly, let us first examine the system of the executive under the 1973 constitution as originally adopted in April 1973.

The Relationship between the President, the Prime Minister and the Cabinet under the 1973 Constitution

Article 41 provides that there be a president of Pakistan who should be head of state and should 'represent the unity of the Republic'.

Among the powers to be given to the president is included the power to grant pardon, reprieve and respite and to remit, suspend or to commute any sentence passed by any court, tribunal or other authority. Under article 216, the prime minister would keep the president informed on matters of internal and foreign policy and on all legislative proposals that the federal government intends to bring to the parliament. It is an accepted convention of the parliamentary government modelled on the British system that the head of state has the right to be informed, besides the right to advise and to 'warn' the cabinet. So article 216 was in accordance with the spirit of the parliamentary system.

The significant article relating to the exercise of powers by the president was article 48 which laid down:

i   In the performance of his functions, the president shall act on and in accordance with the advice of the prime minister and such advice *shall be binding on him* [my italics].

ii The question whether any and if so what advice was tendered to the president by the prime minister 'shall not be inquired into in any court.'

iii The orders of the president would require for their validity the counter-signature of the prime minister. The British parliamentary system as well as parliamentary systems which have developed in many parts of the commonwealth of nations are largely based on unwritten conventions and customs. In theory, the head of state may perform his powers without the advice of the cabinet. But thanks to well-established practices which have grown up over the centuries, there is usually no statutory requirements that the advice of the prime minister or of the cabinet will be 'binding' on the president. The usual expression is that there shall be a council of ministers 'to aid and advise the president' in the discharge of his powers. But in Pakistan, the governor-general under the interim constitution (1947) acted in an arbitrary way by dismissing a prime minister who enjoyed the confidence of the legislature in 1953 and then again, by dissolving the first constituent assembly in 1954. Similar misuse of power by the president took place under

Pakistan's first constitution (1956). So Bhutto was not content to rely only upon unwritten conventions and traditions of the parliamentary democracy modelled on the British system. He made it obligatory on the part of the president to be bound by the advice of the prime minister.

Similarly, the tenure of the prime minister in a parliamentary system is usually provided by expressions such as the 'prime minister and the cabinet will hold the office during the pleasure of the head of the state'. But in practice the head of state does not dismiss a prime minister. The prime minister resigns only when he loses the confidence of the legislature. He remains in office as long as he enjoys the confidence of the legislature. Here again, Bhutto did not rely on well-established conventions and practices but put it in writing: article 91 laid down that the prime minister would be elected by the majority of the total membership of the national assembly and the president would call the person so elected by the majority of the members of the national assembly to assume the office of the prime minister . . . The usual practice in a parliamentary system is that the head of state chooses a prime minister who, in his judgement, will enjoy the confidence of the legislature, but under the 1973 constitution the president had no role in appointing a prime minister except the mere formality of summoning a person who had already been elected as the prime minister by the legislature. Similarly, it was a written provision in the constitution (article 93) that the prime minister 'shall continue to hold office until his successor enters the office of prime minister'. Another feature of the parliamentary system is that members of the cabinet are appointed by the president on the advice of the prime minister but in the case of Bhutto's parliamentary system, it was the prime minister who alone could appoint federal ministers and ministers of state from amongst the members of the legislature (article 92). There was, again, no role of the president in selecting any members of the cabinet, even in a formal sense. Another significant difference between a usual parliamentary system and the one in the 1973 constitution lay in article 90 which said that 'the executive authority of the federation shall be exercised in the name of the president by the federal government, consisting of the prime minister and the federal ministers which shall act through the prime minister who *shall be the chief executive of the federation*' [my italics]. The usual expression in a parliamentary system is 'executive authority of the federation is vested in the president and is to be exercised by him in accordance with the constitution' – such was the case in the 1956 constitution (article 39) as well as in the Indian constitution.

The president could summon and prorogue the parliament (article 54); the president (article 56) might also address the parliament. The president's power to summon and to prorogue the parliament would be exercised on the advice of the prime minister. Similarly, his address to the parliament would be like the speech of the Queen of England, which is prepared and approved by the prime minister. It is a mere formality.

As regards the power to dissolve the parliament, it was specifically laid down under article 58 that the president shall dissolve the national assembly if so advised by the prime minister. Again, the usual practice in a parliamentary system is to give the president the power to dissolve the parliament without mentioning that this power of the president will have to be exercised only when he is advised to do so by the prime minister.

In practice, the president in a parliamentary system dissolves the parliament on the advice of the prime minister just as most of his other powers are exercised on the advice of the prime minister. But occasions may arise when the head of state may have reasons to refuse the prime minister's advice to dissolve the parliament. He may appoint a new one and may dissolve the parliament or continue to retain the new prime minister if he can secure the confidence of the majority in the parliament. Then there may be circumstances when a prime minister who has been defeated in the parliament advises the president to dissolve the parliament. The president may have reason to believe that a new prime minister may be appointed who may continue to function with the confidence of the parliament; under such circumstances the president may refuse the advice of the defeated prime minister to dissolve the parliament. In England during the last hundred and thirty years, there is no instance of a refusal of dissolution by the monarch when advised so by the prime minister. There has been, nevertheless, Sir Ivor Jennings states, a persistent tradition that the monarch could refuse if the necessary circumstances arose.[16]

Similarly, in England as well as in old commonwealth countries such as Australia or Canada where British customs and conventions are firmly established, there have not been any cases where the head of state dismissed a cabinet enjoying the confidence of the parliament, but circumstances may arise when the head of state may remove a prime minister to avoid a national crisis or resolve a serious constitutional deadlock. Again there have been no such instances in

England or in older commonwealth countries during the last century.

In England and in the old commonwealth countries the collective dismissal of a cabinet has become obsolete. Although legally and theoretically the head of the state can dismiss a cabinet, the power is no longer exercised except in cases when a cabinet, as Sir Ivor Jennings says, may subvert the democratic basis of the constitution by unnecessary or indefinite prolongation of the life of the parliament, by a gerrymandering of the constituencies in the interests of his party or by rigging an election. Otherwise the dismissal of a prime minister or the cabinet by the head of the state is not justified. But under the 1973 constitution even in such circumstances as mentioned by Ivor Jennings, the president could do nothing to save either the democratic process or even the country from a serious crisis. Bhutto transferred all the powers exercised by Ayub under the 1962 constitution, which Bhutto also continued to exercise under the 1972 provisional constitution, to the office of the prime minister before he stepped down from the presidency to become prime minister in 1973.

But even in England King George V took the initiative to form a national government in the 1930s when a national crisis as a result of the world-wide economic depression took place after World War I. Such a case arose in Pakistan in July 1977 when the president could probably have resolved the political crisis by removing the prime minister and ordering the dissolution of parliament and a fresh election, which might have saved the country from the imposition of martial law on 5 July 1977. But in the 1973 constitution the president was deprived of such 'reserved' powers in times of crisis, whether political or economic or external.

Similarly, the right of the head of the state to appoint a prime minister in a parliamentary system is a mere formality when there is a clearcut two-party system, one securing the majority of seats and the other having a minority of seats in a general election. The head of the state is certain to invite the leader of the majority to become the prime minister and to form the cabinet. But in cases where there is no clear-cut two-party system, as in many 'new' democracies of the Afro-Asian countries, this power of the head of the state may be of great importance. Even in England, the classic land of a two-party system, the monarch's free choice arises through complications in the political situation. Sir Ivor Jennings maintains that such complications are of more frequent occurrence than is commonly realized.[17]

We may point out the few other significant differences in the powers of the president under the parliamentary system of the 1956 constitution and under the 1973 constitution.

Under the 1956 constitution the discretionary powers of the president were limited and were confined to the making of a few non-controversial but important appointments. The president under the 1956 constitution could, for instance, appoint at his discretion, the chief election commission and other members of the election commission (article 137); he could also appoint, at his discretion, the chairman and members of the federal public service commission (article 186) but under the 1973 constitution the president was denied his discretionary powers even in making these non-political but significant appointments. In making these appointments he would be bound by the advice of the prime minister.

It is a common feature of the parliamentary system that the supreme command of the armed forces is vested in the president – the provision in the 1956 constitution (article 40) was similar. But the 1973 constitution provided that 'the federal government, which means the prime minister and his cabinet, shall have control and command of the armed forces'. Bhutto was not prepared to give up the honour of receiving a 21-gun salute!

From an analysis of the powers of the president under Bhutto's 1973 constitution, one can hardly disagree with Zia that the role of the president under Bhutto's political order was 'ludicrous, meaningless and downright comic'. Zia said, 'When the protagonists of the parliamentary system demanded the establishment of parliamentary government, the government of the day transferred all the dictatorial powers of the president, with some slight modifications, to the office of the prime minister.'[18]

As already stated, President Zia was obviously anxious to have a more balanced division of powers between the president and the prime minister. We shall now examine Zia's constitutional proposals and the national assembly's reaction to these proposals. Zia had to opt for the parliamentary system for the reasons which we have already stated, but he wanted to 'reform' the parliamentary system under the 1973 constitution.

President Zia's Constitutional Proposals

While reviving the 1973 constitution, which was suspended but not abrogated from July 1977, Zia prepared a number of amendments to the constitution. As many as fifty articles of the 1973 constitution were sought to be amended. Zia's proposal related mainly to Islamic provisions with the aim of strengthening the Islamic character of the constitution. As we have already pointed out those amendments relating to the Islamic provisions were approved by the national assembly without any objection.

The only part of the Islamic provisions which were not approved by the national assembly related to empowering the Shariah (Islamic law).

But the more important and more far-reaching were Zia's proposals for restoring some powers of the president which were provided under the 1956 constitution. Let us now examine those proposals.

Article 48 laid down the ways the president could exercise his powers. Bhutto's constitution simply stated that in the discharge of his functions, the president would be bound by the advice of the prime minister. That such advice would be 'binding' on the president. Zia sought to modify article 48 in the following manner:

48 President to act on advice, etc.

1 In the exercise of his functions, the president shall act in accordance with the advice of the cabinet, the prime minister, or appropriate minister:

Provided that the president may require the cabinet to reconsider or consider such advice, as the case may be, either generally or otherwise, and the president shall act in accordance with the advice tendered after such reconsideration or consideration.

2 Notwithstanding anything contained in clause (1), the president shall act in his discretion in respect of any matter in respect of which he is empowered by the constitution to do so.

3 If any question arises whether any matter is or is not a matter in respect of which the president is by the constitution empowered to act in his discretion, the decision of the president in his discretion shall be final, and the validity of anything done by the president shall not be called in question

on the ground that he ought or ought not to have acted in his discretion.

4 The question whether any, and if so what, advice was tendered to the president by the cabinet, the prime minister, a minister or minister of state shall not be inquired into in, or by, any court, tribunal or other authority.

5 Where the president dissolves the national assembly, he shall, in his discretion,

    a appoint a date, not later than one hundred days from the date of the dissolution, for the holding of a general election to the assembly; and

    b appoint a caretaker cabinet.

6 If, at any time, the president, in his discretion, or on the advice of the prime minister, considers that it is desirable that any matter of national importance should be referred to a referendum, the president may cause the matter to be referred to a referendum in the form of a question that is capable of being answered either by 'yes' or 'no'.

7 An act of Majlis-e-Shoora (parliament) may lay down the procedure for the holding of a referendum and the compiling and consolidation of the result of a referendum.

As regards the president's power to dissolve the parliament (article 58), Zia proposed the following change:

2 The president may also dissolve the national assembly in his discretion where, in his opinion, an appeal to the electorate is necessary.

In articles 90 and 91 which dealt with the executive authority of the federation, Zia proposed the following changes:

90 Exercise of executive authority of the federation.
The executive authority of the federation shall vest in the president and shall be exercised by him, either directly or through officers subordinate to him, in accordance with the constitution.
91 The cabinet.
1 There shall be a cabinet of ministers, with the prime minister at its head, to aid and advise the president in the exercise of his functions.
2 The president shall in his discretion appoint from amongst the members of the national assembly a prime minister who, in his

opinion, is most likely to command the confidence of the majority of the members of the national assembly.

3 The person appointed under clause 2 shall, before entering upon the office, make before the president an oath in the form set out in the third schedule and shall within a period of sixty days thereof obtain a vote of confidence from the national assembly.

4 The cabinet, together with the ministers of state, shall be collectively responsible to the national assembly.

5 The prime minister shall hold office during the pleasure of the president, but the president shall not exercise his powers under this clause unless he is satisfied that the prime minister does not command the confidence of the majority of the members of the national assembly.

The changes proposed by Zia under articles 90 and 91 were almost the same as articles 37 and 39 of the 1956 constitution which also provided a parliamentary system.

By another proposal Zia wanted to give the president the power to appoint the provincial governors 'in his discretion' and the advice of the prime minister would not be binding on the president in appointing provincial governors. Zia further proposed that:

the provincial governors, in respect of the following matters shall, subject to the previous approval of the president, act in his discretion, namely:

a   appointment of the chief minister;
b   dismissal of a cabinet which has lost the confidence of the provincial assembly;
c   dissolution of the provincial assembly, when an appeal to the electorate is necessary.

2 The question whether any, and if so what, advice was tendered to the governor by the chief minister, the cabinet or a minister shall not be inquired into in, or by, any court, tribunal or other authority.

3 Where the governor dissolves the provincial assembly, he shall appoint, in his discretion, but with the previous approval of the president, a caretaker cabinet.

4 The powers conferred by this article on the president shall be exercised by him in his discretion.
   (article 105)

By proposing these changes in articles 101 and 105, Zia wanted to make the president able to exercise considerable influence in the politics of the provinces, as exercised by the governor general under the interim constitution (1947) and by the president under the 1956 constitution.

Zia also made proposals to amend article 56 under which the president could address the parliament. His amendments to article 56 were as follows:

2 The president may send messages to either house, whether with respect to a bill then pending in the Majlis-e-Shoora (parliament) or otherwise, and a house to which any message is so sent shall with all convenient despatch consider any matter required by the message to be taken into consideration.

3 At the commencement of each session of the Majlis-e-Shoora (parliament), the president shall address both houses assembled together and inform the Majlis-e-Shoora (parliament) of the causes of the summons.

4 Provision shall be made in the rules for regulating the procedure of a house and the conduct of its business for the allotment of time for discussion of the matters referred to in the address of the president.

Zia made it clear that when he, as the president of the country, addressed the parliament, his speech would not be that of a constitutional figurehead whose speech is prepared and approved by the cabinet, as in England and in some other commonwealth countries. Zia, referring to his constitutional obligation of making an address on the opening day of the parliamentary year, rejected the idea of reading out a speech provided for him by the government. He asked, 'What is the fun in spending crores [ten million is equal to one crore] of rupees on this function if I have read a speech written by someone else? Our circumstances', he added, 'are different from other Western countries and we are not bound to follow their parliamentary practices.'[19]

Under the 1973 constitution the president was not given any veto power, not even a limited one, on bills passed by the parliament. Usually the president is given limited power authorizing him to ask the legislature to reconsider a bill passed by the legislature, but under Bhutto's constitution the president was required to give assent to a bill within seven days and if the president failed to give assent within seven days he would be 'deemed to have assented to the bill' (article 75).

Zia wanted to modify article 75 of the 1973 constitution in a way which would be similar to article 57 of the 1956 constitution relating to the president's power of giving assent to a bill passed by the legislature. Zia's proposed amendments were as follows:

75 President's assent to bills.

1 When a bill is presented to the president for assent, the president shall, within forty-five days
   a assent to the bill, or
   b in the case of a bill other than a money bill, return the bill to the Majlis-e-Shoora (parliament) with a message requesting that the bill, or any specified provision thereof, be reconsidered and that any amendment specified in the message be considered.

2 When the president has returned a bill to the Majlis-e-Shoora (parliament), it shall be considered by the Majlis-e-Shoora (parliament) in joint sitting and if it is again passed, with or without amendment, by the Majlis-e-Shoora (parliament), by the votes of the majority of the total membership of the two houses, it shall be again presented to the president and the president shall assent thereto.

3 When the president has assented to a bill, it shall become law and be called an act of Majlis-e-Shoora (parliament).

We have already pointed out that under article 243 the supreme command of the armed forces was vested in the federal government without specifying that it was 'vested in the president', as was the case under the 1956 constitution (article 40 and also in the Indian constitution). Zia's proposed amendment to article 243 was the addition of a new clause (2A) which clearly stated:

The supreme command of the armed forces shall vest in the president.

We have already stated that Zia wanted to set up a 'national security council'. Its composition including four top army officials and its functions under a new article 152A have been discussed in Chapter II. We have pointed out that the idea of a national security council with four top army officials involved great controversy and opposition. Zia himself acknowledged the fact when he stated: 'People have been saying that is going to some sort of a supreme body which will be able to veto every decision of the assembly and the government . . . that body is, in fact, going to serve as the means through which the armed forces will be able to intervene in the affairs of the state.' Zia added: 'All this is ridiculous, unfounded and condemnable propaganda. There is not an iota of truth in it.'[20] In spite of Zia's assurances, the proposal for a national security council was not, as pointed out earlier, approved by the national assembly. Though Pakistan had experiences of long army rule during three periods of martial law (1958–62, 1969–71 and 1977–85), the people are not prepared to institutionalize the army's role in the political system as they have in Indonesia and Turkey.

Non-controversial but important appointments, like the chairman and members of the election commission and the chairman and members of federal public commissions, used to be made by the president in his discretion under the 1956, but not under Bhutto's 1973, constitution. Zia's proposed amendments gave the president the power to make these appointments 'in his discretion'.

After the introduction of the various amendments to the 1973 constitution through the president order no. 14 of 1985 – 'the revival of the constitution of 1973 order 1985' (ROC) in March 1985, Zia addressed the national assembly and explained the rationale of his proposals for constitutional amendments. Zia told the national assembly:

Now decide for yourself whether wisdom lies in leaving the president to his ludicrous fate like this or conferring upon him some powers. Whatever we have learnt over the past eight years, and the 37 years of our history, can be summed up in these words: Under the requirements of a parliamentary system the prime minister must indeed be an effective head of government, but the president should not be such a powerless person either that he may be a totally ineffective and useless organ of the state. This is the other side of it that merits reform. The constitution is a fundamental charter and a pivot around which the state and its various organs operate. So it is not advisable to tinker with such a fundamental and sacred document. That is one reason why in bringing these amendments we have not disturbed the basic structure of the 1973 constitution. It was parliamentary before and it continues to be parliamentary. But you must be aware that, leaving aside the scriptures, no document can be treated as the ultimate word on any subject. It is to meet the dictates of changing conditions and after benefiting from the experience of the past eight years that we are effecting these changes in the constitution.

And if the elected assembly believes that these amendments are unnecessary and not useful, then it is at full liberty to annul them in accordance with procedure laid down in the constitution.[21]

An analysis of Zia's proposals for constitutional amendments will prove that though Zia retained the parliamentary system, he wanted to make the powers and functions of the head of the state substantially stronger than is the case in the usual form of parliamentary system. The most significant change he sought to introduce was article 48, in which it was provided that the president 'shall act in his discretion in respect of any matter of which he is empowered by the constitution to do so'. The discretionary power of the president, however, was made almost unlimited because it was laid down that 'if any question arises whether any matter is or is not a matter in respect of which the president is by the constitution empowered to act in his discretion, the decision of the president in his discretion shall be final and the validity of anything done by the president shall not be called in question on the ground *that he ought or ought not to have acted in his discretion* [my italics].' The discretionary power of the president as proposed by Zia would make the president's role almost the same as the governor-general and governors of the provinces under the Government of India Act 1935, which was in operation in British India during 1937 to 1947. At the time of independence in August 1947, discretionary powers of the governor general and the provincial governors were abolished under the Indian Independence Act 1947, so that real parliamentary democracy could be established in India and Pakistan after the two states gained independence.

Obviously the national assembly of Pakistan did not approve this particular amendment; similarly, Zia's proposal to enable the president to appoint and dismiss the provincial governors 'in his discretion' was also rejected by the national assembly.

The president's power to dismiss the prime minister was restricted by the national assembly by modifying Zia's proposal with additional words in article 91, under which the president's power to dismiss the prime minister will be effective only when the prime minister is unable to secure a 'vote of confidence' of the national assembly. This puts a serious limitation on the power of the president vis-a-vis the prime minister. As a result of this modification of article 91, the tenure of the prime minister under the present day constitution of Pakistan is more secure than under the 1956 constitution or under the interim constitution, 1947. The president can still dismiss the prime minister only by dissolving the national assembly which he can do 'in his discretion' under article 58. In that case the president, however, is required to hold fresh elections within ninety days (article 224). Similarly, the president can 'in his discretion' refer 'any matter of national importance' to the people through a referendum (article 48). This type of power is not given to the president in a parliamentary system based on the British model.

As a result of strong pressure from the parliament and prime minister as well as from the public, Zia's original purpose to make the president more powerful had to be modified. But still the president under the amended constitution of 1973 enjoys certain powers and responsibilities which are not usually found in the British parliamentary system. Zia is not a mere constitutional figurehead or a ceremonial head of the state. He has been successful in retaining some discretionary powers for himself.

After the national assembly had passed the 8th amendment bill disapproving some of Zia's proposals while retaining some of them, the then law minister, Mr Iqbal Ahmad Khan, who piloted the bill on behalf of the first civilian government installed in 1985 under Zia's rule, told the senate on 28 October 1985 that as a result of new amendments the constitution had created a workable balance between the powers of president and prime minister so that the president could overcome a grave crisis of the magnitude of the summer of 1977 when people took to the streets against the government of the day and shed their blood to get rid of a despotic rule. Under the 1973 constitution the prime minister had unlimited powers.[22]

How should one describe the present political order in Pakistan? It is not a parliamentary system as it exists in England, because the president has some special powers and a significant role, which are not given to the constitutional figurehead of a parliamentary system. It is neither the presidential type as it exists in the United States, as it has a prime minister who is the head of the executive. The prime minister and his cabinet are responsible to the legislature, and the prime minister must have the confidence of the national assembly. He presides over the cabinet meetings; he manages the day to day administration of the country. No executive function can be performed without the prime minister or his cabinet's approval. The prime minister selects the members of the council of ministers. The activities of the various departments of the government are sent to the prime minister for approval or disapproval. The present author had three interviews with the prime minister in 1987–88 and the prime minister, M A Junejo, never missed an opportunity to stress the fact that he was the real executive authority and that Pakistan's present political system offers a more effective and stable parliamentary system than under any of the previous constitutions. He also emphatically asserted that the president had no share in the running of the country's day to day administration.[23]

On the other hand Zia told the present author, in a lengthy thirteen-page typed reply, that he had special obligations and rights with a mandate from the people (referring to the referendum of December 1984) to protect what he termed the 'vital interests of the nation', particularly in defence and security problems as well as in foreign affairs. Above all, Zia felt strongly that he had a real obligation for the Islamization of Pakistani society including the political and economic system. He told the author that under normal circumstances, he had not intervened in the affairs of the government headed by the prime minister. But he made it absolutely clear he would not be a mere constitutional figurehead nor an all-powerful president.[24]

President Zia in his address to the parliament on 7 April 1988 gave his views on the role of the president under the present day constitution of Pakistan; Zia told the parliament:

> The requirements of the United States of America and the United Kingdom are totally different from ours. There are various countries who have their own democratic system quite different from the Western concept of democracy and working satisfactorily. The present president available to you is neither President Ayub Khan (under the 1962 constitution) nor President Fazal Illahi (under Bhutto's 1973 constitution) . . . in the prevailing political situation neither the president nor the prime minister can become a 'master' or 'His Master's Voice'.[25]

The Western diplomats in Islamabad and the present author, during his visit to Islamabad in April–May 1988, could feel that dormant tension had been existing in the relationship between the president and the prime minister. A 'collision of personalities' under the parliamentary system, particularly with a president who had directly received a mandate from the people and who enjoys some special 'reserved' powers, seems inevitable.

The final showdown took place on 29 May 1988; the president dissolved the national assembly in exercise of his powers under article 58 of the present day constitution of Pakistan. He also dismissed Prime Minister Junejo and his cabinet. The provincial legislatures and provincial cabinet were also dismissed.[26] In an address to the nation on the following day, Zia gave the rationale for his dissolving the national assembly and the dismissal of the Junejo cabinet as well as the provincial legislatures and cabinets. Zia told the nation that his actions 'are in conformity with the relevant constitutional provisions and that he intended no deviation from the established democratic process'.[27] Zia had already asked the election commission to prepare for holding general elections within 90 days as required under the constitution. Subsequently Zia also made it clear that the forthcoming elections would be held on a party basis. He has formed a caretaker cabinet with no prime minister at its head which means the caretaker cabinet will function under Zia's control.

Zia made the following allegations against the Junejo government:

1　Law and order in the country had broken down to an alarming extent resulting in tragic loss of human lives.
2　Life, property, honour and security of the citizens was rendered totally unsafe.
3　The integrity and ideology of Pakistan have been seriously endangered and doubts generated in this regard.
4　The president's conscience always pricked that he had not fulfilled his promises regarding the enforcement of Islam made to the people in the referendum of 1984.
5　Public morality had detoriated to an unprecedented level.
6　A situation had arisen in which the government of the federation cannot be carried on in accordance with provisions of the Constitution necessitating an appeal to the election.[28]

The present political system in Pakistan can neither be described as parliamentary democracy as it exists in England nor is it the same as the American presidential system. The French system under de Gaulle's Fifth Republic perhaps offers a closer parallel as the main force in France lies in a strong executive. The French president under article 16 of the Fifth Republic enjoys certain special powers during a period of crisis. But the parallel between the French and Pakistani system is not total.

Wherein lies the legal sovereignty in Pakistan today? The ultimate sovereignty of God is acknowledged in the constitution, but who holds the legal sovereignty in Pakistan? According to Jean Bodin, the French political philosopher who expounded the modern concept of legal sovereignty, and also according to the English political philosopher, Thomas Hobbes, the real sovereignty lies in that organ of the government which has the final control over the other organs of the government. Judged by that criteria, we may conclude our discussion on the political system by saying that the president is the holder of the legal sovereignty in Pakistan.

NOTES

1   *Report of the Constitution Commission (1960–61)*, op. cit., chapters 1 and 2.
2   *The Draft Constitution (1955)*, prepared by Sir Ivor Jennings, is still an unpublished document; the author obtained permission to read it. See also Sir Ivor Jennings, *Approach to Self-Government*, Cambridge, 1956, pp. 18–19.
3   Sidney Bailey, *Parliamentary Democracy in Southern Asia*, London, 1953, pp. 66–67.
4   Clinton Rossiter, *The American Presidency*, New York, 1959, pp. 30 and 36.
5   H I Laski, *American Presidency*, New York, chapter 3.
6   Philip Williams and Martin Harrison, *De Gaulle's Republic*, London, 1960, p. 123.
7   *Report of the Indian Statutory (Simon) Commission*, vol. 3, London, 1930, pp. 6, 7, 11 and 17.
8   See Ayub Khan's interview with the Newspaper Editors on 1 March 1962 in *Dawn*, Karachi, 1962.
9   Ibid.
10 *Round Table*, London, June 1962.
11 Symour M Lipset, 'Some Social Requisites of Democracy, Economic Development and Political Legitimacy', *American Political Science Review*, March 1949.
12 Jinnah's views cited by Zia in *Political Plan Announced*, op. cit., pp. 21–24.
13 *Constitutional Amendments Announced*, address to Nation by President General Mohammad Zia-ul-Haq on 2 March 1985, Government of Pakistan, Islamabad, pp. 16–17.
14 Ibid.
15 *Political Plan Announced*, op. cit., p. 14.
16 Sir Ivor Jennings, *Cabinet Government*, Cambridge, 1937.
17 Ibid.
18 *Constitutional Amendments Announced*, op. cit., p. 15.
19 See President Zia's speech to the parliament on 7 April 1988 in *Dawn*, Karachi, 8 April 1988.
20 *Constitutional Amendments Announced*, op. cit., p. 28
21 Ibid, pp. 18–19.
22 See *Pakistan Times*, 29 October 1985.
23 Based on interviews with Prime Minister Junejo.
24 Based on interviews with President Zia.
25 *Dawn*, 8 April 1988.
26 *The Pakistan Times*, Islamabad, 30 May 1988.
27 Ibid, 31 May 1988.
28 Ibid.

Chapter VI
Federalism in Pakistan

We shall now discuss the problems of federalism in Pakistan as an instrument of national integration. Pakistan, from the very beginning, was created constitutionally as a federation. As long as East Pakistan (now Bangladesh) was part of Pakistan, a federal system was regarded as the 'dictate of geography', because of the separation of East and West Pakistan by more than one thousand miles of foreign territory. Pakistan sought to achieve national unity and integration by offering federal solutions to a geographically unique country. But the federal solution was not adequate to prevent the ultimate separation of the two wings of the country in 1971.

Even after the emergence of Bangladesh, the 1973 constitution of Pakistan opted for a federal system. At the time of framing the 1973 constitution, it was pointed out that 'Pakistan has to have a federal structure. There are different provinces; different peoples, people with different culture; different script; different language; different habit; economies are slightly varied.'[1] Pakistan, therefore, continued the federal form of government assuring autonomy to the provinces, maximum autonomy, in consonance with one united Pakistan under the 1973 constitution.

The then attorney general, Yahya Bakhtiar, claimed that the 1973 constitution 'sought to lay the basis of the federation and not only has provincial autonomy been built into the framework of the unity of the country but new institutions have also been involved; the institution of the common interest which will be responsible for subjects like railways, water and industrial development projects and in this council provinces will be associated with the federal government.'[2]

When the national assembly was debating the federal structure of the country under the 1973 constitutional bill, President Z A Bhutto pointed out that the four federating unites in Pakistan – Baluchistan, North West Frontier, Panjab and Sind – 'are the most difficult provinces in the subcontinent. Always historically they have been a free people . . . [they] have fought always for individuality, personality, freedom . . . they have that tradition; they have that history.' Bhutto concluded that under his 1973 constitution 'the quantum of provincial autonomy has been satisfactorily resolved.'[3]

But unfortunately the controversy over federal authority versus provincial rights has not yet been fully solved in Pakistan. President Zia, while amending the 1973 constitution, did not disturb the delicate balance between the federal and provincial governments. Pakistan is still beset with serious ethnic and racial tensions which threaten the unity of the country. Zia has inherited the problems and prospects of national integration through a federal solution.

At the time of the creation of Pakistan in 1947, its powerful neighbour, the USSR, used to describe Pakistan not 'as a nation' but as consisting of five distinctive nationalities – the Bengalis (then East Pakistan), Baluchis, Pathans, Sindis and Panjabis.[4] The Soviet comments were, no doubt, based on their prejudices and wrath against Pakistan for its pro-Western foreign policy in the 1950s but yet those comments were not entirely baseless. Soon after the emergence of Pakistan in 1947, regional feelings and tensions began to grow, culminating in the disintegration of the country in 1971 when East Pakistan was transformed into an independent state. It was expected that after the acute controversy concerning the federal structure between East and West Pakistan was over, though very tragically, in 1971, the 'new' Pakistan should have no serious problem of national integration. But the problem is not yet over.

Before we discuss the federal structure as it exists in Pakistan today, let us give an account of the growth of federalism in Pakistan since 1947. In our Introduction we have already pointed out that though Pakistan had always a federal constitution – in the interim constitution (1947), in the 1956 as well as in the 1962 constitution – in reality the government was highly centralized. Pakistan had a federal constitution but not federal government.

It began with the interim constitution and the most important feature of the Government of India Act 1935, which became with certain adaptations the interim constitution of Pakistan, was that it invested the provinces for the first time with a separate legal personality. The act of 1935 adopted a method of distribution of legislative powers between the central and the provincial governments which, as it was admitted by the joint parliamentary committee in its report, was without precedent. The seventh schedule to the act contained three legislative lists – the federal, the provincial and concurrent. The first two belonged exclusively to the competence of the federal and provincial legislatures respectively;

both were competent to deal with matters covered by list three. An attempt was thus made to parcel out the entire field of legislation and to obviate the necessity for giving residuary powers to either the federation or its units. Explaining the implications of these devices, Sir Samuel Hoare claimed that during the committee stage of the bill this method had been adopted in preference to a more logical method owing to the sharp cleavage of opinion between the Hindus and the Muslims. Indian opinion was definitely divided between the Hindus who wished to keep a larger area of power in the centre and the Muslims who wished to keep it in the provinces. In some provinces at least, there was a preponderant Muslim majority. They felt they would be able to capture some power in provincial government. The extent of that feeling made each of these communities look with the greatest suspicion to the residuary field. The Hindus demanded that the residuary field should remain with the centre and the Muslims, equally strongly, demanded that the residuary field should remain with the provinces. The device of the three lists was made to limit the residuary powers as far as possible.

An analysis of the relation between the central and the provincial governments under the Government of India Act 1935 would prove that while the act invested the provinces with a separate legal personality, and while sufficient scope was given for regional autonomy, the central government was all-powerful and was fully equipped with powers to carry out its obligations. The centre's predominance was particularly manifested in the administrative and financial relations. The centre retained the ultimate means of controlling and guiding the provinces.

Under the various constitutions a highly centralized federal system was established in Pakistan. The Government of India Act 1935 provided adequate provisions and processes to ensure full predominance of the central authority. Those provisions and processes were fully utilized. The central government's hold in the legislative, financial, administrative and political spheres was so great that for practical purposes, as we have already pointed out, the country's governmental structure could hardly be described as truly federal.

But more significant than anything else was the political control of the central authorities in provincial politics. The provincial governor was appointed by the central authorities and held office during the pleasure of the governor-general. The central government exercised considerable pressure and influence in provincial political scenes through its power of appointment and dismissal of provincial cabinets through the provincial governors.

As pointed out by Professor Wheare, the recent trend in the existing federal systems is towards the increase of the powers and strength of the central government. The chief forces which have caused central governments to increase in strength at the expense of the regions – whether by fuller exploitation of their existing powers or occasionally by the acquisition of new powers – seem to have been four-fold. They are war, economic depression, the growth of social services, and the mechanical revolution in transport and industry. War and economic depression demand unitary control if these problems are to be effectively treated, and they impose a financial strain which only central government has been able to bear.[5] These factors have helped centripetal forces in existing federal systems. But in Pakistan, centrifugal forces had their strength in the circumstances in our Introduction. Hence, we find that the demand for decentralization of power was gaining ground in Pakistan.

The highly centralized federal structure of Pakistan, as described above, was soon attacked and subjected to severe criticism and strain. The centrifugal forces seemed to be getting much stronger than the centripetal forces in Pakistan. Dicey's classic statement relating to the prerequisites of a federation may be repeated here. Federalism requires for its formation two conditions, i.e. on the one hand there must be a body of countries so closely connected by locality, by history, by race or the like as to be capable of bearing in the eyes of their inhabitants an impress of common nationality. On the other hand there must exist a peculiar state of sentiment among the inhabitants of the countries which it is proposed to unite. They must desire union and must not desire unity.[6] One may inquire whether the impress of common nationality as referred to by Dicey is sufficiently strong in Pakistan to uphold the federal experiment or whether the 'peculiar sentiment' he refers to is seriously challenged in Pakistan by centrifugal forces. Unlike the federal systems of the United States or Australia, the sense of distinct nationality was getting stronger and the sense of common nationality was getting weaker in Pakistan.

A federal constitution has certain distinctive characteristics, the most notable of which is the distribution of powers between two sets of government guaranteed by the constitution itself. The actual mode of distribution of powers varies in different federal systems. But there must be a statutory distribution of powers between the central and provincial authorities in a federal constitution. Another characteristic of the federal government is the existence of a common umpire to determine and interpret the distribution of powers. Federal government, as Dicey observed, is legalistic government. Federalism implies a division of power and authority between two sets of government. It is also inevitable that in a federation there will be disputes over the terms of the division of powers. Hence the task of constitutional arbitration is important in a federal system. An arbitrator is required to determine the limitations imposed by the constitution, to check powers which have not been conferred and to authenticate powers which have been granted.[7] This task of umpiring the federal system is usually performed by a supreme court. In the federations of Australia, Canada, India, the United States and West Germany, it is the supreme court which performs this task. Only in Switzerland is this practice not followed where the people performs the functions of deciding whether a federal law is consistent with the constitution. But the task of reviewing state laws is vested with the federal court. It may be mentioned that in some cases the practice of judicial review has developed in a federal system without an explicit provision for it. Even so, it has been accepted, as it is considered an essential attribute of federalism. In the United States, it was established by Chief Justice Marshall in the famous case of Marbury versus Madison about 180 years back. Since then, this power has been criticized, resented, attacked, but never repelled, and in the United States today, the Supreme Court is sometimes described as 'the third chamber' for its role as the umpire and guardian of the constitution.

Another characteristic of a federation is the supremacy of the constitution. Every organ of the state – executive, legislative or judiciary – is subordinate to the constitution. The constitution is regarded as the 'supreme law of the land'.

Judged by these criteria, the federal system in Pakistan as provided under the previous constitutions lacked some of the essential characteristics of the federal systems as noted above. The constitution of 1956, which emerged after years of effort and discussion, had granted provincial autonomy, but it also provided for a strong central government capable of discharging its responsibilities and duties. The administrative and financial relations were hardly changed. The system continued to be more or less the same as provided under the interim constitution. The predominance of the central government continued.

When the reshaping of democracy started in the 1960s with the appointment of a constitution commission in 1960, the problems of the relationship between the centre and the provinces were no less acute than at the time of making the 1956 constitution. As pointed out by the constitution commission, this problem, in fact, continued to be the most serious and difficult task confronting the framers of the constitution in Pakistan.

The constitution commission, having regard to the prevailing circumstances of the country, recommended a federal form of government. The official delegation which represented the Ayub government's views before the constitution commission, recommended a unitary form of government with a central legislature having provincial committees to deal with provincial matters. The commission did not favour the scheme as it considered it unworkable and too complicated. The commission's recommendation for a federal form of government received the approval of the Ayub government and ultimately the federal form was retained.

As pointed out earlier, the distribution of legislative powers under the Government of India Act 1935 was unique in character. It had three lists of powers. Following the model of the 1935 act, the 1956 constitution also divided the lists of subjects into central, concurrent and provincial. In fact, in all the constitutional drafts made in Pakistan, the same procedure for the distribution of powers was followed. Similarly, in India the same method of distribution on the basis of three lists has been followed. The 1962 constitution of Pakistan, however, provided for a much simpler method of distribution of powers. Under the 1962 arrangement, there was only one list of subjects of national importance. All other subjects were left to the provinces. The central government, however, had overriding powers in matters concerning the security of the country, co-ordination between the provinces and economic development.

The crux of the whole relationship between the centre and the provinces in Pakistan lay in the financial sphere. Federalism implies not only an allocation of legislative powers but also financial powers. The federal principle, Professor K C Wheare points out, requires that the central and the provincial governments of a country should be independent of each other within its sphere and should not be subordinate to one another but co-ordinate with each other. Now if these principles, he continues, are to operate not merely as a matter of strict law but also in practice, it follows that the central and provincial governments must each have under its own independent control financial resources to perform its exclusive functions.[8] Each must be financially co-ordinate with the other. The equitable distribution of financial resources between the centre and the provinces in a federal system is, however, one of the most difficult tasks. It raises a number of complex problems and as the authors of the joint parliamentary committee on the Government of India Bill 1935 stated, 'so far as we are aware no entirely satisfactory solution of this problem has yet been found in any federal system'.[9] It is said that in a federation the crucial power is the power to tax.

Taxation in a federal system can be organized in different ways depending upon various circumstances. Broadly speaking there are three variants: (i) All taxes are raised by the component states and a fixed contribution is made to the federal authorities to cover their requirements. This is usually adopted in a confederation and not in a true federal system. It implies an element of subordination of the central authority to the provinces whereas in a federation both sets of government must be co-ordinate and equal in status. (ii) All taxes are raised by the federal authorities and fixed contributions are made to the states. This is again a system which would lead to a position of inferiority for the states as they will be dependent upon the federal government for their financial resources unless there is a statutory provision in the constitution fixing the amount to be given to the provinces of the taxes raised by the central government. (iii) The power to tax is divided betwen the federal government and the component states.

Most federal systems have adopted the third method. Under the Government of India Act 1935 the power to tax was divided between the centre and the provincial governments, although in some cases the taxes were raised by the federation and some part of the net proceeds were given to the provinces. So there was a combination of the second and third methods. The allocation of resources between the centre and the provinces was made under the Government of India Act 1935 on the recommendation of Sir Otto Nemeyer. Under this act the sources of revenue could be classified into three categories (i) provincial sources of revenue, (ii) federal sources of revenue and (iii) certain sources of revenue which would be collected by the central government, but the net proceeds of these sources would be shared between the provincial government and the central government according to the formula recommended by Sir Otto Nemeyer.

During the era of constitution-making particularly in the second constituent assembly, the members from East Pakistan demanded again and again that the constitution should ensure a fair and equitable distribution of the resources in the absence of which provincial autonomy, it was feared, would become a farce.

The constitution of 1956, however, did little in respect of financial autonomy for the provinces. The distribution of the financial resources made under the Government of India Act 1935 was allowed to continue with minor changes. The 1956 constitution, however, provided for a machinery for making recommendations as to the distribution between the federation and the provinces of the net proceeds of the some important taxes such as export duty on jute and cotton, taxes on income and on sales and purchases and any other specified tax, and as to the making of grants by the centre to the provinces. It was also expected to make recommendations for the regulation of the borrowing power of both the federal and the provincial governments. The machinery was the national finance commission which was to be constituted by the president at intervals of not more than five years and was to consist of the central and provincial finance ministers and such other persons as might be appointed by the president on the recommendation of the provincial governors. The national finance commission, however, was not constituted until 1958. When it was constituted in 1958, it was dissolved along with the abrogation of the constitution before it could make any recommendations.

The Ayub government had set up a committee in May 1961 to examine the question of allocation and apportionment of revenues between the central and provincial governments. It was a five-member committee with the secretaries of the ministries of finance and commerce of the central government and finance secretaries to the government of East and West Pakistan. The report of the committee, however, is not yet published.

At a public meeting held in Dhaka on 18 October 1961 President Ayub Khan announced that a commission of impartial people would be appointed to look into the question of equitable allocation of revenues between the central and provincial governments for a balanced development of both East and West Pakistan. The President referred to the complaint that the pace of development in East Pakistan was slower than in West Pakistan and admitted that in certain cases it was 'a genuine complaint'.[10]

In accordance with this announcement made by the president, a ten-man finance commission was appointed in December 1961 with the secretary of the ministry of finance as chairman and several experts on financial and economic matters as members. The commission examined the fiscal relationship between the centre and the provinces. It was expected to prepare an objective report, keeping in view the specific requirements of the centre and the provinces and a harmonious development of both wings through equitable distribution of financial resources. The discussions of the commission were reported to have been marked with disagreement between East and West Pakistan members of the commission and it was understood that two separate reports were submitted to the commission's chairman by two components. The East Pakistan members were reported to have strongly recommended a recasting of the second five-year plan to give more weight to that wing of the country. It was reported that the East and West Pakistan members of the commission had failed to find a common principle regarding allocation of financial resources.[11] In East Pakistan the demand had been that the distribution of the resources should be made on a per capita basis, i.e. on the basis of population.

The divergent reports of the commission were submitted to the president and were discussed elaborately by the cabinet. It finally gave a new award regarding the allocation of the resources between the centre and the provinces. The Finance Minister Mr Shoaib declared on 28 January that under the new allocation of revenues, East Pakistan would roughly receive 11 crores (110 million) and West Pakistan about 2 crores (20 million) in addition to their due share calculated on the existing basis. The finance minister further announced that suitable measures would be taken to ensure the allocation and direction of resources in a manner that disparities in per capita income between provinces and between regions within the provinces were reduced and removed.

The new allocation of the proceeds of the taxes and duties collected and administered by the central government to the provinces were as follows:

1 50% of the income tax including corporation tax as compared to 50% of income tax excluding corporation tax and taxes collected in Karachi under the previous arrangement.
2 60% of the sales tax as against 50% of the sales tax in the previous arrangement.
3 Under the previous arrangement 50% of the excise duties on tobacco, tea, betelnuts were allocated to the provinces; it was now raised to 60%.
4 More significant changes were in respect of export duties on jute and cotton; under the new arrangement 100% of the export duties on jute and cotton would go to the provinces as compared to 62.5% of the export duties on jute allotted to East Pakistan under the previous arrangement. Under the new arrangement both East
•   and West Pakistan would receive a 100% share from the joint pool of export duties on jute and cotton on the basis of population.

The basis of allocation was also changed. According to the new arrangement, income tax and excise duties were broadly distributed in the ratio of 55% to West Pakistan and 45% to East Pakistan and, as regards sales tax, 70% would be on the basis of population and 30% on the basis of incidence, i.e. on the point of collection, and as regards the remaining taxes they would be distributed on the basis of population. As a further relief to the financial position of the provincial governments, it was decided to scale down the debt liabilities incurred by the provinces to the centre up to 1960–61 so that loans outstanding against the provinces would be written down by 50% and consolidated into one loan repayable over 25 years.[12]

There was no doubt that the new fiscal arrangement would increase the financial resources of the provinces and it was also pointed out that this arrangement was fairer to East Pakistan compared to the previous one. The main criticism of the new arrangement was, however, that while it improved the situation with regard to revenue allocation, it did not make any improvement in the sphere of allocation of development funds and foreign exchange without which the disparity between the two wings could not be removed.

As regards the distribution of power to tax between the centre and the provinces, the new constitution had not altered the scheme of distribution as under the interim and the 1956 constitutions. The centre was given, as under the 1956 constitution, power to levy custom duties (excluding export duties), excise duties including duties on salt but not including duties on alcoholic liquor, corporation taxes and taxes on income other than agricultural income, state and succession duties, taxes on capital value of assets, taxes on sales and purchases, terminal taxes on goods or passengers carried by sea or air, and taxes on mineral oil and natural gas. The sources of revenue for the centre were more or less the same under the 1956 constitution. The provincial sources of revenue had not been mentioned in the 1962 constitution just as the legislative powers of the provinces were not mentioned specifically, because any other source which was not specifically given to the centre was given to the provinces under the new arrangement.

The president, however, was to constitute a national finance commission composed of the central finance minister and provincial finance ministers and such other persons as the president might appoint after consultation with the governors of the provinces. The commission should make recommendations to the President as to the distribution between the central and the provincial governments of the proceeds of the following taxes: (i) taxes on income including corporation tax; (ii) taxes on sales and purchases; (iii) export duty on jute and cotton and such other export duties as might be specified by the president and (iv) such excise dutes imposed by the central government as might be specified by the president and any other taxes that might be specified by the president. The commission would also consider the grants-in-aid by the central government to the provincial governments. It might be added here that under article 38 of the 1962 constitution the central legislature might make grants-in-aid to provincial governments. Further, the commission was given the general power of discussing any matters relating to finance.

On the recommendation of the national finance commission, the president would specify by order the share of the proceeds of the above mentioned taxes which would be allotted to each provincial government. The national finance commission's recommendations would be laid before the national assembly and each of the provincial assemblies. The 1956 constitution had also provided for a national finance commission and its composition and functions were more or less the same as under the 1962 constitution. The national finance commission, however, under the 1962 constitution was given an additional function, viz. that it should make a report to the president as to the progress made during a period of the economic development plan, to remove the disparity between the provinces and between different areas within the provinces. It should also make recommendations as to the manner in which the disparity could be removed in the next succeeding plan and its recommendations should be taken into consideration by the national economic council in formulating its plan.

Article 145 of the 1962 constitution provided for a national economic council. The council should be appointed by the president and consisted of such persons as were appointed by the president. The national council under the 1956 constitution consisted of four ministers of the federal government, three ministers of each provincial government and the prime minister who was to be an ex-officio chairman of the council. The function of the council under the 1962 constitution was to review the overall economic development of Pakistan. It was stressed that in formulating the plans, the council should ensure that disparity between the provinces and different areas within a province in relation to income per capita were removed and the resources of Pakistan including resources in foreign exchange were used and allocated in such a manner that the disparity between the provinces would be removed in the shortest possible time, and it had further been stressed that the duty of each government should be to make the utmost endeavour to achieve this object of removing economic disparity between the provinces. As noted earlier, the national finance commission, which was constituted by the president, from time to time would report as to the progress made by the governments to achieve the object of attaining parity in economic development between the provinces and to recommend further steps to attain this objective. In spite of all this emphasis and stress to remove economic disparity between East and West Pakistan under the 1962 constitution, the disparity not only continued to exist but it also increased. This is mainly due to the fact that the real decision-making process in economic issues, as on all other important national problems, was in the hands of a small West Pakistan ruling elite who could not or did not appreciate the gravity of the economic conditions in East Pakistan. The neglect of East Pakistan's economic problems was one of the major factors for the break-up of Pakistan in 1971.

Federal Structure in Pakistan Today

Under article 1 of the 1973 constitution, Pakistan is described as a 'Federal Republic'.

As in the interim constitution (1947) and the 1956 constitution, the present constitution provides elaborate provisions not only relating to the distribution of legislative powers between the federation and provinces but detailed provisions relating to the administrative and financial relations between the federation and provinces.

Distribution of the legislative powers are based broadly on the model as laid down in the Government of India Act 1935, but instead of three lists – federal, provincial and concurrent – there are two lists: the federal list consisting of 59 items and one concurrent list consisting of 47 items, and the federal legislature shall have exclusive power to make laws in respect of any matters in the federal legislative list. The federal and provincial legislatures shall both have power to make laws with respect to any matters in the concurrent legislative list. In all other matters, which are not specifically mentioned either in the federal or concurrent list, a provincial assembly shall have power to make laws. The provincial list is not specified; any matter not specified in either the federal or concurrent list belongs to the provinces. Thus the 'residuary powers' as in the 1956 and 1962 constitutions belong to the provinces. This is done to satisfy the demand for maximum autonomy for provinces. The process of decentralization has been allowed to an extent which is unusual with many new federal constitutions, particularly of Afro-Asian countries. The federal constitution of India, for instance, shows a strong tendency towards centralization of authority and administration. The Indian constitution has been described as 'Quasi-Federation' by Professor K C Wheare. This trend towards centralization of power and authority in the new federal systems had its roots in recent developments, particularly in economic and defence spheres. A modern government can hardly fulfil the wider objectives of social welfare services or full employment unless it has the power of legislation over the whole economic and fiscal field. Similarly, the nature of modern warfare is forcing a federal government to extend its sphere of legislation. It is for this reason, as pointed out by Professor Max Beloff, that each new federation created since World War II has tended to allot more powers to the centre and with 'old' federations like the American and Australian 'the centralising tendency has been steadily at work and with ever increasing speed.'[13] Eminent experts on federalism have expounded the view that a federal system could hardly be expected to work satisfactorily and smoothly without this process of centralization in a modern complex society. Yet the Pakistan government had to provide maximum room for decentralization in view of the fact that the four provinces in Pakistan, as already pointed out, are very conscious of their regional rights. Pakistanis seem to feel more at home in calling themselves 'Panjabis', 'Pathans', 'Baluchs' or 'Sindis' rather than 'Pakistanis', so the constitution had to satisfy their regional demands and aspirations.

The powers of the provinces may look impressive when one confines oneself to the distribution of legislative powers, but when one examines the administrative and financial aspects of the federal versus provincial authorities, dominance of the former is clearly manifested; even in the legislative sphere, if there is any inconsistency between the federal and provincial laws in the concurrent list, the federal act shall prevail and the act of the provincial assembly 'shall to the extent of repugnancy be void' (article 143). The federal legislature is also empowered to legislate on any matter which has not been spelled out in either a federal or concurrent list, if two or more provincial assemblies request the federal legislature to pass any law in any subject not enumerated in either federal or concurrent list.

A provincial assembly, however, can subsequently amend or even repeal such a law.

It is, however, in the administrative sphere that the dominance of the federal government over the provincial governments is clearly demonstrated. The governor of a province is not elected by the people of that province as he is elected in the United States of America. The provincial governors are appointed and dismissed by the president on the advice of the prime minister. This power of appointment and dismissal of provincial governors by the federal government is of great importance in influencing provincial politics in Pakistan. The provincial chief minister is supposed to exercise the executive power of a province since the form of government in the provinces is a parliamentary one, as at the federal level, yet the provincial governors, like the president of Pakistan at the national level, can exercise a lot of influence and power through various constitutional devices as in the previous constitutions in Pakistan since 1947. Hence, the power to appoint and to dismiss a provincial governor by the federal government enables the federal authority to exercise considerable influence in provincial politics. In the most recent past – April 1988 – the chief minister of Sind was removed, though a formal vote of no-confidence had not been passed against him by the Sind provincial assembly. The new chief minister, Akhter Ali G Kazi, did no doubt get a vote of confidence once he was chosen by the provincial governor. But the whole episode illustrated the influence, if not intervention, of the federal government in the politics of a province. Commenting on the episode, an able commentator in Pakistan's oldest English language paper *Dawn* wrote:

In a durable federal set up, how should Chief Ministers in the provinces be changed between general elections? Should that be done by the federal rulers or by provincial assemblies or voters? In fact, who should decide that a mid-term change in the stewardship of a province has become imperative, and how to bring that about smoothly, in harmony with not merely the form of the Constitution but also its spirit?

Our brief but embattled history testifies that the manner in which the change in the chief minister-ship of Sind has been brought about, now along with the supense or stalemate that preceded that, is only the latest link in a long and unhappy chain in the centre–province relations. In a State which was conceived on the basis that its constituent units would be 'sovereign and autonomous' central leaders during the last 39 years have been instrumental in bringing about change in the provincial chief ministers in violation of the basic principles of provincial autonomy.

In fact, almost all the changes in provincial leadership over the decades – from that of Mr M A Khuhro to Syed Ghous Ali Shah in Sind, Mr Fazlul Haq in East Pakistan and Khan Abdul Qayyum Khan in the Frontier – had been brought about not through no confidence motions in provincial assemblies but through central intervention. And Khan Wali Khan argues that all that began with the removal of Dr Khan Saheb's ministry in the Frontier immediately after the birth of Pakistan by the central leaders.[14]

The administrative relations between the centre and the provinces are therefore little changed. The federal system shows in this sphere marked tendencies towards unified control and authority. It is the constitutional duty of the federal government to protect each province against external aggression and internal disturbance. Although the maintenance of law and order is a provincial subject, the federal government is vested with the ultimate responsibility of ensuring the peace and safety of the country which is the primary duty of any national government, be it under a unitary or a federal system. No central government can afford to neglect this vital function. The federal government is also entrusted with the task of ensuring that the government of each province is carried on in accordance with the provisions of the constitution. Under article 149, a provincial government is obliged to exercise its executive authority in such a way as to ensure compliance with acts of parliament and existing laws applying to that province. The central government makes laws in the federal and concurrent lists which would apply to the provinces. Although these laws might be administered by the federal authority itself, yet the constitution enjoins upon the provincial authorities the duty of giving due effect to the federal laws prevailing or applying to the provinces, and not impeding or prejudicing the exercise of the executive authority of the federation. The federal government is entitled to give directions to a province with regard to the duties of the provincial authority under this article, and is further entitled to give directions to a province in the following matters:

a as to the construction and maintenance of communications declared to be of national or military importance.

b as to the manner in which the executive authority of the province was to be exercised for the purpose of preventing any grave menace to the peace or tranquillity or economic life of Pakistan or any part thereof.

c as to the carrying into execution in the province of any act of parliament in the concurrent list.

Articles 149 and 151 are very similar to article 126 of the Government of India Act 1935, as adopted in Pakistan which gave sweeping powers to the federal government to exercise control and give directions to a province.

There is one important provision in the constitution which enables the federal government to constitute the provincial governments as its agents. The president may with the consent of a provincial government entrust, either conditionally or unconditionally, to that government or to its officers functions in relation to any matter to which the executive authority of the federation extends (article 145). The practice of delegation to provincial governments or their servants the duty of executing the orders of the federal government was exercised under the Government of India Act of 1935. The federal government did not have a sufficient number of officers in the provinces to execute its laws or orders hence the necessity of such delegation, and the framers of the constitution also allowed this process of delegation to provincial governments to continue, thus permitting the federal government to utilize the 1973 provincial executive machinery for the enforcement of federal laws.

The federal government may acquire any land situated in a province or ask the provincial government to acquire the land on its behalf for any purpose connected with a matter included in the federal or concurrent list. The price of the land again would be mutually settled or determined by a tribunal appointed by the chief justice (article 152).

Turning to the financial aspect of the federal system, we find that the 1973 constitution has not made any significant changes in the distribution of revenues between the federation and the provinces. The major sources of income have been assigned, as under the three previous constitutions – interim, 1947, 1956 and 1962 constitutions – to the federation, and the provinces have been left without sufficient resources. A national finance commission has been set up under article 160 which is required to recommend to the president as to the distribution of the net proceeds of the important taxes such as income tax, corporation tax, taxes on the sale and purchases of the goods imported, exported, produced, manufactured or consumed, export duties on cotton and other items, excise duties, etc. The national finance commission consists of the federal and provincial financial ministers and such other persons as may be appointed by the president after consultation with the governor of the provinces. It is required to make recommendations to the president 'at intervals not exceeding five years'.

So while the 1973 constitution left the existing distribution of the financial resources almost intact, provisions are being made for a fresh distribution of revenues in accordance with the requirements and responsibilities of federal and provincial governments. Similar provisions for a national finance commission were provided under the 1956 and 1962 constitutions.

As provinces have not been given sufficient financial resources, article 160 provides that the president may make 'grants in aid' of the revenues of the provinces in need of consistence. Grants from the federal government to the component states form part of the financial arrangements in many existing federal systems as, for example, in Canada, Australia, Switzerland and the United States. But a grant, as Professor Wheare maintains, cannot be regarded as an independent source of revenue if it is to depend upon the goodwill or discretion of the central authority. Grants at the discretion of the federal authority may be used to bring pressure of control over the units, which may be a departure from true federalism. It may leave the units legally free but financially bound to the chariot-wheels of the federation. The history of the three decades (1947–77) in Pakistan reveals such possibilities. Fiscal dependence may spread to other fields.

Power to raise revenue by borrowing is normally given both to the centre and to provincial governments in most existing federal systems. Following this tradition, the 1973 constitution of Pakistan conferred this power on both the central and the provincial governments. Parliament is empowered to set limits to the borrowing of money by the central government on the security of the federal consolidated fund (article 115). A provincial legislature, similarly, may regulate the borrowing of money by the provincial government on the security of the provincial consolidated fund (article 116); the federal government may make loans to the provinces or give guarantees in respect of loans missed by the provinces.

The financial resources of the provinces under the federal system in Pakistan are still inadequate to make them free from federal control. The demand for autonomy in the financial sphere continues to be heard both inside and outside the provincial legislatures. There are, however, some encouraging developments in the country from the standpoint of national integration; there are the gigantic efforts, made by the federal government under President Zia, for rural development. Rural development is one of the most important objectives of Pakistan's development strategy today. The vast majority of the Pakistani population (70 per cent) live in rural areas. A large part of unemployment is concentrated in the villages, particularly in less developed parts of the country.

Under the present development strategy, the rural economy targets are sought to be reached through a variety of programmes, cutting across many sectors. The programmes affecting rural life fall under two broad areas, which are: (i) raising agricultural productivity and income from agriculture and allied vocations (ii) extension of physical and social infrastructure – construction of roads, supply of water, village electrification, better health and educational facilities.[15] Great stress is being given to the rapid development of lesser developed areas in provinces like Baluchistan and Sind where there have been separatist movements because of widespread discontentment over economic issues. The unhappy experiences former East Pakistan, Bangladesh, have influenced efforts to remove discontentment in Baluchistan and Sind so as to avoid any further disintegration of the country. Both in Baluchistan and Sind there were secessionist movements. In Sind, a movement for 'Sindidesh' after the model of Bangladesh had developed. There were allegations of India's encouragement and help in Sind, but the Zia government took both firm action and positive steps towards rapid development of the rural areas in Sind. This led to an improvement in the situation. A similar strategy of the combination of firm action and economic development was adopted in Baluchistan where in the 1970s the political unrest was quite serious.

The process of political integration should be carried on in such a way as to allow sufficient room for self expression and self development of the federating units. The great unifying force of Islam and the fear of Indian aggression are there; it requires able and wise leadership to utilize the federal system in the task of developing common national consciousness without which federalism can hardly be expected to work. In spite of ethnic conflicts and tensions, there is a sense of 'belonging together' which should make federalism successful in Pakistan. Professor K C Wheare points out that federalism offers devices through which differing nationalities may unite and while retaining their distinct sub-national existence create a new sense of common nationality.[16] There is no reason why it should not happen in Pakistan among a group of people who are bound together by a common spiritual and cultural heritage and the common aspiration of an ideological polity. Much will depend on the way in which socio-economic development of the country is carried out. President Zia seems to be fully conscious of the delicate and urgent problems of national integration in Pakistan. Sectional factors like race, language and region have great significance in the politics of the 'new' democracies in the emergent countries of Asia and Africa. The social order in these countries is characterized by a lack of integration. This is due in part to the ethnic, religious, racial and cultural pluralism characteristic of the societies, in part to the limited and uneven operation of the process of modernity.[17]

NOTES

1 *National Assembly of Pakistan* (Constitution-making) *Debates*, op. cit., 31 December 1972, p. 5.
2 Ibid, 10 April 1973.
3 Ibid, p. 2468.
4 For details, see *Central Asian Review*, London, no. 1, 1957.
5 K C Wheare, *Federal Government*, London, 1953, third edition, pp. 253–4.
6 Cited in Macmahen, *Federalism Mature & Emergent*, New York, 1955, p. 6.
7 Bowie and Friederich, *Studies in Federalism*, New York, 1954, p. 115.
8 *Federal Government*, op. cit., chapter vi.
9 *Report of the Joint Select Committee on Indian Constitutional Reforms* (in the British parliament), London, 1934.
10 *Dawn*, Karachi, 19 October 1961.
11 *Morning News*, Dhaka, 20 January 1962.
12 Ibid, 23 March 1962.
13 See Max Beloff, 'The federal solution in 25 applications to Europe, Asia and Africa', *Political Studies*, Oxford, June 1959.
14 *Dawn*, Karachi, 18 April 1988.
15 For details see *Pakistan 1986*, op. cit., pp. 64–65.
16 See *Federal Government*, op. cit., concluding chapter.
17 G A Almoved and J S Coleman, *The Politics of the Developing Areas*, op. cit., p. 535.

Chapter VII
Ingredients of Democracy

Whenever there is a military rule under martial law, the basic rights of citizens such as freedom of speech and expression, of assembly and association are either suspended or taken away; similarly, the powers of the judiciary in respect of the enforcement of basic rights of the citizen are also curtailed; political parties are either suspended or abolished. All these usual components of a military rule were associated with the emergence of martial law regimes in Pakistan in 1958–62, 1969–71 and in 1977–85. So when the process of restoration of democracy started in 1983, the issues of fundamental rights, independence of the judiciary and revival of political parties were raised and debate began about how to revive these basic elements of democracy in the proposed constitutional reforms.

Fundamental Rights in Pakistan

Following the practice of many modern constitutions, the constitution of Pakistan includes a lengthy list of fundamental rights. The ideas that 'rights are prior to the state' and that every citizen must enjoy certain inalienable and fundamental rights which even the state authorities cannot or should not encroach upon are not new phenomena; they are as old as humanity itself. The theorists of the doctrine of national law were always inspired by such ideas and from time to time they have been expressed in such documents as the Magna Carta of 1215, the Habeas Corpus Act of 1679, the Bill of Rights of 1689, the American Declaration of Independence in 1776 and the French declarations of the Rights of Man in 1789. Today, they have also gained international recognition and status in the declaration of 'Human Rights' as adopted by the United Nations General Assembly on 10 December 1948.

There was no bill of rights under the interim constitution. The views of the British constitutional experts who made the

Government of India Act 1935 were against the incorporation of such a bill in the constitution itself. But after independence, the preponderance of views in Pakistan as in other new democracies was in favour of a bill of rights being incorporated in the constitution. The experience under the rule of law during the British rule in India was not always happy because the British practice in the dependent territories differed from that found in the United Kingdom. During the movement for freedom, the idea of a bill of rights as incorporated in the constitution of the United States of America and in many other modern constitutions appealed very much to the nationalist leaders. It was, therefore, natural that the nature and content of fundamental rights should have engaged the attention of the framers of the constitution. In Pakistan, it had attracted the attention of the framers of the constitution from the very beginning of their assignment in 1947; a committee on the fundamental rights of the citizens and on matters relating to minorities was set up at the inaugural session of the first constituent assembly in August 1947. In fact, there were weighty arguments in favour of fundamental rights being defined and inserted in the proposed constitution. In a country like Pakistan where the English tradition of democratic practices is lacking, where public opinion is not yet articulate or powerful, the need for such a declaration is imperative. Further, since Pakistan has religious minorities, it is necessary to define and protect their rights so as to prevent the majority from interfering with the rights of individuals irrespective of caste, creed or religion. The interim report of the committee on fundamental rights was accepted in 1950 long before the adoption of any other laws of the constitution. The main idea was, to quote the words of Liaquat, 'to respect the dignity of man'. The fundamental rights as adopted by the first constituent assembly included familiar liberties such as equality of status, of opportunity and before the law; social, economic and political justice; and freedom of thought, expression, belief, faith, worship and association. The fundamental rights were guaranteed to Muslim and non-Muslim citizens without any discrimination or distinction. No concept of 'second class' citizens could be found in the list of these rights which were to be enforced by the law courts.

The second constituent assembly retained all these rights, liberties and the liberal principles and ideals behind them. They, however, made changes improving the content of some of the rights. The constitution of 1956 laid great importance and emphasis on fundamental rights by asserting that if any existing law or custom or usage having the force of law on constitution day was inconsistent with any provision of the fundamental rights, it would be void to the extent of inconsistency, and similarly no authority in Pakistan whether federal government, national assembly, the provincial government, the provincial legislature, or any local authority was competent to make any law, regulation, or any order which might be repugnant to any provisions of fundamental rights and if any such law, regulation or order was made it would to the extent of repugnancy be void (article 4). Thus the democratic concept of limited government, that is, government that rules by law is itself ruled by law, was established. The judiciary was given power to enforce the fundamental rights and the courts were to decide if a law was repugnant to any provisions of the fundamental rights.

Familiar democratic rights and freedoms such as freedom of speech and expression, of assembly and association, of movement and of profession were all provided in the constitution. Similarly, they were restricted with the usual qualifications. With regard to civil rights, familiar rights such as the right to life, liberty and property were granted, again with the usual qualifications and safeguards. Most of the constitutions which guarantee such liberties have found it necessary to make qualifications in respect of enjoyment of such rights. Similar qualifications could be found in the constitution of 1956 as well. An important provision from the standpoint of civil liberty was provided under article 7, which laid down that a person arrested should not be detained in custody without being informed, 'as soon as may be', of the grounds for such arrest, and such a person should not be denied the right of legal consultation and defence. Further, a person arrested or detained in custody was given the right to appear before the nearest magistrate within a period of twenty-four hours and no further detention was allowed except on order of the magistrate.

Such safeguards were, however, not applicable to an enemy alien or any person who might be arrested or detained under any law provided for 'preventive detention'.

The most serious restrictions on civil liberties were, however, under the Security of Pakistan Acts which provided for preventive detention. Provisions for preventive detention cannot be found in democratic countries like England and the United States, except during an emergency such as war or armed invasion. Preventive detention with certain safeguards was provided in England during World Wars I and II under the Defence of the Realm Act of 1914 and under the Emergency Powers (Defence Act) 1938, but no provision for such detention in time of peace is allowed. The provision for preventive detention in the Indo–Pak sub-continent has a long history behind it. The British authorities exercised this power to control the unrest connected with liberation movements. It is, however, curious to find that after independence, both Pakistan and India and also Bangladesh have retained provisions for preventive detention even in times of peace. Both at the centre and in the provinces security acts were passed. The federal legislature exercised its power by enacting the Security Act of 1952. Although the act was meant for a temporary period of three years it was extended again and again. The central government was given power to detain any individual with a view to preventing meetings, from acting in any manner prejudicial to the defence or to the security of Pakistan or the maintenance of public order. Within one month after detention, a person was to be informed of the grounds for detention, but the government was entitled to withhold facts which it considered to be against the interest of the public.

The person detained had to be given the earliest opportunity for making a representation against the detention order to the authority. The grounds of detention were usually the conclusions drawn from the facts coming before the government from the police and other sources of information and no ground could be withheld. Further the grounds supplied had to furnish the detainee with sufficient information to enable him, if he chose, to make a written representation against the order requiring his detention. The ground also had not to be too vague. The court could order the release of the detainee if the grounds supplied were irrelevant to the purpose of detention set out in the security act.

The whole idea of detention under the security act was not to punish a person for having done something illegal but to intercept him before he did it. 'The order is founded not on proof of guilt by legal evidence but on the subjective satisfaction of an authority, empowered under the statute that his detention is necesary to prevent him acting to the prejudice of the security of Pakistan or of a province or of the maintenance of the public order or for such other reason as the Statute lays down.'[1]

The expediency of the detention order was not within the control of a court but it could release the detainee if the statute was not complied with within three months from the issue of the detention order; the case had to be laid before an advisory board which would consist of two persons qualified to be high court judges and appointed by the government. The board was entitled to scrutinize the grounds of detention and also to call for any additional information; but it was not permitted to hear oral evidence by the detainee or his counsel or his witness. On receipt of the report of the advisory board the government was to pass an order which it would consider 'just and proper'. However, the government was to review all cases of detention every six months.

The security act should be applied not only to individuals but also to political parties or other organizations and newspapers.

Preventive detention is incompatible with the spirit and practices of a free democratic state. It must, however, be pointed out that Pakistan from its inception has been beset with threats to its existence as an independent state. Internal and external threats to the security of the country created situations which were not conducive to the growth of free institutions. As pointed out by a Western scholar, 'Some security from the prospect of foreign aggression is necessary in order to permit the luxury of active opposition which attempts to frustrate the policies of government.'[2] As a result of the serious crisis and threats through which the country had to pass, stringent measures against subversive and anti-social action were found necessary. The prime minister of Pakistan said 'The safety and integrity of Pakistan comes first, the liberty of the individual comes later' (*Constituent Assembly Debates*, vol. i, 1951). It was, however, not the security acts themselves which were challenged but the way in which these were applied. It was alleged that the security acts were applied against political opponents by the ruling party and in this process of political persecution of rival parties no government in Pakistan could be entirely exonerated. In 1962 when martial law was lifted and the demand was made for the release of all political detainees, a statement was made on behalf of the government revealing the number of persons detained under the security acts by the so-called 'elected' governments under parliamentary democracy (1947–58).

FUNDAMENTAL RIGHTS UNDER THE 1962 CONSTITUTION

When the new constitution was in the process of being framed, the demand for the incorporation of a bill of rights as it was incorporated under the 1956 constitution was almost unanimous. The constitution commission found that a preponderance of opinion (98.39%) was in favour of a bill of rights being incorporated in the new constitution and being made enforceable by the courts as in the

1956 constitution. The constitution commission discussed, in great detail, two aspects of fundamental rights: (1) should these be incorporated in the constitution (2) should the courts be trusted with the responsibility of seeing that no law is made which is contrary to the basic right of the citizens? In both cases, the commission gave an affirmative answer to these questions. However, the 1962 constitution followed the commission's recommendation only in the first of these questions. When the report of the commission was examined by Ayub's cabinet sub-committee a suggestion was made that the substance of fundamental rights be laid down within the constitution as 'principles of law-making': but they should not be enforceable by the courts. Ultimately this particular suggestion won the approval of those who finally drafted the constitution. The constitution laid down fifteen principles known as 'principles of law-making' which sought to maintain most of the fundamental rights as guaranteed under the 1956 constitution, such as freedom of speech and expression, of assembly and association, of movement and profession subject to usual safeguards, but these 'principles of law-making' were mere pious declarations and there was no remedy if these principles were violated. It was perhaps meaningless to formulate and declare a long list of rights without providing machinery to enforce them. As it has been said very rightly, from the standpoint of law and the science of jurisprudence, nothing is a 'right' unless it is enforceable in the courts of law.

The framers of the 1962 constitution tried to justify the new method by citing the case of Britain, where parliament is the custodian of these rights. But in the absence of the great English tradition, we cannot safely rely on the English method of protecting the basic rights of the citizens. It is because of this realization that the first and the second constituent assemblies as well as the constitution commission favoured and strongly recommended the powers of the courts to enforce the basic rights. The authors of the 1962 constitution referred to the alleged defects of the judicial review in the United States and they seem to have put the issue in the form of a choice between a judge's interpretation of the constitution and the people's interpretation. President Ayub, while introducing the constitution, said, 'Fundamental rights have been secured in the constitution without the complication of all laws never reaching the stage of complete certainty, because they remain perpetually susceptible to challenge in the court of law.'[3] According to President Ayub, the legislature was to be preferred in the matter of guaranteeing basic rights, on the grounds that only the rich minority can go to the courts. But the president's preference in this matter was shared neither by the intelligentsia nor by the people.

As soon as the constitution was published, there was vehement criticism against the curtailment of the powers of the courts in the matter of the fundamental rights of the citizens. No feature of the constitution was more severely attacked or criticized than this particular provision. The issue of fundamental rights had created a storm of controversy and insistent demands were made on behalf of the people to make these 'principles of law-making' justiciable and enforceable by the courts, and this was a burning topic of the political scene in Pakistan in the early 1960s.

In response to public demand and pressure, a bill was introduced by the government which would make these rights justiciable but with certain important reservations. A bill on fundamental rights was introduced in the national assembly during its session in March 1963. The effect of the proposed amendment was to convert the 'principles of law-making' in the 1962 constitution into constitutional restrictions on the power of a legislature, so that the decision whether the legislature, in making a law, had safeguarded fundamental rights would be vested in the law courts. If any legislature passed a law repugnant to or inconsistent with any of the fundamental rights enumerated in the 'principles of law-making' the court would have the power to declare any such law void. This would give the court the same power as under article 4 of the 1956 constitution which put an embargo on the legislature not to pass any bill violating fundamental rights. Thus the amendment sought to make the courts, rather than the legislature, the custodian of fundamental rights. The law minister claimed that the amendment would virtually incorporate a bill of rights in the constitution and it would also enlarge the jurisdiction of the courts, which would be entrusted with the task of enforcement of the rights.

FUNDAMENTAL RIGHTS UNDER THE PRESENT POLITICAL ORDER IN PAKISTAN

When the process of reshaping democracy began in Pakistan in 1972–73 after the withdrawal of the military from politics, the idea of incorporating fundamental rights in the proposed constitution was taken up seriously. While introducing the 1973 constitutional bill in parliament, the then law minister, Mr Hafeez Pirzada, claimed that 'all the fundamental rights in the previous constitution have been continued.' He further claimed that there had been greater stress on 'human dignity – inviolable', and the absolute right of private property had been modified so that 'the country could embark upon the path of socio-economic justice being given to the people.'[4]

When President Zia began his turn of reshaping democracy in Pakistan, particularly in the context of his great emphasis on Islamization of the constitution, there were some doubts whether his constitutional reforms as proposed in the 8th amendment (1985) to the 1973 constitution would modify the modern concept of a bill of rights giving all citizens, irrespective of religion, sex, race, etc., certain basic rights which even the state authorities cannot or should not encroach upon. In one or two reports which preceeded Zia's constitutional proposals of 1985, there was reference to 'rights of citizens' in an Islamic state. But the consensus of all those reports, which were engaged in formulating constitutional proposals for the 'Islamic system of government' or 'Form and system of the government in Pakistan from the Islamic point of view', was that Islam puts great emphasis on human rights and rule of law. Under the Shariah (the Islamic laws) even the highest state authority is subject to the rule of law.

So the present constitution in Pakistan does not make any modifications or changes in the contents of the fundamental rights of the citizens. We shall discuss the status of human rights in Pakistan both from the standpoint of constitutional provisions and from actual practice.

Part II of the 1973 constitution as amended under the 8th Amendment Act 1985 provides an impressive list of fundamental rights. The first provision dealing with fundamental rights – article 8 – lays down that any law or any custom or usage having the force of law, in so far as it is inconsistent with the fundamental rights, shall, to the extent of such inconsistency, 'be void'; the state shall not make any law which takes away or abridges the fundamental rights and any law made in contravention of article 8 shall, to the extent of such contravention, 'be void'. But there is a qualifying sub-clause – article 8 (B) – which protects certain laws specified in the first schedule of the constitution. The laws specified in the first schedule include, among others, the Land Reforms Act 1974 and 1975, Economic Reforms Regulation 1972; the Distribution of Property Regulation 1974, the Settlement of Disputes of Immovable Property Regulation 1974 and 1975. Some of these laws and regulations as protected under the constitution are essential for economic welfare and justice for the people. So the qualifying sub-clause is not a limitation on the fundamental rights. The fundamental rights are not applicable to members of the armed forces, of the police or of such other forces as are charged with the maintenance of public order under article 199. The superior courts have been given power for the enforcement of the fundamental rights. The fundamental rights shall not be suspended, except as expressly provided by the constitution when a state of emergency is declared under article 232 the fundamental rights shall remain 'suspended' (article 233).

The fundamental rights under the amended 1973 constitution include all the democratic rights and freedoms as provided under the first constitution of Pakistan (1956) and the liberal principles and ideals behind them. The familiar and basic rights, such as freedom of speech and expression, of assembly and association – 'subject to any reasonable restrictions imposed by law in the interest of sovereignty or integrity of Pakistan, public order or morality' (article 17). Freedoms of movement and profession are also included. As regards civil liberties, familiar rights such as right to life, liberty and property are granted with the usual qualifications and safeguards. Most of the modern constitutions which guarantee such fundamental rights find it necessary to make qualifications in respect of the enjoyment of basic rights.[5]

There are some difficulties and problems in defining and inserting fundamental rights in a constitution. The framers of a constitution may or at least ought to know the current political, economic and social problems, but they are not expected to have 'the gift of prophecy' and hence do not know the problems that may crop up in the future. The risks, therefore, are that the fetters which are placed today on the state authorities may prove to be an excellent weapon in the hands of vested interests in the next generations. There have been such cases in a country where fundamental rights have been incorporated in the constitution. The right to private property was regarded as one of the important fundamental rights in the eighteenth century, but by the twentieth century it has been recognized that absolute ownership of private property may create obstacles in achieving an equitable and fair economic order; some limitations on the right to own private property are now regarded as essential in order to establish a welfare state. These problems and difficulties led Professor Wheare to say that an ideal constitution should contain few or no declarations of basic rights, though the ideal system of law should define and guarantee many rights.[6] But as we have already explained, in a third world country like Pakistan there are weighty reasons for the incorporation of fundamental rights in the constitution for safeguarding individual freedom and liberty.

Turning back to the contents of the fundamental rights in the present-day constitution of Pakistan, we may point out some important provisions of the basic rights:

a Security of person – no person shall be deprived of life and liberty save in accordance with law (article 9).

b Slavery is non-existent and forbidden and no law shall permit or facilitate its introduction in any form (article 11).

c The dignity of man and, subject to law, the privacy of home shall be inviolable.

d All citizens are equal before the law and are entitled to equal protection of the law and there shall be no discrimination on the basis of sex alone (article 25). There have been apprehensions that in an Islamic state like Pakistan, women will suffer some discrimination or will not have equal status. But in accordance with the true spirit of Islam, there is no discrimination against women.

e Similarly, adequate provisions have been made to safeguard the rights of religious minorities on their status as citizens. Except the provision that the presidency is reserved for the Muslims, there is not a single instance of discrimination against any religious community (articles 20, 21 and 22). This is again, as explained earlier, in tune with the spirit of toleration of religious minorities in Islam.

IMPORTANT LIMITATIONS ON FUNDAMENTAL RIGHTS

We have shown that there were some limitations on the enjoyment of certain basic rights in the form of security acts, preventive detention, limitations on freedom of speech, and on the right to own private property in the previous constitutions in Pakistan. Similar limitations and qualifications are provided in the 1973 constitution also.

(I) Preventive detention: we have explained the definition and concept of preventive detention. Let us examine the provisions for arrest and detention, including preventive detention, under the present-day constitution in Pakistan. Article 10 lays down:

1 No person who is arrested shall be detained in custody without being informed, as soon as may be, of the grounds for such arrest, nor shall he be denied the right to consult and be defended by a legal practitioner of his choice.

2 Every person who is arrested and detained in custody shall appear before a magistrate within a period of twenty-four hours of arrest, and no person shall be detained in custody beyond the said period without the authority of a magistrate.

3 Nothing in clauses (1) and (2) shall apply to any person who is arrested or detained under any law providing for preventive detention.

4 No law providing for preventive detention shall be made except to deal with persons acting in a manner prejudicial to the integrity, security or defence of Pakistan or any part, thereof, or external affairs of Pakistan, or public order, or the maintenance of essential supplies or services. No such law shall authorize the detention of a person for a period exceeding three months unless the appropriate review board has, after affording him an opportunity of being heard in person, reviewed his case and reported, before the expiration of the said period, that there is, in its opinion, sufficient cause for such detention, and, if the detention is continued after the said period of three months, unless the appropriate review board has reviewed his case and reported before the expiration of each period of three months, that there is, in its opinion, sufficient cause for such detention.

'The appropriate review board' means –

a in the case of a person detained under a federal law, a board appointed by the chief justice of Pakistan and consisting of a chairman and two other persons, each of whom is or has been a judge of the supreme court or a high court; and

b in the case of a person detained under a provincial law, a board apppointed by the chief justice of the high court concerned and consisting of a chairman and two other persons, each of whom is or has been a judge of a high court.

The opinion of a review board shall be expressed in terms of the views of the majority of its members.

5 When any person is detained in pursuance of an order made under any law providing for preventive detention, the authority making the order shall, within fifteen days from such detention, communicate to such person the grounds on which the order has been made, and shall afford him the earliest opportunity of making a representation against the order.

The authority making any such order may refuse to disclose facts which the said authority considers to be against the public interest to disclose.

6 The authority making the order shall furnish the appropriate review board with all documents relevant to the case unless a certificate, signed by a secretary to the government concerned, to the effect that it is not in the public interest to furnish any documents, is produced.

7 Within a period of twenty-four months commencing on the day of his first detention in pursuance of an order made under a law providing for preventive detention, no person shall be detained in pursuance of any such order for more than a total period of eight months in the case of a person detained for acting in a manner prejudicial to public order and twelve months in any other case:
provided that this clause shall not apply to any person who is employed by, or works for, or acts on instructions received from, the enemy, or who is acting or attempting to act in a manner prejudicial to the integrity, security or defence of Pakistan or any part thereof, or who commits or attempts to commit any act which amounts to an anti-national activity as defined in a federal law or is a member of any association which has for its objects, or which indulges in, any such anti-national activity.

8 The appropriate review board shall determine the place of detention of the person detained and fix a reasonable subsistence allowance for his family.

9 Nothing in this article shall apply to an enemy alien.

(II) The limitations on freedom of speech – article 19 – provides:
Every citizen shall have the right to freedom of speech and expression, and there shall be freedom of the press, subject to any reasonable restrictions imposed by law in the interest of the glory of Islam or the integrity, security or defence of Pakistan or any part thereof, friendly relations with foreign states, public order, decency or morality or in relation to contempt of court, commission of or incitement to an offence.
Private property: articles 23 and 24 provide a long list of restrictions on the ownership of private property.

Every citizen shall have the right to acquire, hold and dispose of property in any part of Pakistan, subject to the constitution and any reasonable restrictions imposed by law in the public interest.

1 No person shall be deprived of his property save in accordance with the law.

2 No property shall be compulsorily acquired or taken possession of save for a public purpose, and save by the authority of law which provides for compensation thereof, and either fixes the amount of compensation or specifies the principles or/and the manner in which compensation is to be determined and given.

3 Nothing in this article shall affect the validity of:

a any law permitting the compulsory acquisition or taking possession of any property for preventing danger to life, property or public health

b any law permitting the taking over of any property which has been acquired by, or come into the possession of, any person by any unfair means, or in any manner, contrary to law

c any law relating to the acquisition, administration or disposal of any property which is or is deemed to be enemy property or evacuee property under any law (not being property which has ceased to be evacuee property under any law)

d any law providing for the taking over of the management of any property by the state for a limited period, either in the public interest or in order to secure the proper management of the property, or for the benefit of its owner

e any law providing for the acquisition of any class of property for the purpose of:

i providing education and medical aid to all or any specified class of citizens

ii providing housing and public facilities and services such as roads, water supply, sewerage, gas and electric power to all or any specified class of citizens

iii providing maintenance to those who, on account of unemployment, sickness, infirmity or old age, are unable to maintain themselves

f any existing law or any law made in pursuance of article 253 (providing maximum limits as to property).

4 The adequacy or otherwise of any compensation provided for by any such law as is referred to in this article, or determined in pursuance thereof, shall not be called in question in any court.

Under the first constitution of Pakistan (1956), it was provided under article 15 that 'No person shall be deprived of his property save in accordance with law.' The state, however, might acquire private property for a public purpose and under the authority of a law which provided for compensation, by either fixing the amount or specifying the principles on which the compensation was to be determined. In the draft constitution as presented to the second constituent assembly it was further provided that no such law should be called into question in any court on the grounds that the compensation provided by law was not adequate. But these words were not acceptable to the big landlords of West Pakistan, who raised a hue and cry about it. Mr Malik Firoz Khan Noon could even see the emergence of a communist state in Pakistan through such a clause: 'If this provision was passed Pakistan would overnight become a Communist state and this will be the final nail in the coffin of the present government.'[7] Mr Noon could perhaps have well added that such a clause might be 'the final nail in the coffin' of landlordism in Pakistan which constituted a serious menace to the growth of free democratic institutions in West Pakistan. In the assembly, while the big landlords from West Pakistan defended landlordism, the members from East Pakistan sought to bring amendments providing for the abolition of feudalism and landlordism even without compensation. Pakistan inherited from the British a bad type of land tenure system with all its economic and political evils; whereas in East Pakistan landlordism was abolished in 1951, nothing substantial was done in West Pakistan. It was a pity that the 1956 constitution, instead of paving the path to abolition of this rotten system, seemed to have given it a constitutional basis, and its abolition by future legislation might prove to be more difficult. Such difficulties may easily be imagined from the interpretation by the court of the word 'compensation' in the constitution in a case (Jibendra vs. East Pakistan) as 'market value of the property acquired'. It would be well-nigh impossible to pay the market value of big landed properties in West Pakistan and the 1956 constitution thus gave a fresh lease of life to this out-dated and thoroughly rotten system.

While the debate on the 1973 constitution was going on in 1972–73, the then law minister, A Hafeez Pirzada, stated that property might have to be abridged. He added: 'That means that property can be acquired with or without compensation and once it is acquired, even if compensation is granted under the law, the award of that compensation shall be final and no court shall have jurisdiction to inquire the adequacy, or otherwise, of the compensation.' Pirzada claimed that the 1973 constitution had evolved 'a system in the constitution which shall not provide for impediments in the way of socio-economic reforms and any progressive action that were to be taken.'[8]

Political Parties

Our discussion on fundamental rights will not be complete without a reference to the status of political parties in Pakistan.

Political Parties

Both Ayub Khan and Zia-ul-Haq thought of introducing democracy in Pakistan on a non-party basis. The constitution commission, appointed by Ayub in 1960–61, categorically rejected the idea of having democracy without political parties. It wrote: 'It is almost truism that democracy without political parties is unthinkable.' The commission quoted with approval the remarks of Lord Bryce that political parties are far older than democracies; that 'no one has yet shown how democratic government could get on without parties'. Ayub had to concede the right of formation of political parties; finally he himself organized a political party and became its president. But under the Political Parties Act 1962, Ayub put a number of restrictions on political parties. Similarly, Zia's reservations about political parties in an 'Islamic democracy' had to be withdrawn. Political parties are allowed to function in Pakistan, though there are some limitations on the formation of political parties on the grounds of national security and integrity of Pakistan. We shall now examine the status of political parties in the present-day political system in Pakistan.

Under article 17 of the present constitution of Pakistan it is stated: every citizen, not being in the service of Pakistan, shall have the right to form or be a member of a political party, subject to any reasonable restrictions imposed by law in the interests of the sovereignty or integrity of Pakistan and such law shall provide that where the federal government declares that any political party has been formed or is operating in a manner prejudicial to the sovereignty or integrity of Pakistan, the federal government shall, within fifteen days of such declaration, refer the matter to the supreme court whose decision on such reference shall be final.

President Zia revived the Political Parties Act 1962 by an ordinance on 17 October 1978 – ordinance number xli of 1978. It was further elaborated by two other ordinances – ordinance number xliii of 1978, dated 30 August 1979, and ordinance number liii, dated 27 September 1979. Under the Political Parties Act 1962 as amended by

Zia, a political party has to operate under some restriction and has to be registered by the election commission. The act provides:

1 Every political party in existence at the commencement of the Political Parties (Amendment) Ordinance 1979 shall, within one month of such commencement, and every political party formed after such commencement shall, within one month of being formed, apply to the election commission for registration.

2 An application shall be made on behalf of a political party by such person and in such form, and shall be accompanied by such documents besides a copy of its constitution, a list of the names of its office-bearers at the national level and a statement of its total membership in each province, as the election commission may, by notification in the official Gazette, specify.

3 The election commission shall register a political party applying for registration if the commission is satisfied that the political party:

   a has published a formal manifesto, that is to say, the party's foundation document or constitution giving its aims and objectives and provided therein for elections of its office-bearers being held periodically

   b believes in the ideology of Pakistan and the integrity and sovereignty of Pakistan

   c has submitted its accounts.

4 If a political party which has been registered:

   a fails to submit its accounts

   b fails to hold election of any of its office-bearers within the time allowed by, and in accordance with, its constitution and rules

   c propagates any opinion, or acts in any manner, prejudicial to the ideology of Pakistan, or the sovereignty, integrity or security of Pakistan, or morality, or the maintenance of public order, or the integrity or independence of the judiciary of Pakistan or which defames or brings into ridicule the judiciary or the armed forces of Pakistan.

   d receives any aid, financial or otherwise, from the government or any political party of a foreign country, or any portion of its funds from foreign nationals

   e does or omits to do any such act or thing as would have resulted in registration being refused to it in the first instance, then, without prejudice to any action that may be taken in respect of the political party, the election commission may, after giving the political party an opportunity of showing cause against the action proposed to be taken, cancel its registration.

5 The cancellation of the registration of a political party shall be notified by the election commission in the official Gazette.

6 A political party which has not been registered or the registration of which has been cancelled shall not be eligible to participate in an election to a seat in a house of parliament or a provincial assembly or to nominate or put up a candidate at any such election.

The political parties in Pakistan reacted sharply against the registration of a party under the amended Political Parties Act 1962 as revived by Zia in 1978–79. When Zia proposed a number of amendments to the 1973 constitution in 1985, which we have already discussed in our previous chapters, the Political Parties Act was not incorporated in the constitution itself. The 8th amendment bill of 1985 did not make any provision for incorporating the act into the constitution. When the present author asked the then law minister, Iqbal Ahmad Khan, about this omission, he told him that it was 'perhaps by mistake'.

Zia had to pay for this alleged omission. The principal opposition party, the Pakistan People's Party (PPP), never got itself registered under the Political Parties Act and as such it did not or could not participate in any election. Recently in June 1988, it made an appeal to the Pakistan supreme court against the provision of registration of political parties under the act of 1962, as amended by Zia in 1977–78. The court declared the Political Parties Act void on the ground that it violated the fundamental right to form a political party (article 17 – sub-clause 2).

Enjoyment of certain basic rights by the citizens is one of the very important safeguards against arbitrary actions by either executive or legislative bodies in a 'new' democracy like Pakistan. The concept of fundamental rights is based on the inherent rights of citizens to lead a free life in a free society. There cannot be any compromise on basic rights and freedoms. The need for fundamental rights to be incorporated in the constitution of the country has been recognized from the very inception of Pakistan in 1947. The government should not be niggardly in giving fundamental rights to the citizen. It is a pity that even today, after the four decades of its creation, Pakistan's problem over certain rights, such as freedom from arrest, under security acts or under preventive detention, or the right to form political parties, is still not resolved.

PRINCIPLES OF POLICY

The framers of the various constitutions of Pakistan, such as the 1956 and 1962 constitutions, laid down a number of 'principles of policy' to serve as a guide for the state authorities which may help the growth and development of a better society, in which these principles based on social, political and economic justice may be fully realized. The principles are not an integral part of the constitution to be enforced by the law courts like other provisions. But the framers of various constitutions in Pakistan still felt that these principles should at least be inserted in the constitution so that it might serve as the manifesto of the state which should be guided by these principles. These principles, like many other ideas and institutions in the country's constitution, are based partly on Islamic principles and partly on Western democratic philosophy. The idea of 'principles of policy' is found in the constitution of Eire (1973) and the constitutions of several new democracies of Afro-Asian countries, most notably in the Indian constitution (1950), the largest democracy in the world.

The 1973 constitution of Pakistan contains such principles of policy. Some of these principles relate to the Islamic character of the constitution which we have already discussed in our chapter on the process of Islamization in Pakistan. We may now refer to other principles of policy relating to socio-economic justice and welfare. They are as follows:

(I) The state shall encourage local government institutions composed of elected representatives of the areas concerned and in such institutions special representation will be given to peasants, workers and women.

(II) The state shall discourage parochial, racial, tribal, sectarian and provincial prejudices among the citizens.

(III) Steps shall be taken to ensure full participation of women in all spheres of national life.

(IV) The state shall safeguard the legitimate rights and interests of minorities, including their due representation in the federal and provincial services.

(V) The state shall:

    a promote, with special care, the educational and economic interests of backward classes or areas

    b remove illiteracy and provide free and compulsory secondary education within the minimum possible period c make technical and professional education generally available and higher education equally accessible to all on the basis of merit

d ensure inexpensive and expeditious justice

e make provision for securing just and humane conditions of work, ensuring that children and women are not employed in vocations unsuited to their age or sex, and provide maternity benefits for women in employment

f enable the people of different areas, through education, training, agricultural and industrial development and other methods, to participate fully in all forms of national activities, including employment in the service of Pakistan

g prevent prostitution, gambling and the taking of injurious drugs, and printing, publication, circulation and display of obscene literature and advertisements

h prevent the consumption of alcoholic liquor other than for medical and, in the case of non-Muslims, religious purposes

i decentralise the government administration so as to facilitate expeditious disposal of its business to meet the convenience and requirements of the public.

(VI) The state shall:

a secure the well-being of the people irrespective of sex, caste, creed or race, by raising their standard of living, by preventing the concentration of wealth and means of production and distribution in the hands of a few to the detriment of general interest, and by ensuring equitable adjustment of rights between employers and employees, and landlords and tenants

b provide for all citizens, within the available resources of the country, facilities for work and adequate livelihood with reasonable rest and leisure

c provide for all persons employed in the service of Pakistan or otherwise, social security by compulsory social insurance or other means

d provide basic necessities of life, such as food, clothing, housing, education and medical relief, for all citizens, irrespective of sex, caste, creed or race, as are permanently or temporarily unable to earn their livelihood on account of infirmity, sickness or unemployment

e reduce disparity in the income and earnings of individuals, including persons in the various classes of the service of Pakistan

f eliminate riba as early as possible.

(VII) The state shall enable people from all parts of Pakistan to participate in the armed forces of Pakistan.

(VIII) The state shall endeavour to preserve and strengthen fraternal relations among Muslim countries based on Islamic unity, support the common interests of the peoples of Asia, Africa and Latin America, promote international peace and security, foster goodwill and friendly relations among all nations, and encourage the settlement of international disputes by peaceful means.

Judiciary

An independent judiciary is also regarded as a fundamental ingredient of democracy. Thanks to the beneficent legacy of the British concept of justice, the predominance of the legal spirit, as Dicoy pointed out, may be described as a special attribute of English institutions, the respect for the judiciary is significant in Pakistan. It is also the legacy of the Islamic concept of justice; the concept of legal sovereignty has been strong in the annals of Islam. When Pakistan's first constitution (1956) was adopted, the then law minister claimed 'the independency of the judiciary is a principal very dear to the people of this country'.[9] Similarly at the time of adoption of the 1973 constitution, the law minister claimed that 'Independence of the judiciary has not only been ensured but it has been reinforced.'[10]

While the working of democratic institutions in Pakistan such as cabinet, parliament and political parties were far from satisfactory and had received rude set backs under the direct or indirect authoritarian regimes, the role of the judiciary in Pakistan has a better record. Even the military rulers have shown some regard to the judiciary; similarly, judges of the supreme court and high courts have demonstrated courage and independence in upholding the rule of law.

Under the present constitution in Pakistan, as amended by President Zia, the judicial system of the 1973 constitution has largely been maintained. His introduction of the federal Shariah court has, however, added a new factor to the judicial system though it has not affected the independence of the judiciary, particularly in respect of the enforcement of the fundamental rights of the citizens. We have already referred to the concept and role of the Shariah court.

Before we discuss the judicial system in Pakistan today, let us first review the judicial system in Pakistan under previous constitutions (1956 and 1962).

THE JUDICIARY UNDER THE CONSTITUTION OF 1956

Adequate provisions were made in the constitution of 1956 to ensure the independence of judges so that 'justice is given in Pakistan in a real and unpolluted form'.[11] The efficiency and independence of the judicial system depends, to a great extent, upon the method of appointment, tenure of service and salary of the judges. The framers of the constitution in Pakistan thought it desirable to include the organization of the judicial system in the constitution itself. Provisions relating to the judiciary occupied considerable length in the 1956 constitution. The aim of constitutional safeguards in the organization of the judiciary was to secure its independence as being fundamental to both the Islamic and Western conceptions of justice.

Though the supreme court under the 1956 constitution was the successor of the federal court in the interim constitution, its jurisdiction was in some respects wider. It was asserted by an English jurist that its jurisdiction is 'without parallel in the Commonwealth'.[12] Apart from expressed constitutional or statutory provision, there was no limit to its jurisdiction in matters decided by the high courts. The law it would lay down was binding on courts in Pakistan. As supreme tribunal it was the sole judge of its jurisdiction. And there was no judicial means of challenging its exercise. The judgment of the supreme court was binding on all courts in Pakistan, and all executive and judicial authorities throughout the country would act in accord with the supreme court, and all directions, orders, decrees or writs issued by that court were to be executed as if they were issued by the high courts of the appropriate province.

Like its predecessor, the federal court, the supreme court was entrusted with the task of interpreting the constitution. It was specifically given the power to adjudicate in any dispute between:

a The federal government and the government of one or both provinces
b The federal government and the government of a province on the one side and the government of the other province
c The governments of the provinces, if and in so far as the dispute involve any:
   i question of legal right
   ii question as to the interpretation of the constitution.

The 1956 constitution of Pakistan thus departed from the principle of parliamentary supremacy as exists in England and accepted the principle of judicial review as exists in the federal systems of Australia, Canada, and the United States. The constitution was made the 'supreme law of the land' and the 'judiciary was made the guardian of the constitution'. Similar was the position under the interim constitution when after independence, the right of appeal to the privy council was abolished. In fact, in all the constitutional drafts which had been presented to the country from time to time, there was hardly any difference of opinion as to the role and status of the judiciary.

The writ jurisdiction of the superior courts which was introduced in July 1954 was retained under the 1956 constitution. Under article 170 each high court had power throughout the territories in relation to which it would exercise jurisdiction to issue to any person or authority, orders, or writs including writs in the nature of habeas corpus, mandamus, prohibition, quo-warranto and certiorari for the enforcement of any of the fundamental rights guaranteed under the constitution or for any other purpose. The writ jurisdictions of the superior courts in Pakistan constitute a perpetual reminder to the executives to exercise restraint and caution as imposed under the laws of the land. The courts exercise this power in a beneficial and befitting manner, and thus have earned the confidence and trust of the people.

THE JUDICIARY UNDER THE 1962 CONSTITUTION

When President Ayub decided to restore constitutional government and the new constitution was in the process of being made, there was an almost universal demand to restore the full jurisdiction and powers of the courts which restressed and emphasized the fact that independence of the judiciary should be maintained as had been the practice for a long time, and any inroad into it that was found necessary during the martial law period should not be treated as a precedent. The constitution commission had recommended all the safeguards to ensure the independence of the judiciary as was done under the 1956 constitution.

Like many other recommendations of the constitution commission, its recommendations relating to the judiciary were radically changed by Ayub's cabinet sub-committee and those who gave the final touches to the 1962 constitution. It has to be made clear, however, that there seemed to be no threat or challenge to the independence and integrity of the judiciary in the 1962 constitution.

Adequate measures were taken to retain the independence of the judiciary. It was encouraging to note that the government recognized the fact that for democratic government, the proper functioning of the judiciary was just as important as the proper functioning of the executive and the legislature. It was stated, 'It is, therefore, necessary to uphold and ensure the independence of the judiciary as they are the guardians of the rule of the law.'[13] The security of the tenure of office and other conditions of the services which give trust and confidence to the judiciary were retained in the constitution. The method of removal of judges of the superior courts was, however, different from that of the 1956 constitution. Under the constitution the judges of the supreme court would hold office till the age of 65 years unless, of course, they were removed from office on the ground of misbehaviour or infirmity of mind or body by an order of the president, upon an address by the national assembly praying for such a removal. Under the constitution, the president would appoint a council to be known as the supreme judicial council consisting of the chief justice of the supreme court, the two next most senior judges of the supreme court, and the chief justice of each high court. If, on information received from the council, or from other sources, the president was of the opinion that a judge of the supreme court or of a high court was incapable of performing duties of his office by reason of physical or mental incapacity, or might have been guilty of gross misconduct, the president would direct the council to enquire into the matter, and the president might remove the judge from the office if the council would report to do so. The method of removal of the judges under the 1962 constitution could be compared with the one as recommended by the first constituent assembly in its draft constitution of 1954. Perhaps the idea behind the new method was that legislatures in Pakistan were not yet mature and competent enough to decide the issues relating to the removal of the judges. It was suggested in some quarters that for a long time to come legislatures would not have the requisite integrity and competence to sit in judgment over a superior judge. There was something to be said in favour of this view. In any case, the new method as provided under the 1962 constitution did not in any way constitute a threat to the independence of the judiciary.

As to the powers of the judiciary, the 1962 constitution had restricted its jurisdiction in certain vital matters. The 1962 constitution had departed from the well-established system of umpiring the constitution by the judiciary. Under the 1962 constitution, the task of umpiring the federal system was not given to the courts. No law could be challenged in a court on the grounds that the legislature by which it was made lacked power. This is an acceptance of the principle of parliamentary supremacy as it exists in England, and it is a departure from the system of judicial review as it exists in the United States of America. Under both the interim and the 1956 constitutions, the judiciary had power to adjudicate upon the vires of the legislative provisions.

It would not, however, be correct to say that the judiciary had no part in interpreting the constitution. The original power of the supreme court included jurisdiction in any dispute between the central government and a provincial government, or between two provincial governments (article 57). Similarly, the appellate jurisdiction of the supreme court provided that an appeal from a judgment decree, order or sentence, should lie as of right if the high court would certify that the case involved a substantial question of law as to the interpretation of the constitution (article 58). These two articles (57 and 58) seem to be in conflict with article 133, which laid down that responsibility of deciding whether a legislature had power under the constitution to make a law was that of the legislature itself, and that the validity of a law could not be called into question on the grounds that the legislature by which it was made had no power to make the law. How could the judiciary settle the disputes between the central and a provincial government, or interpret the constitution if it had no power to decide the legality of enactment passed by any legislature?

While the power of the judiciary to adjudicate on the legality of enactment passed by the legislature seemed to have been taken away, the judicial control over the executive seemed to have been fully maintained. As to the judicial review of executive action, the 1962 constitution has faithfully preserved, in a substantial manner, the jurisdiction of the courts, on the lines of the common law of England. The substance of the former writ jurisdiction which was greatly valued and cherished in Pakistan was preserved under the 1962 constitution, although it did not mention the English names of habeas corpus, mandamus, certiorari and quo-warranto. Article 98 of the constitution laid down that a high court of a province might, if it was satisfied that no other adequate remedy was provided by law:

a on the application of any aggrieved party, making an order.

   i directing a person performing in the province functions in connection with affairs of the centre, the province or a local authority to refrain from doing that which was not permitted by law to do or to do that which he was required by law to do

ii declaring that any act done or proceeding in the province by a person performing functions in connection with the affairs of the centre, the province or a local authority, had been done or taken without lawful authority and was of no legal effect

b on the application of any person could make an order

i directing that a person in custody in the province be brought before the high court so that the court might satisfy itself that he was not being held in custody without lawful authority or in unlawful manner

ii requiring any person in the province holding or purporting to hold a public office to show under what authority of law he held that office.

This particular article was an important provision under the 1962 constitution for the protection of individual rights and liberties and this can be compared with section 223-A of the interim constitution and article 170 of the 1956 constitution. The implication of this power of the courts to review executive action was explained by Justice Mourshed as follows:

It is not the use of the executive powers but their misuse which the courts will intervene to prevent. The courts will insist that such powers must be exercised genuinely for the purposes for which they are conferred and not for any extraneous purpose.

He goes on to point out that if the powers of the executive are exercised in a way which is plainly unreasonable the courts will infer that it is not a genuine exercise of power. The courts, according to him, will prevent the executive from exceeding the bounds of its authority. Whenever a power is conferred, the courts will intervene to see that such power is exercised with a fundamental fairness and in accordance with the well-established principles of substantial justice.[14] It was highly encouraging and reassuring from the standpoints of the free institutions in the country that the constitution had granted this power to the judiciary and that the judges took such a view of the courts' role in checking arbitrary action by the executive. The decision of the Dacca high court, and of the supreme court of Pakistan, in declaring the order of the president which enabled the ministers to retain their seats in the legislature ultra vires, proved that the courts under the 1962 constitution played an effective and important role.

THE JUDICIAL SYSTEM IN PAKISTAN TODAY

The Judiciary in Pakistan consists of different tiers of courts, starting from the civil and criminal courts at tehsil/taluka level and going up to the supreme court – the highest judicial authority in the country.

Supreme Court

Appeals lie to the supreme court of Pakistan from judgments and orders of all the high courts in the country, as also from the federal Shariah court. The supreme court has concurrent writ jurisdiction similar to the high courts. It also has jurisdiction to answer references made to it by the government, as well as to settle cases of dispute among provincial governments and between the latter and the federal government (articles 184–185, 186 and 188).

High Courts

There is a high court in each of the four provinces of Pakistan. The Islamabad Capital Territory falls within the jurisdiction of the Lahore high court of the Panjab. The high courts have original writ jurisdiction, and appeals from judgements and orders made therein lie to the supreme court. Subject to such appeals the decisions of the high courts are final.

The high courts hear appeals arising out of judgements and orders made by the district judges on the civil side and the sessions judges on the criminal side. Death sentences awarded by the sessions judges have to be confirmed by the high courts before they are carried out even if no appeal is filed by the convicted persons. The high courts have also revisional jurisdiction in civil and criminal cases, and they can exercise this jurisdiction, not only on the application of a party, but also on their own. A high court has the overall control of all the civil and criminal courts in the province (articles 199, 208 and 203).

District and Sessions Judges

In every district of a province there is a district and sessions judge who has both civil and criminal jurisdiction. While exercising civil jurisdiction he acts as a district judge, and for criminal cases as a sessions judge. The sessions judges are assisted by the additional sessions judges who have the same civil and criminal jurisdiction, except the administrative powers which vest in the district and sessions judge.

On the criminal side, the sessions judges try murder cases or cases in which the death penalty is prescribed. They also try most of the cases under the Hudood Laws (Islamic Penal Code). Appeals from their judgments and orders in Hudood cases lie to the federal Shariah court, and in other cases to the high courts. The district and sessions judges exercise appellate jurisdiction over judgements and orders of the subordinate courts. At the lower tier going down to tehsil level, there are senior civil judges, administrative civil judges and civil judges for civil cases, and magistrates and sub-divisional magistrates for criminal cases.

Special Courts and Tribunals

To deal with specific types of cases, special courts and tribunals are constituted. These are: special courts for trial of offences in banks; special courts under the Banking Companies (Recovery of Loans) Ordinance 1979, Special Courts under the Customs Act 1969, Special Traffic Courts, courts of special anti-corruption judges (at federal and provincial levels), commercial courts, drug courts, labour courts, insurance appellate tribunal, income tax appellate tribunal and service tribunals.

Appeals from the special courts lie to the high courts, except in the case of labour courts and special traffic courts, which have separate forums of appeal. The tribunals are high-powered judicial bodies consisting of members of the judiciary and those dealing with the specific subjects concerned. Appeals from decisions of the tribunals lie to the supreme court of Pakistan.

Speedy and Inexpensive Justice

Steps have been taken to overcome the problems of inordinate delays in dispensing justice and the enormous cost involved in litigation – a legacy of the past. The number of high court judges, additional sessions judges and magistrates has been increased. The disposal of cases under Islamic laws by the federal Shariah court is quick, most criminal appeals being decided within a maximum period of two months.[15]

The most novel feature of the judicial system in Pakistan today is the creation of the 'federal Shariah court'. We have discussed its role and functions in our chapter on Islamization in Pakistan. A new chapter 3A has been added under part vi (dealing with the jurisdiction) of the constitution. The Shariah court was orginally introduced by President Zia under president's order no. 1 of 1980, which was further added and amended by president's order no. 5 of 1982, president's order no. 7 of 1983, president's order no. 2 of 1984 and president's order no. 14 of 1985. These presidential orders relating to the federal Shariah court have been incorporated in the constitution by adding the new chapter 3A of part vi of the 1973 constitution. This part gives details relating to the composition, functions and role of the Shariah court (articles 203A, 203B, 203C, 203D, 203DD, 203E, 203F, 203G and 203H).

The Shariah court consists of not more than eight Muslim judges including the chief justice to be appointed by the president. The chief justice shall be a person who is or has been or is qualified to be a judge of the supreme court or who is or has been a permanent judge of a high court. The judges, not more than four, shall be persons each one of whom is or has been or is qualified to be a judge of a high court and not more than three shall be ulema (religious teachers) who are well-versed in Islamic law.

As we have already stated, the main role of the federal Shariah court is to determine if any of the existing laws in Pakistan are or are not repugnant to Islamic injunctions. On the basis of this role, about 500 laws in Pakistan have either been modified or annulled.

From June 1962 the federal Shariah court has also undertook *suo moto* examination of federal as well as provincial laws, and notices are issued to the public in general to assist the Shariah court in this task.

The most significant aspect of the judicial system in Pakistan today is the preservation of the supremacy of the supreme court of Pakistan even over the jurisdiction of the federal Shariah court: article 203/F provides that 'any party to any proceedings before the Federal Shariah Court, aggrieved by the final decision of the Federal Shariah Court in such proceedings, may, within sixty days of such decision, prefer an appeal to the Supreme Court'.

An appeal shall lie to the supreme court from any judgement, final order or sentence of the federal Shariah court:

a if the federal Shariah court has on appeal reversed an order of acquital of an accused person and sentenced him to death or imprisonment for life or imprisonment for a term exceeding fourteen years; or, on revision, has enhanced a sentence as aforesaid

b if the federal Shariah court has imposed any punishment on any person for contempt of the court.

An appeal to the supreme court from a judgement, decision, order or sentence of the federal Shariah court in a case to which the preceding clauses do not apply shall lie only if the supreme court grants leave to appeal.

For the purpose of the exercise of the jurisdiction conferred by this article, there shall be constituted in the supreme court a bench to be called the Shariah appellate bench and consisting of:

a three Muslim judges of the supreme court

b not more than two ulema to be appointed by the president to attend sittings of the bench as ad hoc members thereof from amongst the judges of the federal Shariah court or from out of a panel of ulema to be drawn up by the president in consultation with the chief justice.

Notwithstanding the establishment of the federal Shariah court, President Zia has maintained the independence and the supremacy of the country's highest court whose decisions will be final and 'all executive and judicial authorities throughout Pakistan shall act in aid of the supreme court' (article 190). There seems to be no threat or challenge to the independence and integrity of the judiciary in the present political order in Pakistan. Zia's process of Islamization has not affected the judicial system because 'Rule of Law' is fundamental in a true Islamic state which is Zia's cherished goal for Pakistan.

NOTES

1 Alan Gledhill, *The British Commonwealth – The Development of its Laws and Constitutions, Vol. 8 Pakistan*, London, 1957, p. 130.
2 Keith Callard, *Pakistan – A Political Study*, London, 1957, p. 352.
3 President Ayub's Speech on 1 March 1962; see *Dawn*, Karachi, 2 March 1962.
4 *National Assembly of Pakistan: (Constitution-Making) Debates*, op. cit., 31 December 1972, p. 8.
5 See Ivor Jenning, *Approach to Self-Government*, Cambridge, 1957.
6 K C Wheare, *Modern Constitutions*, London, 1951, pp. 101–2.
7 *Dawn*, Karachi, 28 January 1956.
8 *National Assembly of Pakistan: (Constitution-Making) Debates*, op. cit., 31 December 1972, pp. 5 and 9.
9 *Debates of the (second) Constituent Assembly*, op. cit., 7 January 1956.
10 *National Assembly of Pakistan (Constitution-Making) Debates*, op. cit., 28 January 1973.
11 *Debates of the (second) Constituent Assembly*, 7 January 1956.
12 Alan Gledhill, op. cit., p. 213.
13 *A Pledge Redeemed*, Karachi, Government of Pakistan, March 1962, p. 2.
14 Justice S M Mourshed, 'Md. Hossain, V & General Manager East Bengal Railway', *PLD*, Dhaka, 1961, p. 22.
15 See for details *Pakistan 1986*, op. cit., pp. 51–55.

Chapter VIII
Conclusion

We have discussed and examined the constitutional and political developments in Pakistan after the tragic events of 1971, when the country was dismembered into two parts – East Pakistan becoming an independent state, Bangladesh, and the erstwhile West Pakistan forming the new and smaller Pakistan. Pakistan was the largest Muslim state till 16 December 1971. Though smaller in size and population, Pakistan still occupies a central position in the world of Islam. Pakistan is also highly strategically important in regional and global politics. After his first visit to the Middle East and South Asia, the late US Secretary, Foster Dulles, stated: 'Communist China borders on northern territories held by Pakistan and from Pakistan's northern border one can see the Soviet Union. Pakistan flanks Iran and the Middle East and guards the Khyber pass, the invasion route from the north into the subcontinent.'[1] Many people, in particular, the Indians thought that Pakistan had become a lost case after the tragic events of 1971 in the subcontinent. But Pakistan though, smaller in size and population, is a highly important country in South Asia and in the world of Islam. Pakistan's fraternal relations with the Islamic countries are based on shared values of culture and history, and are nourished by a common faith and spiritual heritage. Though ties have continued to expand, and constitute a central pillar of her foreign policy, Pakistan has made consistent efforts to promote solidarity among the Islamic ummah and for the advancement of Islamic causes. With its deep commitment to the promotion of Islamic solidarity, Pakistan played a significant role in the establishment of the Organization of Islamic Conference (OIC) in 1970, and hosted the Second Islamic Summit in Lahore in 1974. It has also endeavoured to contribute to the strengthening of various organs and agencies of OIC, such as the Islamic Solidarity Fund. In October 1980, the president of Pakistan was accorded the unique honour of addressing the UN General Assembly on behalf of the entire Islamic world.

As an Islamic country, Pakistan has supported the cause of

Muslims – particularly the struggle of the people of Palestine and Afghanistan.

The central theme of our work has been to examine the great experiment of an 'Islamic democracy' in Pakistan. We have discussed elaborately the relationship between the state and religion in Islam. We have also analysed the process of Islamization of Pakistani society including its political, legal and economic order under President Zia since 1977. Simultaneously, Zia has taken steps towards the transition of his military regime into a civilian democratic government. The transition from military rule to a democratic one started in 1983, and it was completed in December 1985 when the longest martial law in Pakistan's history was lifted. An elected civilian government and elected legislature began functioning, both at the national and provincial levels. The civilian prime minister, M K Junejo, claimed, 'We will be able to bury martial law forever'. We are, however, not so sure that martial law is buried forever in Pakistan. But, after eight years of military rule, 'Pakistan', it is claimed, 'basks in the sunshine of democracy and a representative government.' A completely civilian cabinet, comprising elected members of the national parliament, has been sworn into office. Fundamental rights of citizens, suspended for over 20 years, have been restored. The press is free, courts are independent. Pakistan has a fully fledged democratic order.[2]

The advent of this democratic era is not a sudden development. It is the culminating point of a phased, well-thought-out and carefully implemented political programme announced by President Zia-ul-Haq in August 1983. The president has been moving slowly and cautiously towards the goal of constitutional rule.

The lifting of martial law after eight and a half years was the most remarkable achievement of the newly elected government. But that was not enough. After the Indo-Pak War of 1965, the people of Pakistan lived under a state of emergency, with their fundamental rights suspended. For twenty long years, they had not seen what the constitution had guaranteed them. Even in the days of elected governments claiming to be the champions of democracy, the Pakistani nation was made to live under emergency rule. This sorry state of affairs changed on 30 December 1985.

Simultaneously with the withdrawal of martial law, the civilian government lifted the state of emergency and restored fundamental rights and freedoms of the people.

Announcing this, Mr Junejo declared: 'These rights are the foundation of democracy, a symbol of a democratic society and an emblem of the greatness of the nation and the people. You are now the custodians of these rights.'[3] Simultaneously, as a result of President Zia's various reforms towards Islamization in Pakistan, visible changes are taking place in the socio-economic, educational, judicial and political spheres of Muslim society in Pakistan.

This great experiment of blending Islam and democracy in Pakistan is of great significance and importance to the entire world, particularly to the world of Islam. The experiment deserves the attention and thought of anybody who is interested in understanding Islam as a factor in the contemporary world. A mounting religious fervour or a resurgence of Islam has been sweeping the Muslim world. Muslims all over the world – from Indonesia in the East to Senegal in the West – are discovering their roots and reassessing the political power of the Islamic way of life. The resurgence of Islam has become the subject of great debates among Westerners, orientalists, political philosophers, youth and students.[4] In the early 1950s, Pakistanis were engaged in deciding the role of Islam in their political order. After lengthy and wide discussion, the framers of the constitution were successful in producing a constitution (the 1956 constitution) which was a commendable synthesis of modern needs and Islamic values. The broad principles of the teaching of Islam were woven into the fundamental pattern of a modern democratic state, just as the broad ideals of Judaeo-Christian ethics have provided the basic notions in several Western democracies. The framers of Pakistan's first constitution in 1956 gave a rational and dynamic interpretation of Islamic ideals, and therefore they had no difficulty in creating a state in which social justice, rule of law and equality were guaranteed to all citizens, Muslim and non-Muslim. Pakistan was set up as a democratic state with its ethical aspect via Islam. Democracy became an aspect of its Islamicness, a part of the definition of the Islamic state. The experiment of 'an Islamic democracy' as provided in the 1956 constitution was, however, not fulfilled by the subsequent political developments in the country. The real power was exercised by a small ruling elite composed of top civil and military officials. This group, who captured political power by a number of factors which have been explained in our work, had no faith either in democracy or in Islamic values and ideals. So the trial of 'Islamic democracy' came to a sad end. Democracy was buried in a formal way in 1958. The political order set up under the 1962 constitution was based on 'controlled democracy' and the Islamic provisions were put in 'cold storage'. Then came the tragic happenings in Pakistan in 1971 resulting in the dismemberment of

Pakistan. East Pakistan became the independent state of Bangladesh whose constitution was declared as 'secular', and where democracy was also formally ended in 1975 when a one-party dictatorship was set up by amending the constitution – the 4th amendment in 1975. So one part of undivided Pakistan became secular and a one-party dictatorship. West Pakistan then became the 'new' Pakistan. The 'new' Pakistan continued to be an 'Islamic Republic' and there was also a parliamentary system of government under a democratic constitution (the 1973 constitution). But Z A Bhutto, like his authoritarian predecessors, had no enthusiasm for Islam or for democracy. So there was neither true democracy – only a parody of democratic institutions existed – nor were any worthwhile steps taken to implement the Islamic provisions of the 1973 constitution.

It was left for a military ruler, General Mohammad Zia-ul-Haq to get the Islamic provisions of the 1973 constitution reactivated and enlarged. Zia also started a comprehensive scheme lasting for a period of eighteen months – August 1983 to December 1985 – for the transformation of his military rule into a democratic civilian one. The great experiment of an Islamic democracy has, therefore, begun, in the real sense, in Pakistan. This time, the experiment is of much greater significance and importance because President Zia really means business as far as his ideal of the Islamization of Pakistani society and government is concerned. In the past, as we have stated in this work, the Islamic provisions of the various constitutions were merely in the form of an ideal and not a proclamation of any reality. No significant move was taken, for instance, to bring the existing laws of the country into conformity with Islamic injunctions as laid down in the Quran and in Islamic law, the Shariah, but Zia has already taken steps to bring the existing laws of the country into conformity with Islamic injunctions. He has set up the federal Shariah court which has changed or amended or nullified about five hundred existing laws of the country on the grounds of those laws being repugnant to the Quranic injunctions. Similarly, there is now no way to pass a bill by the parliament which will be against the Islamic injunctions. Zia has also introduced far-reaching reforms for Islamization of the country's economic order by changing the banking and taxation systems and by taking fiscal measures. Significant changes have already taken place in other spheres of Pakistani society and in the political order to give substance to the Islamic provisions of the country's existing constitution.

Does it mean that Pakistan is becoming a 'fundamentalist' state? Zia strongly refutes it. In fact, if a country adopts true Islamization as laid down in the Quranic injunctions, there is no room for what is called 'fundamentalism'. This is a term, Zia rightly points out, coined by those who fail to understand the true nature of an Islamic state. What Zia has been trying to achieve in Pakistan is not a narrow concept of a fanatical religious system, his aim is to implement Islam in its correct perspective and proper meaning. Zia has not accepted, for instance, that there is no room for a legislature in an Islamic state as extremists believe. Nor has he agreed that women should not be given the right to vote as suggested by the board of Talimat-i-Islammiah, which was set up by the first constituent assembly of Pakistan to advise on matters arising out of the 1949 'Objective Resolution' – whose meaning and significance have been explained in our work.

Zia is committed, as we have shown, to having a socio-political system in Pakistan which would fully conform to Islamic principles and must at the same time fulfil present day requirements. Zia rightly thinks that there is no contradiction between the two because Islam is a progressive and enlightened religion. We have quoted Zia's significant remarks, made while announcing his 'political plan' for the transfer of powers to an elected civilian government, that 'when God revealed the Holy Quran for the guidance of mankind, it was not only for any particular period but for all times to come.' 'The Quran', he continued, 'provides only the guiding principles and leaves out many things.' 'Where the Quran', Zia concluded, 'is silent the Muslims have the option of resorting to *Ijtihad*' (individual judgement and consensus).[5] Zia believes in the adjustment of a particular case to the requirements of a particular situation at a given time.

So, President Zia had no difficulty in introducing a democratic political system while keeping the fundamental principles of Islam intact.

We have discussed and analysed the democratic system introduced by Zia in Pakistan through an elected parliament in 1985. The big question is whether the present-day political order in Pakistan may be described as a democratic one. No constitution or political order is perfect. So is the case with Pakistan's present political system. Pakistan's present constitution may differ from some varieties of democracy as they exist in Western countries like Britain, France or the United States of America. But that should not lead a political scientist to make the conclusion that Pakistan, or for that matter any political system in the new democracies of Afro-Asian countries, is undemocratic. A constitution, as the father of political science, Aristotle, would say, is like a vest which has to be fitted to the body for which it is meant. The carbon copy of any particular form of democracy is not the last word on free institutions. There are, however, certain basic ingredients of democracy such as free and fair elections at periodical intervals in accordance with the provisions of the constitutions and held under the supervision of an independent election commission, the existence of more than one political party so that the electorate may freely chose who should govern the country for the next four or five years, enjoyment of certain basic human rights by all citizens including religious and racial minorities and, of course, including women. The government should be responsible to the people, and the wishes of the people should be executed by their elected representatives in legislatures as well as in the executive branch of the governmental machinery. The third organ, the judiciary, must be independent and should have the powers to enforce the basic rights of the citizens. Judged by these criteria, the constitution and political order in Pakistan today may be safely described as a democratic one. When President Zia installed the elected civilian governments both at federal and provincial levels in 1985, he really transferred the full powers and authorities to the elected bodies. The prime minister is the holder of the executive authority, and parliament enjoys full freedom in making laws, subject only to Islamic law, the Shariah, which has been declared, 'the supreme law of the land'. No doubt, the president of Pakistan enjoys certain special powers and functions which one may not find in a parliamentary system on the British model. But as long as the fundamental requisites of democracy are preserved, and as long as the constitutional process is maintained, it will be fair to describe the system as democratic.

Democracy in the new Afro-Asian country is, however, beset with many limitations and problems.[6] The real problem in Pakistan, as in most of the other newly independent countries of Asia and Africa, is that Western political institutions were imposed on people from above and did not grow from the bottom. The socio-economic conditions in which democratic ideas and practices evolved in the West are lacking in new democracies. These countries are economically backward. Most of the people live in rural areas; they are largely poor and illiterate. In a country like Pakistan the basic problem is how to further economic development while preserving democratic values and traditions– President Zia has also added the preservation of Islamic values and tradition as a fundamental requirement.

Thomas Jefferson's remarks that 'if a nation expects to be ignorant and free, it expects what never was and never will be', can hardly be challenged. Democracy, as R M MacIver points out, is the only system that has faith in the free mind but a free mind is the product of education. Because democracy trusts its citizens, it makes, MacIver continues, 'higher demands on them, on their reason, on their integrity, or their faith, than does any other system.'[7] This can, however, be expected only when the masses have achieved a minimum level of education. In its absence, public opinion cannot be well organized or articulate. No democracy can function satisfactorily, however impressive its machinery may be, without an effective public opinion as a source of ideas for criticism of the government and the opposition, as well as for an instrument for the generation of alternative policies.[8]

The problem of national integration is also a big challenge for democracy in Pakistan. Pakistan is still beset with ethnic and racial conflicts. Pakistan has been working very hard to achieve national integration through federal solutions, and also Zia expects, through the application of the unifying force of Islam. The fate of democracy or, for that matter the fate of an Islamic democracy, depends on the development of a sound foundation among the people. They may be termed as the infrastructure of democracy which means that the movement for democracy must grow with education and enlightenment as well as with economic improvement.

It is perhaps too early to predict how far the great experiment of 'Islamic democracy' in Pakistan will succeed, and whether it will have a better future than the early modest experiment of Islamic democracy in the 1950s. President Zia's sincerity and dedication to both Islamic and democratic values and traditions are beyond doubt. The present author, after his extensive research and discussions with the Pakistani leaders including the intelligentsia, professionals like journalists, university professors and experts on Islamic and democratic theories, is convinced that the present regime in Pakistan headed by President Zia is determined to make Islamic democracy in Pakistan a great success. It is, therefore, worth watching and observing this new and great experiment in the combination of Islamic and democratic values.

NOTES

1 See Foster Dulles' speech of 29 May 1953, *Documents on International Affairs, 1953*, London, 1956, pp. 258–259.
2 *Pakistan Times*, Islamabad, 17 October 1985.

3 *Pakistan Functioning Democracy*, Islamabad, Government of Pakistan, n.d., pp. 3–5.
4 For details see Flora Lewis, 'Upsurge in Islam', *New York Times*, 28, 29, 30 December 1979.
5 *Political Plan Announced*, op. cit., pp. 20–21.
6 See the present author's *Democracy in Pakistan*, Canada, 1963, chapter 11 – 'Dilemmas of Democracy', pp. 270–296.
7 R M MacIver, *The Rampart We Guard*, New York, 1950, p. 51.
8 See the working paper from a seminar on 'South and Southeast Asia has second look at Democracy' in New Delhi in 1961, cited in *Democracy in Pakistan*, op. cit., p. 273.

Epilogue

Since the manuscript of this work was sent to the publishers in late July 1988, a great tragedy has taken place in Pakistan: President Mohammad Zia-ul-Haq was killed in an aircraft explosion on 17 August 1988. Zia was the architect of Pakistan's transition from military to civilian rule – the theme of the present volume. At his death, Zia had been in power just over eleven years (1977–88), making him the longest serving ruler since Pakistan was created in 1947. He was the 'strong man' of South Asia. Like any other successful person, Zia was a controversial figure. He left behind a large number of admirers both at home and abroad. No other Pakistani leader except the two earliest ones – Quaid-e-Azam Muhammad Ali Jinnah and the first prime minister, Liaquat Ali Khan – had such an honourable death, mourned by both his countrymen and world leaders. The US Secretary of State, George Schultz, who led the US Delegation to Zia's state funeral, described Zia as a 'martyr' for the cause of freedom fighters in Afghanistan. Zia, as we have pointed out in this volume, was a great champion of the rights and aspirations of the world of Islam. He was never tired of working for the unity and solidarity of the Islamic ummah, he was held in high esteem in the Muslim countries as a devout Muslim and as a great statesman. He was also highly respected in the West, particularly in the United States and the United Kingdom, for his courage, convictions and diplomatic skills. Zia was one of the first world leaders who raised his voice against the Soviet invasion of Afghanistan in December 1979. In early January 1980, soon after the Soviet military intervention against its weak South Asian neighbour, Afghanistan, the present author had a lengthy interview with President Zia. Zia considered the Soviet actions in Afghanistan as a great danger for Moscow's expansionist designs in South and South West Asia. He said that Russia seemed to have a big strategic plan for global domination. He pointed out that although land-locked, Afghanistan provides the Soviets with a base of operations and for a cluster of pressure points that extend from the tip of Indo-China across central Asia through the Arabian peninsula, and to the horn of Africa. Czarist and Communist Russia's expansionist designs towards a 'warm water' port in the Indian Ocean have a long history behind them. Zia gave unqualified assistance to the freedom-fighters in Afghanistan for eight years (1980–88). As the *Washington Post* wrote in its editorial in August 1988, 'Without his [Zia's] bold and courageous stance, the Kremlin's decision to evacuate Soviet troops would have been unthinkable.' The *Economist* wrote on 20 August 1988, 'Zia, the sometimes confused human being, will be recalled with affection. Zia, the soldier, has a decent place in the momentous recent history of the region. He did more than most to save it from Russia. That is not a bad epitaph.'

But Zia had also many adversaries both inside and outside Pakistan. Pakistan's main opposition party (PPP) leader Benazir Bhutto bluntly stated that she did not regret Zia's death. Outside Pakistan, Dr Henry Kissinger said, 'Zia's death is an immediate and important benefit to the Soviet Union and the Afghan government.'[1] Kissinger might have added 'to the Indian government also'. The US government felt it necessary to warn Moscow and New Delhi that it would continue its 'strong support' of Pakistan in the wake of Zia's death. Why did Washington feel it necessary to tell Moscow and New Delhi about its continued 'strong support' of Pakistan? Does the United States apprehend any design by Pakistan's meddlesome neighbours? The Soviet newspaper *Pravda* on 28 August 1988 made most uncharitable attacks on the late president of Pakistan. What were Zia's 'crimes'? According to *Pravda*, Zia used to help those whom *Pravda* described as the 'most reactionary and militant Afghan Mujahideen [freedom fighters]'. No doubt, Zia was determined to overthrow the Soviet puppet regime in Kabul so that the people of Afghanistan might choose a truly representative government. Zia's death is not only a great loss for Pakistan but it is also a big loss for the smaller nations of South Asia, as Pakistan under Zia had been a 'bulwark' against the Indo-Soviet grand strategy for expansionist designs in South and South West Asia. The most pertinent question concerns the impact of Zia's death on Pakistan's political stability and socio-economic progress. 'His death at 64 leaves a vacuum that could incite turmoil . . . it was his mission to impose unity on a fractious country.'[2] We have discussed how Zia's various socio-economic reforms gave Pakistan important assets; 'a free market orientation led to annual economic growth of more than 7 per cent – a remarkable achievement in Pakistan. In short, Pakistan has enjoyed some good years.'[3] His 18-month long plan for the transfer of power from military to civilian rule has been discussed thoroughly in our work. It gave Pakistan a form of representative government which may not be the same as the British parliamentary system or the American presidential system. But Zia's choice of 'Islamic democracy', as he used to take pride in describing his political order, has the essential ingredients of a democratic state, such as periodical elections in accordance with the provisions of a written constitution, the existence of more than one political party, independence of the judiciary and the role of the judiciary in enforcing the fundamental rights of the citizens guaranteed by the constitution itself. Zia must be given credit for transforming a military regime into civilian rule by peaceful means. This was not a small achievement for a country like Pakistan which had experienced military rule for about 25 years out of its 41 years of existence. 'He turned out to be a well informed ruler who relied less on intimidation than had any of his predecessors.'[4]

The present author had his two final meetings with President Zia between 9 and 15 August 1988. The author spent almost a whole day with Zia on 10 August, first having a lengthy discussion on the Pakistan political order that he had set up; then participating in a lunch-cum-press conference given by Zia for top newspaper men and finally having dinner on the same evening. Zia had already been given a copy of the manuscript of our work; the author found enough opportunities to discuss the various aspects of Pakistan's present political system. Zia repeatedly assured the author that the constitutional process which he took so much care to develop under his 18-month long plan for the transfer of power would be maintained at any cost. He described the present constitutional set-up in Pakistan as his 'baby' and categorically told the author, 'I cannot afford to kill it.'[5]

Zia has left behind a potential vehicle for peaceful transition. After Zia's death the transfer of power has been surprisingly smooth. In accordance with the provisions of the constitution (article 49) the civilian chairman of the senate, Ghulam Ishaq Khan, took over as the acting president of the country. He retained the caretaker cabinet appointed by Zia after his dissolution of the national assembly and dismissal of the Junejo cabinet on 29 May 1988. Zia had already announced the date for fresh elections to be held on 16 November 1988. The acting president, Ghulam Ishaq Khan, has already given assurances that the elections would be held on schedule. 'The elections can become the salvation of the nation if the military supports them and if the opposition parties proceed with wisdom and restraint.'[6] The new chief of the Pakistan army, General Mirza Aslam Beg, pledged support for elections scheduled for 16

November 1988 and warned against 'any ill-planned steps' by the army in the greater interest of the country. He also assured the interim civilian government of the army's full co-operation.[7]

The superior courts in Pakistan are confronted with a number of cases involving constitutional issues. Zia created regulations to the effect that if any political party had not registered under the Pakistan Political Parties Act, it would not be eligible to participate in any elections. The Pakistan People's Party (PPP) refused to register itself under the act. It challenged the Zia government's limitations on political parties. The supreme court gave its verdict in favour of the PPP and held the view that non-registration under the Political Party Act would not disqualify any party since the constitution itself gives citizens the right to form political parties (article 17). Then Zia made the decision that the forthcoming elections scheduled to be held in November 1988 would be held on a non-party basis as in the 1985 elections. Again the PPP challenged Zia's decision. Zia's contention was that the constitution did not specify whether elections should be on a party basis or not. The appeal from the PPP is yet to be decided by the court. Zia told the present author on 14 August that he would abide by the decision of the court, and the new president, Mr Ghulam Ishaq Khan, reaffirmed that the court's decision on the issue would be honoured. Finally, Zia's actions to dissolve the national assembly and to dismiss the Junejo cabinet have also been challenged. A group of opposition leaders belonging to Mr Junejo's party have made a formal appeal to the court challenging Zia's action on 29 May 1988 dissolving the national assembly and dismissing the Junejo cabinet. The decisions of the courts on these two constitutional cases will have a great impact on the political developments in Pakistan between now and the November elections.

More important and significant is the fact that politics in a developing country like Pakistan which is surrounded by hostile neighbours are vulnerable to 'foreign-linked factionalism: where there are linkages between internal political factors and the international environment.'[8] Zia applied himself with vigour and devotion to ridding the Afghan people of the Soviet puppet regime in Kabul. He gave every help and assistance to the Afghan people to achieve the right of self-determination. His great aim was that the people of Afghanistan should establish an Islamic republic by their free choice. Zia told the present author during the final meeting with him just three days before his tragic death that if the people of Afghanistan established an Islamic state (he had no doubts that given a free choice the Afghanis would opt for an Islamic state) it would be a great accomplishment for the world of Islam. Iran and Pakistan are already Islamic republics and a third adjoining Islamic republic would be a great source of strength for the Islamic ummah in which Zia was a passionate believer.

But Zia's zeal for a third Islamic state in Kabul was an anathema to both Moscow and New Delhi. The Indian prime minister, Rajiv Gandhi, had openly stated that an Islamic republic in Afghanistan would be regarded as a security threat to India. How the choice of a neighbouring country for a particular form of government can be termed as a 'threat' to its more powerful neighbour is difficult to explain; of course, it is in accordance with the 'Brezhnev Doctrine' of the Soviet Union under which the Kremlin would not tolerate any form of government in Eastern Europe if it were not acceptable in Moscow. Similarly, there is the 'Indira Doctrine' under which the late Indian prime minister, Mrs Indira Gandhi, would not accept any political development in any South Asian country which was not approved in New Delhi. Both the Soviet Union and India seem to be eager to have a sphere of influence in their neighbouring regions. A third Islamic republic near the Soviet Central Asian Republics was also not acceptable to Moscow. Both Moscow and New Delhi were most unhappy with Zia's unqualified support for the freedom fighters in Afghanistan and his pro-Western foreign policy, in particular, his special relationship with the United States. There are reasons to believe that Zia's death was not unwelcome both in Moscow and New Delhi. Many believe that Zia did not die in an ordinary plane accident. There are strong suspicions in many quarters that Zia's plane accident was a case of sabotage. The spokesman of the Pakistan government, Mr Riaz Muhammad Khan, said, 'Personally I am 100 per cent sure – not 99 per cent – that it was sabotage. Zia was the man who was targeted.'[9]

Pakistanis and many foreigners speculated that the plane was struck by a surface to air missile or more likely blown up by a bomb planted aboard and detonated by remote control. The investigation into the causes of the accident is not yet final, but according to a preliminary report of the Pakistan air force the plane was shot down by a missile.

If that is the case, it must have the blessing of some neighbouring foreign countries. During the past few months, Moscow has issued increasingly strident warnings to Pakistan to stop allowing arms for the Afghan freedom fighters. Only days before Zia's death, the Kremlin declared that Pakistan's actions could 'no longer be tolerated' and implied that some sort of reprisal was 'imminent'.[10]

India also has been giving warnings to Pakistan for Zia's alleged support to the Sikh's separatist movement in the Indian Panjab province.

According to the *Economist*, 'Whether he [Zia] was murdered and if so who killed him, may help decide which way things go.'[11] There are political forces inside Pakistan including a faction within the PPP who are opposed to Zia's all-out support for the freedom fighters in Afghanistan and to his special relationship with the United States. Obviously, both Moscow and New Delhi would like to see a regime emerging in post-Zia Pakistan not so friendly to the West and not so totally committed to the cause of the Afghani people. On the other hand, the Pakistan army, which is a very important factor in the political dynamics of Pakistan, would not like to see a regime emerging which is pro-Moscow or pro-India. 'Pakistan cannot accept a Soviet dominated Afghanistan on one border and India on the other . . . The geo-political realities remain even if Zia is gone,' said a US Defence Department official.[12]

So, ultimately the choice in post-Zia Pakistan may be between a left-oriented civilian government or a new martial law regime. The type of democratic institutions Zia tried to develop in Pakistan after 1985 requires an able and strong leadership; with Zia's death, that stewardship is gone for the fragile democracy in Pakistan. Zia's departure is likely to create a vacuum in internal politics in Pakistan as well as in international relations in South and South West Asia.

NOTES

1 'Who killed Gen Zia?', *Newsweek*, 29 August 1988.
2 *New York Times*, 18 August 1988.
3 'The Danger now is a Weakened Pakistan', Daniel Pipes, *International Herald Tribune*, 19 August 1988.
4 Ibid.
5 Based on the author's final interview with Zia on 10 and 14 August 1988.
6 *New York Times*, 18 August 1988.
7 *International Herald Tribune*, 26 August 1988.
8 Alan Dowty, op. cit.
9 *Time*, 29 August 1988.
10 Ibid.
11 *The Economist*, 20 August 1988.
12 *Time*, 29 August 1988.

Appendix I

An Ordinance[1] for the Enforcement of Shari'ah

WHEREAS the Principles and Provisions set out in the Objectives Resolution have been incorporated in the Constitution of the Islamic Republic of Pakistan as substantive part thereof;

AND WHEREAS the Objectives Resolution provides that the Muslims shall be enabled to order their lives in the individual and collective spheres in accordance with the teachings and requirements of Islam as set out in the Holy Qur'an and the Sunnah;

AND WHEREAS it is necessary to carry out the purposes of the Objectives Resolution and provide that all existing laws shall be brought in conformity with the Injunctions of Islam as laid down in the Holy Qur'an and Sunnah;

AND WHEREAS the National Assembly is not in session and the President is satisfied that circumstances exist which render it necessary to take immediate action;

NOW, THEREFORE, in exercise of the powers conferred by clause 1 of Article 89 of the Constitution of the Islamic Republic of Pakistan, the President is pleased to make and promulgate the following Ordinance:

1 Short title, extent and commencement–
   (1) This Ordinance may be called the Enforcement of Shari'ah Ordinance, 1988.
   (2) It extends to the whole of Pakistan, and it shall have effect notwithstanding anything contained in any other law, or any custom or usage having the force of law.
   (3) Nothing contained in this Ordinance shall affect the personal laws of the non-Muslims.
   (4) It shall come into force at once.

2 Definitions – In this Ordinance, unless there is anything repugnant in the subject or context, –
   a 'appropriate Government' means, –
      i in relation to any matter enumerated in the Federal Legislative List or the Concurrent Legislative List in the Constitution or any matter which relates to the Federation, the Federal Government; and
      ii in relation to any matter not enumerated in either of the said Lists or any matter which relates to the Province, the Provincial Government;
   b 'court' means a court subordinate to a High Court;
   c 'Mufti' means a Muslim scholar well-versed in Shari'ah appointed under this Ordinance to assist the Supreme Court, a High Court or the Federal Shari'at Court in the interpretation of Shari'ah;
   d 'Objectives Resolution' means the Objectives Resolution referred to in Article 2A of the Constitution and reproduced in the Annex thereto;
   e 'Shari'ah' means the Injunctions of Islam as laid down in the Holy Qur'an and Sunnah.

Explanation–As envisaged in Article 227 of the Constitution, in interpreting the Shari'ah with respect to the personal law of any Muslim sect, the expression 'Qur'an and Sunnah' shall mean the Qur'an and Sunnah as interpreted by that sect.

3 Supremacy of Shari'ah – Shari'ah shall be the supreme source of law in Pakistan and *Grund Norm* for guidance for policy making by the State and shall be enforced in the manner and as envisaged hereunder.

4 Court to decide cases according to Shari'ah
   (1) If a question arises before a court that a law or provision of law is repugnant to Shari'ah, the court shall, if it is satisfied that the question needs consideration, make a reference to the Federal Shari'at Court in respect of matters which fall within the jurisdiction of the Federal Shari'at Court under the Constitution and that Court may call for and examine the record of the case and decide the question within sixty days:

Provided that, if the question relates to Muslim personal law, any fiscal law or any law relating to the levy and collection of taxes and fees or banking or insurance practice and procedure, the court shall refer the question to the High Court which shall decide the question within sixty days:

Provided further that no question as to the repugnancy or otherwise to Shari'ah shall be entertained by the court in respect of a law or provision of law already examined by the Federal Shari'at Court or the Shari'at Appellate Bench of the Supreme Court and found not to be repugnant to Shari'ah.

(2)   The second proviso to sub-section (1) shall not affect the jurisdiction of the Federal Shari'at Court and the Shari'at Appellate Bench of the Supreme Court to review any decision given or order made by it.

(3)   The High Court may, either of its own motion or on the petition of a citizen of Pakistan or the Federal Government or a Provincial Government or on a reference made to it under the first proviso to sub-section (1), examine and decide the question whether or not any law relating to Muslim personal law, any fiscal law or any law relating to the levy and collection of taxes and fees or banking or insurance practice and procedure or any provision of such law, is repugnant to Shari'ah:

Provided that while examining and deciding the question, the High Court shall call for and hear the views of experts having specialized knowledge in the field to which the question relates and of such other persons as the High Court may deem fit.

(4)   Where the High Court takes up the examination of a law or provision of law under sub-section (3), and such law or provision of law appears to it to be repugnant to Shari'ah, the High Court shall cause to be given to the Federal Government in the case of a law with respect to a matter in the Federal Legislative List or the Concurrent Legislative List in the Constitution or to the Provincial Government in the case of a law with respect to a matter not enumerated in either of those Lists, a notice specifying the particular provisions that appear to it to be so repugnant, and afford to such Government adequate opportunity to have its point of view placed before the High Court.

(5)   If the High Court decides that any such law or provision of law is repugnant to Shari'ah, it shall set out in its decision –

    a   the reasons for its holding that opinion; and

    b   the extent to which such law or provision is so repugnant;

    and specify the day on which the decision shall take effect:

Provided that no such decision shall take effect before the expiration of the period within which an appeal therefrom may be preferred to the Supreme Court or, where an appeal has been so preferred, before the disposal of such appeal:

Provided further that the decision of the High Court shall not take effect until the expiration of a period of at least six months from the date of the decision:

Provided further that the High Court may, on the petition of Federal Government or a Provincial Government showing sufficient cause for not implementing the decision, extend the time for a period not exceeding three months.

(6)   The High Court shall have power to review any decision given or order made by it under this section.

(7)   The jurisdiction conferred on the High Court by this section shall be exercised by a Bench of not less than three Judges.

(8)   Where a question referred to in sub-section (1) or sub-section (3) arises before a Single or Division Bench of the High Court, it shall be referred to a Bench of not less than three Judges.

(9)   Any party aggrieved by the final decision of the High Court in any proceedings under this section may, within sixty days of such decision, prefer an appeal to the Supreme Court:
Provided that an appeal on behalf of the Federation or of a Province may be preferred at any time after the decision but not later than six months of the day on which the decision shall take effect and such extended period as may be allowed by the High Court under sub-section (5).

(10) Nothing contained in this Ordinance nor decisions made thereunder shall affect any proceedings pending before any Court or Tribunal or any sentences passed or orders made, judgements pronounced, decrees passed, liabilities incurred, rights accrued, assessments made, amounts recovered or declared payable under any law by any Court or Tribunal or authority before the commencement of this Ordinance.

Explanation – For the purposes of this sub-section, the word 'Court' or 'Tribunal' shall mean any Court or Tribunal established by or under any law or the Constitution at any time before the commencement of this Ordinance and the word 'authority' shall mean any authority established under any law for the time being in force.

(11) No court or tribunal including the High Court shall adjourn or stay any proceedings whether pending or initiated after the commencement of this Ordinance by reason only that the question whether a law or provision of law is repugnant to the Shari'ah has been referred to the High Court or the Federal Shari'at Court or that the High Court has otherwise undertaken examination of this question under this section and all such proceedings shall continue and the point in issue therein shall be decided in accordance with the law for the time being in force.

5   Ulema to be appointed as Judges, etc.
   (1)   Experienced and qualified *ulema* shall be eligible to be appointed as judges, and *amicus curiae* in the court.
   (2)   Persons well-versed in Shari'ah from reputable institutions of Islamic learning and *Deeni Madaris* in Pakistan or abroad, recognized by the appropriate Government for this purpose shall, notwithstanding anything contained in any other law for the time being in force, be eligible for appearing before the court for interpretation of Shari'ah in accordance with the rules to be framed for this purpose.
   (3)   The President shall, in consultation with the Chief Justice of Pakistan, the Chief Justice of the Federal Shari'at Court and the Chairman of the Council of Islamic Ideology, make rules for the purpose of sub-section (1) specifying the qualifications and experience required for appointment of judges, and *amicus curiae* in the courts.
   (4)   Persons holding graduate and post-graduate degrees in law and Shari'ah from the universities or International Islamic University, Islamabad, shall, notwithstanding anything contained in any other law for the time being in force, be eligible for being enrolled as advocates in accordance with the rules to be framed for this purpose.
   (5)   The provisions of the section shall not affect in any manner whatsoever the right of the advocates enrolled under the law relating to legal Practitioners and Bar Councils to appear in various courts, tribunals and other authorities including the Supreme Court, a High Court or the Federal Shari'at Court.

6   Appointment of Muftis
   (1)   The President shall, in consultation with the Chief Justice of Pakistan, the Chief Justice of the Federal Shari'at Court and the Chairman of the Council of Islamic Ideology, appoint in his individual judgement as many Muftis as he may deem fit for rendering such assistance as may be required of them by the Supreme Court, the High Court and the Federal Shari'at Court.
   (2)   A Mufti appointed under sub-section (1) shall hold office during the pleasure of the President and shall receive such remuneration as is for the time being admissible to a Deputy Attorney General for Pakistan.
   (3)   It shall be the duty of a Mufti to give advice to the Federal Government upon such legal matters involving interpretation of Shari'ah, and perform such other duties as may be referred or assigned to him by the Federal Government; and in the performance of his duties he shall have the right of audience in the Supreme Court, and the High Court while exercising jurisdiction under this Ordinance and in the Federal Shari'at Court.
   (4)   A Mufti shall not plead for any party but shall state, expound and interpret Shari'ah relevant to the proceedings as far as may be known to him and submit to the Court a written statement of his interpretation of Shari'ah.
   (5)   The Ministry of Justice and Parliamentary Affairs in the Government of Pakistan shall deal with the administrative matters relating to the Muftis.

7   Teaching of and training in Shari'ah
   (1)   The State shall make effective arrangements for the teaching of, and training in, Shari'ah and Islamic jurisprudence and the holding of refresher programmes at regular intervals in the Federal Judicial Academy, Islamabad, or other similar institutions for the members of the subordinate judiciary.
   (2)   The State shall make effective arrangements for providing education and training in various branches of Islamic law in order to ensure the availability of manpower trained in the administration of justice according to Shari'ah.
   (3)   The Chief Justice of Pakistan shall make rules for the participation of the Judges of Superior Courts in seminars and programmes connected with Shari'ah.
   (4)   The State shall take effective measures to include courses in Shari'ah in the syllabi of the law colleges in Pakistan.

8   Islamization of economy
   (1)   The State shall take steps to ensure that the economic system of Pakistan is constructed on the basis of Islamic economic principles, values and priorities.
   (2)   The President shall, within thirty days from the commencement of this Ordinance, appoint in his individual judgement a permanent Commission consisting of economists, jurists, *ulema*, elected representatives and such other persons as he may deem fit, and appoint one of them to be its Chairman.
   (3)   The Chairman of the Commission shall have the powers to appoint such consultants as he may deem necessary.

(4) The functions of the Commission shall be –

   a   to undertake the examination of any fiscal law or any law relating to the levy and collection of taxes and fees or banking or insurance practice and procedure to determine whether or not these are repugnant to Shari'ah;

   b   to make recommendations to bring such laws, practices and procedures in conformity with Shari'ah;

   c   to recommend the methods for such changes in the economic system of Pakistan so as to achieve the social and economic well being of the people as envisaged in Article 38 of the Constitution; and

   d   to suggest the manner and actions including suitable alternatives by which the system of economy as enunciated by Islam may be brought into effect.

(5) The Commission shall submit its reports, from time to time, to the Federal Government.

(6) A comprehensive report containing recommendations of the Commission shall be submitted to the Federal Government within a period of one year from the date of its appointment.

(7) The Commission shall have the power to conduct its proceedings and regulate its procedure in all respects as it may deem fit.

(8) All executive authorities, institutions, and local authorities shall act in aid of the Commission.

(9) The Commission shall monitor the process of Islamization of the economy and bring cases of non compliance to the notice of the President.

(10) The Ministry of Finance and Economic Affairs in the Government of Pakistan shall deal with the administrative matters relating to the Commission.

9   Islamization of education –

(1) The State shall, for a comprehensive and harmonious development as an Islamic society, take steps to ensure that the educational system of Pakistan is based on Islamic values of learning and teachings.

(2) The President shall, within thirty days from the commencement of this Ordinance, appoint in his individual judgement a permanent Commission consisting of educationists, jurists, *ulema* and elected representatives and such other persons as he may deem fit and appoint one of them to be its Chairman.

(3) The Chairman of the Commission shall have the powers to appoint such consultants as he may deem necessary.

(4) The functions of the Commission shall be to examine the educational system of Pakistan to achieve the objective referred to in sub-section (1) and make recommendations in this behalf.

(5) The Commission shall submit its reports, from time to time, to the Federal Government.

(6) A comprehensive report containing recommendations of the Commission shall be submitted to the Federal Government within a period of one year from the date of its appointment.

(7) The Commission shall have the power to conduct its proceedings and regulate its procedure in all respects as it may deem fit.

(8) All executive authorities, institutions and local authorities shall act in aid of the Commission.

(9) The Commission shall monitor the process of Islamization of education and bring cases of non compliance to the notice of the President.

(10) The Ministry of Education in the Government of Pakistan shall deal with the administrative matters relating to the Commission.

10 Mass media to promote Islamic values

Steps shall be taken by the State so that the mass media promote Islamic values.

11 Laws to be interpreted in the light of Shari'ah

For the purpose of this Ordinance –

i   while interpreting the statute law, if more than one interpretation is possible, the one consistent with the Islamic principles and jurisprudence shall be adopted by the Courts, and

ii   where two or more interpretations are equally possible, the interpretation which advances the Principles of Policy and Islamic provisions in the Constitution shall be adopted by the Courts.

12 Expeditious codification of Islamic Law

(1) The Council of Islamic Ideology shall take urgent steps to fulfil its functions as envisaged in sub-clauses (c) and (d) of clause (1) of Article 230 of the Constitution.

    (2)   The State shall take early steps to place the recommendations made to it by the Council of Islamic Ideology, before the Parliament for the purpose envisaged in clause (4) of Article 230 of the Constitution.

13 Continuance of International financial obligations

Notwithstanding anything contained in this Ordinance or any decision given thereunder, the financial obligations incurred or which may be incurred, and contracts made or which may be made, before or after the commencement of this Ordinance, between a National Institution and a Foreign Agency shall continue to remain valid, binding and operative and no court including the High Court and the Supreme Court shall have any jurisdiction to pass any order or make any decision under this Ordinance in respect of such obligations and contracts.

Explanation – In this section, the expression 'National Institution' shall include the Federal Government or a Provincial Government, a statutory corporation, company, institution, body, enterprise or any person in Pakistan and the expression 'Foreign Agency' shall include a foreign Government, a foreign financial institution, foreign capital market including a Bank and any foreign lending Agency, including an individual.

14 Fulfilment of existing obligations

Nothing contained in this Ordinance or any decision made thereunder shall affect the validity of any financial obligations incurred including under any instruments, whether contractual or otherwise, promises to pay, or any other financial commitment made by or on behalf of the Federal Government or a Provincial Government or a financial or statutory corporation or other institution to make payments envisaged therein, and all such obligations, promises and commitments shall continue to remain valid, binding and operative.

15 Rules

The appropriate Government may, by notification in the official Gazette, make rules for carrying out the purposes of this Ordinance.

NOTE

1   *Enforcement of Shari'ah Ordinance 1408 AH/1988 AD*, The Islamic Republic of Pakistan, Islamabad, 1988.

Selected Bibliography

Abernathy, G L, Pakistan, *A Selected Annotated Bibliography*, New York, 1960, rev. ed.
Ahmad, Manzooruddin, *Pakistan: The Emerging Islamic State*, Karachi, 1966.
Ahmad Mushtaq, *Government and Politics in Pakistan*, Karachi, 1959.
Alburuni, A H, *Makers of Pakistan and Modern Muslim India*, Lahore, 1950.
Ali Ameer, *The Spirit of Islam*, London, 1935.
Ali Choudhury Mohd, *Emergence of Pakistan*, New York, 1967.
Almond, G A, and Coleman, J S, *The Politics of the Developing Areas*, Princeton, 1960.
Ambedkar, B R, *Pakistan or Partition of India*, Bombay, 1946.
Andrus, J R, and Mohammad, A R, *The Economy of Pakistan*, Stanford, 1958.
Arnold, Sir T W, *The Preaching of Islam*, London, 1913.
Ansari, Muhammad Fazl-ur-Rahman, *The Quranic Foundation and the Structure of Muslim Society*, Karachi, 1973, second impression, 1977, vols. I and II.
Asad, Muhammad, *The Principles of State and Government in Islam*, Berkeley, 1961; new edition, 1980, Gibraltar.
Bailey, S D, *Parliamentary Government in Southern Asia*, London, 1953.
Bhutto, Zulfikar Ali, *The Myth of Independence*, Lahore, 1969.
Bhutto, Z A, *The Great Tragedy*, Karachi, 1971.
Birdwood, Lord, *India and Pakistan: A Continent Decides*, New York, 1954.
Braibanti, Ralph, *Research on the Bureaucracy of Pakistan*, Durham, 1966.
Brohi, A K, *Fundamental Law of Pakistan*, Lahore, 1958.
Brown, W N, *The United States and India and Pakistan, Bangladesh*, Harvard University Press, 1972.
Burke, S M, *Mainsprings of Indian and Pakistani Foreign Policies*, Minneapolis, Minn., 1979.
Burki, Shahid Javed, *Pakistan Under Bhutto 1971–77*, New York, 1980.
Callard, Keith, *Pakistan – A Political Study*, London, 1957.
Callard, Keith, *Political Forces in Pakistan 1947–59*, New York, 1959.
Campbell, Robert D, *Pakistan: Emerging Decocracy*, Princeton, 1963.
Choudhury, G W, *Democracy in Pakistan*, Dacca and Vancouver, 1963.
Choudhury, G W, *Pakistan's Relations with India*, London, 1968.
Choudhury, G W, *Documents and Speeches on the Constitution of Pakistan*, Dacca and Vancouver, 1967.
Choudhury, G W, *Constitutional Development in Pakistan*, second edition, London, 1969.
Choudhury, G W, *The Last Days of United Pakistan*, Bloomington, Indiana, 1974.
Choudhury, G W, *India, Pakistan, Bangladesh and the Major Powers: Politics of a Divided Sub-Continent*, New York, 1975.
Cohen, Stephen P, *The Pakistan Army*, Berkeley, 1984.
Coupland, R C, *The Indian Problem*, London, 1944.
Cumming, John, ed., *Political India 1832–1932*, London, 1932.
Cronin, Richard P, *The United States, Pakistan and the Soviet Threats to Southern Asia*, Washington D C Congressional Research Service, Library of Congress, September, 1985.
Cutteridge, William P, *Military Institutions and Power in New States*, London, 1964.
Feldman, H, *A Constitution for Pakistan*, Karachi, 1956.
Feldman, H, *Crisis to Crisis: Pakistan 1962–69*, London, 1972.
Finer, S E, *The Men on Horseback*, London and New York, 1962.
Gibb, H A R, *Modern Trends in Islam*, Chicago, 1947.
Gledhill, Alan, *The British Commonwealth: The Development of its Laws and Constitutions*, vol. VIII– Pakistan, London, 1957.
Goodnow, Henry Frank, *The Civil Service of Pakistan*, New Haven, 1964.
Gwyer, M, and Appadorai, A, *Speeches and Documents on the Indian Constitution 1921–47*, vols. I and II, London, 1957.
Hakim, Khalifa A, *Islamic Ideology*, Lahore, 1945.
Haq, Mahbubul, *The Strategy of Economic Planning: A Case Study of Pakistan*, Lahore, Oxford, 1963.
Iqbal, Sir Mohd, *The Reconstruction of Religious Thought in Islam*, London, 1934.
Iqbal, Mohamed, *Law of Preventive Detention in England, India and Pakistan*, Lahore, 1955.
Jahan, Rounaq, *Pakistan Failure in National Integration*, New York, 1972.

Janowitz, M, *The Military in the Political Development of New Nations*, Chicago, 1964.

Jennings, Sir Ivor, *Commonwealth in Asia*, Colombo, 1949.

Jennings, Sir Ivor, *Constitutional Problems in Pakistan*, Cambridge, 1957.

Jennings, Sir Ivor, *Approach to Self-Government*, Cambridge, 1956.

Jennings, Sir Ivor, *Problems of New Commonwealth*, Durham, 1958.

Jinnah, Mohammad Ali, *Selected Speeches and Statements of the Quaid-i-Azam Mohammad Ali Jinnah: 1911–34 and 1947–48*, Lahore, 1966.

Jinnah, Mohammad Ali, *Quaid-i-Azam Speaks*, Karachi, n.d.

Johnson, J J, ed., *The Role of the Military in Under Developed Countries*, Princeton, 1962.

Khan, Major-General Fazal Muqueem, *The Story of the Pakistan Army*, Dacca, 1963.

Khan, Mohammad Ayub, *Friends Not Masters: A Political Autobiography*, London, 1967.

Khan, Mohammad Ayub, *Speeches and Statements*, 6 vols., Karachi, 1961–64.

Khelli, Shirin Tahir, *The United States and Pakistan: The Evolution of an Influence Relationship*, New York, 1982.

Lumby, W E R, *The Transfer of Power in India*, London, 1954.

Maniruzzaman, Talukder, *Military Withdrawal from Pakistan: A Comprehensive Study*, Cambridge, Mass., 1987.

Maron, Stanley, *Pakistan Society and Culture*, New Haven, Human Relations Area File, 1957.

Maudoodi, S A A, *Islamic Law and Constitution*, Karachi, 1955.

Mawdudi, Abul A'La, *Towards Understanding Islam*, translated and edited by Khurshid Ahmad, London, reprinted 1981.

Mawdudi, Abul A'La, *The Islamic Way of Life*, edited by Khurshid Ahmad and Khurram Murad, London, 1986.

Mawdudi, Abul A'La, *Islamic Perspectives: Studies in Honour of Sayyed Abul A'La Mawdudi*, edited by Khurshid Ahmad and Zafar Ishaq Ansari, London, Jeddah, 1979.

Menon, V P, *The Transfer of Power in India*, London, 1957.

Metz, W S, *Pakistan: Government and Politics*, New Haven, Human Relations Area File, 1956.

Moon, Penderel, *Divide and Quit*, Berkeley, 1962.

Mosley, Leonard, *The Last Days of the British Raj*, New York, 1962.

Mukerjee, Radha Kamal, *Democracies of the East*, London, 1923.

Munir, Justice M, *Construction of the Islamic Republic of Pakistan*, All Pakistan Legal Decisions, Lahore, 1965.

Murshed, Justice S M, *The Judiciary, Law and the Legal Profession in a Democratic State*, Dacca, 1962.

Nasir, Sheikh Ahmad, *Some Aspects of the Constitution and Economics of Islam*, Woking, Surrey, England, 1957.

Newman, K J, *Essays on the Constitution of Pakistan*, Dacca, 1956.

Nizami, Majid, *The Press in Pakistan*, Lahore, 1958.

Qureshi, I H, *Pakistan as Islamic Democracy*, Karachi, n.d.

Qureshi, I H, *Islamic Elements in the Political Thought of Pakistan*, Mimeographed, 1960.

Qureshi, I H, *The Pakistan Way of Life*, London, 1956.

Qureshi, I H, *The Muslim Community in the Indo-Pakistan Sub-Continent*, Monton Press, 1962.

Rahman, Justice Tanzil-ur-, *Islamisation in Pakistan*, Islamabad, Council of Islamic Ideology, Government of Pakistan, May 1984.

Rahman, Justice Tanzil-ur-, *Introduction of Zakat in Pakistan*, Islamabad, Council of Islamic Ideology, Government of Pakistan, 1980

Rosenthal, Erwin I J, *Islam in the Modern National States*, Cambridge, 1966.

Rosenthal, Erwin I J, *Political Thought in Medieval Islam*, Cambridge, 1958.

Saiyid, M H, *Mohammad Ali Jinnah*, Lahore, 1945.

Sen Gupta, Bhabani, *Soviet-Asian Relations in the 1970s and Beyond: An Interperceptional Study*, New York, 1976.

Sharif, M M, ed., *A History of Muslim Philosophy*, vols. I and II, Karachi, reprinted in 1983.

Sherwani, H K, *Studies in Muslim Political Thought and Administration*, Lahore, 1945.

Smith, W C, *Modern Islam in India*, London, 1946.

Smith, W C, *Pakistan as an Islamic State*, Lahore, 1951.

Smith, W C, *Islam in the Modern World*, Princeton, 1957.

Smith, W C, *The Muslim League 1942–45*, Lahore, 1945.

Stephens, Ian, *Pakistan*, London, 1962.

Stephens, Ian, *Pakistanis*, London, 1968.

Syed, Anwar Hussain, *Pakistan: Islam, Politics and National Solidarity*, New York, 1982.

Syeed, Khalid Bin, *Politics in Pakistan: The Nature and Direction of Change*, New York, 1980.

Syeed, Khalid Bin, *The Political System of Pakistan*, Karachi, 1967.

Symonds, R, *The Making of Pakistan*, London, 1949.

251

Taseer, Salmaan, *Bhutto: A Political Biography*, London, 1979
Tinker, Hugh, *Ballot Box and Bayonet*, London, 1964.
Tinker, Hugh, *Experiment with Freedom: India and Pakistan 1947*, London, 1967.
Tinker, Hugh, *India and Pakistan: A Political Analysis*, London, 1962.
Von Vorys, Kari, *Political Development in Pakistan*, Princeton, 1965.
Wallbank, T W, *A Short History of India and Pakistan*, New York, 1958.
Weekes, Richard V, *Pakistan: Birth and Growth of A Muslim Nation*, Princeton Van Nostrand, 1964.
Wheeler, Sir R E M, *The Five Thousand Years of Pakistan*, Royal India and Pakistan Society, 1950.
Wilbur, Donald N, *Pakistan: Its People, Its Society, Its Culture*, New Haven, Human Relations Area
    File, 1964.
Wilcox, Wayne Ayres, *Pakistan: The Consolidation of a Nation*, New York, 1963.
Williams, Rushbrook, *The State of Pakistan*, London, 1962.
Wilson, Patrick, *Government and Politics in India and Pakistan 1885–1955*, Berkeley, 1956.
Wolpert, Stanley, *Jinnah of Pakistan*, New York, 1984.
Ziring, Lawrence, *Pakistan: The Enigma of Political Development*, London, 1980.

PUBLIC DOCUMENTS
Annual Reports of the State Bank of Pakistan, Karachi, 1948–88.
Basic Democracies: Rules and Ordinances 1959–60, Karachi, Government of Pakistan Press.
Constituent Assembly Debates, legislature, official reports, Karachi, Government of Pakistan Press,
    1947–56.
Constituent Assembly Debates, official reports, Karachi, Government of Pakistan Press, 1947–56.
Constitution of Pakistan, as promulgated by President Ayub in 1962.
Constitution of the Islamic Republic of Pakistan, as passed by the Second Constituent Assembly on 29
    February 1956, Karachi, Government of Pakistan Press, 1956. Debates of the Provincial
    Assemblies, 1947–58 and 1962–63.
Constitution-Making in Pakistan 1973, printed by the manager, Printing Corporation of Pakistan
    Press, Karachi, 1973.
Fundamental Principles of an Islamic State, a manifesto drawn up by the ulema of Pakistan, Karachi,
    Jamaat-e-Islami, 1954.
Pakistan Law Digest, Lahore, Government of Pakistan Press.
Proceeding of the Seminar on 'South and South-East Asia Has a Second Look at Democracy', New Delhi,
    Congress for Cultural Freedom and Indian Institute of Public Administration, 1961.
Proceedings of the Seminar on 'Representative Government and Public Liberties in the New States', The
    Congress for Cultural Freedom, Rhodes, 1958.
Proposals for Indian Constitutional Reform, comd. 4268, 1932.
Report of the Constitution Commission, Government of Pakistan Press, 1961.
Report of the Court of Inquiry, Punjab Disturbances, 1953, Lahore, Government of the Punjab Press,
    1954.
Report of the Electoral Reform Commission, Karachi, 1956.
Report of the Franchise Commission, The Gazette of Pakistan Extraordinary, 23 August 1963.
Report of the Indian Statutory Commission, vols. I– III, 1980.
*Report on the Financial Enquiry Regarding Allocation of Revenues between the Central and Provincial
    Governments*, by Sir Jeremy Raisman, Karachi, Government of Pakistan Press, 1952.
The Constitution of the Islamic Republic of Pakistan, as passed by the National Assembly of Pakistan
    on 10 April 1973 and authenticated by the President of National Assembly on 12 April 1973,
    Karachi, printed by the manager, Printing Corporation of Pakistan Press, n.d.
The Final Report of the Basic Principles Committee, Karachi, Government of Pakistan Press, 1952.
The Government of India Act 1935, as modified up to 7 April 1955.
The Interim Report of the Basic Principles Committee, Karachi, Government of Pakistan Press, 1950.
The National Assembly of Pakistan: Constitution-Making Debates 1972–73.
The Report of the Basic Principles Committee, as adopted by the Constituent Assembly 1954, Karachi,
    Government of Pakistan Press, 1954.
US Security Interests and Policies in Southwest Asia, Hearings, Senate Foreign Relations Committee,
    96th Congress, Washington DC, US GPO, 1980.

RECENT DOCUMENTS AND SPEECHES ON THE PROCESS OF WITHDRAWAL OF MARTIAL LAW AND ON THE PROCESS OF ISLAMIZATION IN PAKISTAN, 1977–88

Ansari Commission's Report on Form of Government, Islamabad, Printing Corporation of Pakistan Press, August 1983.

Comparative Statement of the Constitution As It Stood Before 20 March 1985 and As It Stands After Date, After Eighth Amendment of December 1985, Government of Pakistan, Ministry of Justice and Parliamentary Affairs, Justice Division, printed by the Printing Corporation of Pakistan Press, Islamabad, n.d.

Comparison of Related Articles of 1973 Constitution (as on 4 July 1977), The Revival of the Constitution of 1973 Order, 1985, President's Order no.14 of 1985, 8th Amendment Bill 1956 Constitution and Indian Constitution, Islamabad, President's Secretariat, printed by the Printing Corporation.

Constitutional Amendments Announced, address to nation, President Mohammad Zia-ul-Haq, Rawalpindi, 2 March 1985, Ministry of Information and Broadcasting, Islamabad, Goverment of Pakistan.

Constitutional Recommendations for the Islamic System of Government, Council of Islamic Ideology, Government of Pakistan, Islamabad, June 1983.

Democratic Institutions will be Fortified, address to nation, Prime Minister Mohammad Khan Junejo, Islamabad, Ministry of Information and Broadcasting, Government of Pakistan, 31 March 1985.

Enforcement of Shariah, address to nation, General Mohammad Zia-ul-Haq, President, Islamic Republic of Pakistan, and *Text of Enforcement of Shariah Ordinance*, Islamabad, Ministry of Information and Broadcasting, Government of Pakistan, 15 June 1988.

General Elections: Announcement of Dates, address to nation, President Mohammad Zia-ul-Haq, Rawalpindi, 12 January 1983, Islamabad, Ministry of Information and Broadcasting, Government of Pakistan, 1985.

Martial Law Lifted: Constitution Fully Restored, address to Majlis-e-Shoora (parliament) by President Mohammad Zia-ul-Haq on 30 December 1985, Islamabad, Ministry of Information and Broadcasting, Government of Pakistan, October 1987.

Pakistan Functioning Democracy, Islamabad, Ministry of Information and Broadcasting, Government of Pakistan, Printing Corporation of Pakistan Press, September 1987.

Political Plan Announced, address of President Zia at the Seventh Session of Federal Council, 12 August 1983, Islamabad, Ministry of Information and Broadcasting, Government of Pakistan, August 1983.

Report of the Special Committee of the Federal Council on the Form and System of Government in Pakistan from Islamic Point of View, Islamabad, Federal Council, Majlis-e-Shoora, Secretariat, July 1983.

Report on Zakat and Ushr Fund Management in the Islamic Republic of Pakistan by Monzer Kahf, Jeddah, Islamic Development Bank, Islamic Research and Training Institute, unpublished, confidential, July 1987.

Revival of the Constitution of 1973 Order, 1985, President's Order no.14 of 1985, Islamabad, Ministry of Justice and Parliamentary Affairs, Government of Pakistan, 17 March 1985.

The Constitution of the Islamic Republic of Pakistan, as modified up to 30 December 1985, Islamabad, Ministry of Justice and Parliamentary Affairs, Justice Division, Government of Pakistan, printed by Printing Corporation of Pakistan, n.d.

The Federal Council (Majlis-e-Shura) Order 1981, President's Order no.15 of 1981, Islamabad, printed by the manager, Printing Corporation of Pakistan Press, 1981.

The Laws (Continuance in Force) Order, 1977 CMLA, Order no.1 of 1977, Islamabad, Printing Corporation of Pakistan Press, 1981.

The Political Parties Act, 1962 in Election Commission of Pakistan: Election Laws as modified up to 20 January 1985, Islamabad, Election Commission Office, 1985.

The Provisional Constitution Order, 1981 CMLA, Order no.1 of 1981, Islamabad, Printing Corporation of Pakistan Press, 1981.

The Referendum Order, 1984, Islamabad, Ministry of Law and Parliamentary Affairs, Government of Pakistan, 12 December 1984.

Vital Step Towards Democracy, address to National Assembly, President Zia, 17 October 1985, Islamabad, Ministry of Information and Broadcasting, Government of Pakistan, October 1985.

Index

Abdul Qayyum Khan 197
Abida Hussain, Mrs 73
Advisory council of Islamic
   ideology 114, 130, 134
Afghan crisis 42 et seq., 56
Afghanistan 232, 239, 242-44
Agha Shah 43
Akbar, Emperor 87
Akhter Ali G Kazi 196
Al-Azhar of Egypt 135
All-India Radio 32
Allama Iqbal 7
Allama Syed Suleman Nadvi 78
Ameer Ali 109
Amir-e-Mumlakat 145 et seq.
Ansari 57, 82, 90, 107, 144
Ansari Commission 60, 83, 114,
   144 et seq., 164
Armed forces 44, 57, 210
Atomic bomb, Pakistan's 47
Australia, federal system of 16
Austro-Hungarian empire 121
Awami League 8, 28
Ayub Khan 7, 19, 23, 29, 33, 83,
   154, 165, 170, 180, 190, 207, 216,
   223
Azad Jammu and Kashmir Local
   Government Ordinance 1979 52

Baluchistan 8, 23, 36, 67, 183, 200
Baluchistan Local Government
   Ordinance 1979 52
Bangladesh 9, 10, 30, 33, 160,
   165, 183, 205, 231, 234
Bangladesh, Islamic constitution
   of 83
Banking Companies (Recovery of
   Loans) Ordinance 1979 228
Basic Democracy 23, 28
Basic Principles Committee
   (BPC) 12, 13
Beloff, Max 195
Bench registries of federal Shariah
   court 131
Bengali Mukti Bahini (the
   Bengali freedom fighters) 33
Bengalis, lack of power 165
Bhutto, Benazir 56, 240
Bhutto, Z A 8, 9, 23, 24, 25, 30,
   31, 33, 35, 41, 46, 64, 125, 126,
   128, 160, 161, 165, 168, 170, 171,
   183, 234
Bill on fundamental rights 208
Board of Ulema 128
Bodin, Jean 181
Brezhnev Doctrine 243
British approach to fundamental
   rights 207
British authorities and power of
   detention 205
British India, constitutional
   machinery of 21
British parliamentary system
   153, 159, 167
British Raj 20, 45
Bryce, Lord 52, 216
Brzezinski, Dr 43
Buckley, James 43
Buddhists in Pakistan 120
Bureaucratic rule in Pakistani
   politics 22

Cantonments Act 1924 52
Capital Territory Local
   Government Ordinance 1979 52
Carter administration 57
Carter, Jimmy 42, 43
Central government 186, 199
Chadar and Char-Deewari 65
Chairman of the joint chiefs of
   staff committee 61
Chief election commissioner 61
Chief justice of Pakistan 61
Chief Martial Law Administrator
   order no.1 of 1977 33
China 10, 42, 44
Chittagong Hills tract 119
Choudhry Mohammad Ali 20,
   127
Christians in Pakistan 120
Chundrigar, I I 127
Civil liberties 204, 210
Civil war in Pakistan (1971) 9
Commission for monitoring
   process of Islamization 151, 152
Commission on finance, Ayub
   government 190 et seq
Committee on fundamental
   rights of the citizens 203
Congress 6, 7
Constituent assemblies 7
Constitution commission
   1960-61 84, 128, 148, 216
Constitution commission of
   1980-81 154 et seq
Constitution commission 160,
   188, 206, 207, 223
Constitution, 1956 18, 169, 187,
   190, 203
Constitution, 1962 29, 156, 160,
   188, 207
Constitution, 1973 24, 71,
   140 et seq., 167, 199, 219
Constitution-making in Pakistan
   10, 60
Cornwallis, Lord 21
Council of Islamic ideology 39,
   40, 114, 126, 127, 128, 130, 133,
   164
Council of Ministers 13
Customs Act 1969 228

Dacca (Dhaka), disturbance in
   provincial legislature 28
Dacca high court 226
The Daily Muslim 64
Dawn, 196
Defence of the Realm Act of
   1914 204
Democracy 62, 51 et seq., 88,
   117, 235, 237
Democrats, American 43
Detention, powers of preventive
   204 et seq.
Development programmes 65
Dhimmis 123
Dicey 187
Dismemberment of Pakistan in
   1971 10
Distribution of Property
   Regulation 1974 209
District judges 227
District agencies 62

Divine Right of Kings 107
Dulles, Foster, US Secretary 231

East Pakistan 183, 190
Economic growth in Pakistan 240
Economic Reforms Regulation
   1972 209
Economist 28, 240, 244
Education 65, 219, 220
8th Amendment Act 1985 209,
   218
Eire, constitution of 219
Election commission 34, 66, 217,
   218
Elections for local bodies 61
Eligibility of candidates for the
   assemblies 69
Emergency Powers (Defence Act)
   1938 204
Ethnic conflict in Pakistan 48
Excise duties, distribution
   of 192

Fakar Imam 73
Fazal Illahi 180
Fazlul Haq 197
Federal constitution of India 195
Federal government,
   administrative powers 197
Federal government, power over
   provinces 196
Federal legislature 195
Federal Shariah court, 131 et seq.,
   150, 221, 227, 228, 230, 234
Federal structure in Pakistan 184,
   194 et seq
Federalism, conditions for 186
Federally Administered Tribal
   Areas, Local Government
   Regulation 1979 52
Fida Commission Report,
   1983 56, 114
Fifth five-year plan (1978-83) 35
Fiqh 134
First five-year plan 16
Freedom of speech, limitations
   on 213
French constitution 158
French president, powers of 181
Fundamental rights for non-
   Muslims 203
Fundamental rights 202 et seq.

Gandhi, Indira 32, 46, 243
Gandhi, Rajiv 46, 243
General elections 1977 25
General elections 1985 66 et seq.
Geneva Accord 45
George III 165
George V 170
Ghulam Ishaq Khan 241, 242
Ghulam Mohammad 19, 20, 21,
   156
Government of India Act 1935 6,
   7, 15, 121, 153, 159, 163, 178,
   184 et seq., 194, 198, 203
Governor general, powers of 178
Greco-Roman tradition in
   Western political thought 111

Habeas Corpus Act 202
Haig, Alexander 43
Harvard Advisory Group 28
Head of the Islamic State (*Amir al-Mo'minin*) 94
Head of the state 118, 120
High Courts 223, 227
Hindus 6, 7, 87, 119, 124, 185
Hoare, Sir Samuel 185
Hobbes, Thomas 182
House of Parliament and Provincial (Election) Order 1977 68
House of the People 13
House of Units 13
Hudood Laws (Islamic Penal Code) 40, 130 et seq., 228

Ijtihad 115, 235
Income tax, distribution of 192
Income, Pakistan's per capita 48
Income-tax Ordinance 1979 133
India 7, 31, 40, 46, 47, 63, 205
Indian constitution (1950) 219
Indian Independence Act 1947 6, 7, 153
Indian National Congress 10
Indira Doctrine 243
Indo-Pakistan war, 1971, 10, 23, 31, 33, 47, 165
Interim constitution order of 1947 163, 179, 218
Iran, constitution of 118
Iskander Mirza 19, 20
Islam, as social gospel 81
Islam, resurgence of 233
Islamabad Capital Territory 227
Islamic atom bomb 42, 57
Islamic concept of justice 221
Islamic Conference Organization (OIC) 44
Islamic democracy 51, 57, 110, · 111, 232, 241
Islamic law, training in 133
Islamic provisions in the constitutions 114 et seq.
Islamic Republic of Pakistan 61, 84, 125
Islamic Research Institute 128, 148
Islamic research organization 114
Islamic welfare state 65
Islamization – *Nifaz-i-Nizam-i-Islam* 56, 74, 129 et seq., 150 et seq.
Islamization of financial institutions in Pakistan 37
Islamization of banking 37 et seq
Islamization of the country's laws 23, 40
Izafi zila qazis 133

Jahandad Khan 75
Jamaat-e-Islam 64
Jefferson, Thomas 237
Jennings, Sir Ivor 156, 169, 170
Jews 122
Jinnah, Mohammad Ali 6, 7, 10, 14, 17, 18, 58, 77, 86, 88, 115, 120, 154, 155, 239
Judaeo-Christian tradition in Western democracy 111, 233
Judges, tenure of 224
Judicial system 223 et seq., 227, 236
Judiciary, independence of 141, 221, 224
Judiciary, power to enforce fundamental rights 204
Junejo, Mohammad Khan· 73, 180, 232

Juris-consults 132
Justice, speedy dispensation of 228

Karachi 67
Karachi Bar Association 88
Kemal Atatürk 85
Khalifas 110, 125
Khan Saheb 197
Khatt-e-Naskh 147
Khawaja Khairuddin 25
Khawaja Nazimuddin 13, 89, 128
Khuhro, M A 197
Khwaja Muhammad Safder 73
King Abdul Aziz University of Saudi Arabia 134
Kissinger, Henry 240
Krishak Sramik (peasants and workers) party 28

Lahore high court of the Panjab 227
Land Reforms Act 1974 and 1975 209
Landlordism in Pakistan 215
Language differences in Pakistan 12, 17
Laski 158
League of Nations 121
Legal Frame Work Orders (LFO) 8, 23
Legislature, financial power of 156
Legislature, role of 155
Liaquat Ali Khan 10, 13, 19, 20, 116, 117, 118, 143, 154, 203, 239
Lindsay, Professor 21
Local government institutions 51, 52, 54 et seq.
Lucknow Pact of 1916 6

MacIver, R M 237
Magna Carta 202
Mahbub Ul Haq 31
Majlis-e-Shoora 54, 55, 73, 146 et seq
Maktab schools 65
Malik Firoz Khan Noon 215
Marshall, Chief Justice 187
Martial law lifted, 1985 et seq 74
Martial law regime, first 27
Martial law regime, third (1977-1988) 25, 33
Maulana Abul A'la Mawdudi 79, 107
Metropolitan Corporations 53
Michels 21
Military rule, reasons for 27, 50
Minorities in Pakistan 123, 144
Minorities, religious in Islamic State 62, 67, 119 et seq.
Minorities, rights of 219
Mirza Aslam Beg 241
Mirza 19, 21, 27
Mohammad Ali Formula 14
Mohammad Iqbal, Sir 108
Mohammad Shahabuddin 20
Montagu-Chelmsford Reforms (1919) 121
Morley-Minto Reforms 121
Mosca 21
Moscow 46
Mourshed, Justice 226
Movement for the Restoration of Democracy (MRD) 56, 64
Muftis 151
Muhammad Asad 82
Muhammad Zafrullah Khan, Sir 81
Mujibur Rahman 8, 9, 31, 32, 83, 160, 161

Municipal corporations/committees 53, 62
Municipal Training and Research Institute, Karachi 54
Munir, Justice 86, 128
Muslim Family Laws Ordinance 1961 53
Muslim League 11, 16, 27, 73

Nasser 30
National Assembly 67 et seq.
National Centre for Rural Development, Islamabad 54
National economic council 193
National finance commission 190, 198, 199
National Security Council 61, 71, 72, 148, 176
Nehru, Jawaharlal 10, 27
Nemeyer, Sir Otto 189
New Delhi 46
Newspapers and the security act 206
Nifaz-i-Nizam-i-Islam: see Islamization
Nifaz-i-Shariah' 129
Nominations to assemblies 67
North West Frontier Province 8, 23, 52, 54, 183
Northern Areas Local Government Order 1979 52
Nuclear device, India's 47
Nuclear Non-Proliferation Treaty 48

Objectives resolution of 1949 113, 117, 122 et seq., 147, 150, 235
Oligarchy in Pakistan 22
Organization of Islamic Conference (OIC) 41, 42, 231

Pagara, Pir 64, 73
Pakistan (Provincial Constitution) Order 1947 11
Pakistan as homeland for Indian Muslims 7
Pakistan as Islamic state 233
Pakistan Muslim League 64
Pakistan National Congress 119
Pakistan People's Party (PPP) 8, 56, 64, 218, 242, 244
Pakistan Political Parties Act 242
Pakistan-US relationship 42, 47
Palestine 232
Panchayat system 53
Panjab Local Government Ordinance 1979 52
Panjab 8, 23, 46, 54, 63, 64, 183
Parliamentary system 59, 160, 168
Parsis in Pakistan 120
Partition of India 7
Peasants, representation of 219
People's Republic of China
Persian Gulf 42
Pirzada, A Hafeez 128, 208, 215
Police and fundamental rights 210
Political Parties (Amendment) Ordinance 1979 217
Political Parties Act 1962 35, 68, 69, 143, 216, 218
Political parties and the security act 206
Political parties, banned in 1977 34
Political Plan 57, 62, 64 et seq., 162
Pravda 240
Preamble to the 1973 constitution 116

President, as supreme commander of armed forces 176
President, financial power of 156
President, power of veto 175
President, power to address parliament 175
President, power to appoint the provincial governors 174
President, power to dismiss the prime minister 178, 179
President, powers of 167 et seq.
President, powers of pardon 142
President, qualifications of 142 et seq.
President, role of 166
Presidential system 59, 157, 162
Preventive detention 211 et seq.
Prime minister, dismissal of 170
Prime minister, role of 168 et seq.
Private property 210 et seq.
PRODA (Public and Representative Offices Disqualification Act) 22
Provincial assemblies 68 et seq.
Provincial councils 55
Provincial governor, appointment of 185
Provincial governors 61, 196
Provincial governors, powers of 178
Provisional Constitution Order 34, 54, 55

qarz-e-hasna (interest-free loan to needy persons) 37
Qazi courts 133 et seq.
Quaid-e-Azam University, Islamabad 134
Quranic sources 89 et seq.
Qureshi, I H 81, 108

Rahman, T W 135
Reagan, Ronald 43
Referendum, 1984 63 et seq., 165, 173, 180
Regional aspirations in Pakistan 195
Religious minorities, fundamental rights of 203, 211
Report of the board of *Talimat-i-Islamiah* 148
Report of the Council of Islamic Ideology 135 et seq.
Report of the Court of Enquiry for the Panjab disturbances of 1953 86
Report of the Special Committee of the Federal Council 139 et seq.
Republic Party 27
Republicans, American 43
Revenues, allocation of 191 et seq.

Revival of the Constitution of 1973 order 1985 71
Riaz Muhammad Khan 243
Riba, interest 37, 129
Roman [sc. Byzantium] empire 77, 78
Round Table Conferences 121
Round Table (London) 160
Rural development 200
Russian empire 121

Saudi Arabia 44, 118
Scheduled Castes Federation 119
Scheme for Financing Locally Manufactured Machinery 38
Schultz, George 239
Second Islamic Summit, Lahore 231
Security of Pakistan Acts 204, 205
Senate 68 et seq.
Sessions Judges 227
Settlement of Disputes of Immovable Property Regulation 1974 and 1975 209
Shahabuddin 84
Shariah (Islamic law) 37, 85, 108, 109, 129, 141, 149 et seq., 172, 209, 234
Shariah appellate bench 230
Shariah benches 40, 131
Shariah faculty, Islamic University 134 et seq.
Shariah Ordinance 15 June 1988 150 et seq.
Sharif, M M 82
Shiah community 36, 81
Sikh's separatist movement 46, 244
Simon Commission 121, 158 et seq.
Sind 8, 23, 36, 53, 54, 62, 67, 183, 196, 200
Sind Local Government Ordinance 1979 52
Sixth five-year plan 35, 61
Slavery 211
Smith, W C 80, 109, 111, 125
Social security, provision of 220
South Asia, nuclear weapons-free zone 48
Sovereignty in an Islamic state 90
Soviet Union 10, 40, 44, 46, 184, 243
Special Courts 228
Sri Lanka, democracy in 20
State Bank of Pakistan 28, 37, 38, 39
Subrahmaniyam, K 32
Suharwardy 20
Sukkur 67
Superior courts, writ jurisdiction of 223
Supreme court 187, 222 et seq.
Supreme court in USA 187

Supreme judicial council 224
Syed Ahmed, Sir 6
Syed Ghous Ali Shah 197

Talimat-i-Islammiah, board of 235
Taxation in a federal system 189
Taxes, distribution of 199
The Times (London) 22
Town Committees 53, 62
Toynbee, Arnold 28
Tribunals 228

U Thant 31
Ulema 89, 109, 123, 149
Union councils 52, 62
United Front 17
United Nations 45, 47
UN Charter 32, 46
UN General Assembly 41, 44, 202, 231
UN sponsored talks on Afghanistan 46
United States 10, 14, 40 et seq., 56
US aid programme for Pakistan 43, 44
US Congress 56, 160
US Pakistan security relationship 43
US, federal system of 16
US, presidential form of government 155, 158
US, Zia's special relationship with 244
Urdu as official language of Pakistan 17
Ushr 36, 129, 150
USSR: see Soviet Union

Vietnam 46

Wali Khan 197
Washington Post 240
Wealth, distribution of 220
Wealth-tax Act 1983 133
Wheare, K C 186, 188, 195, 199, 201, 210
Wifaq 64
Women 62, 211, 219
Workers, representation of 219
World Bank 44

Yahya Bakhtiar 183
Yahya Khan, President 9, 19, 23, 29 et seq., 165

Zakat and Ushr Ordinance 18 of 1980 133
Zakat 36, 118, 129, 150
Zia-ul-Haq: see under subject
Zia-ur-Rahman 161
Zila qazis 133
Zila/District Councils 53

3 1544 0 8935115 9

White Plains Public Library, WP.,NY.

954.91 C
Choudhury, G. W. 1926-
Pakistan

WHITE PLAINS PUBLIC LIBRARY

WHITE PLAINS, N. Y.

JUL 31 1990

ADULT